A Thomistic Christocentrism

THOMISTIC RESSOURCEMENT SERIES

Volume 17

SERIES EDITORS

Matthew Levering, Mundelein Seminary

Thomas Joseph White, OP, Pontifical University
of Saint Thomas Aquinas

EDITORIAL BOARD

Serge-Thomas Bonino, OP, Pontifical University
of St. Thomas Aquinas

Gilles Emery, OP, University of Fribourg (Switzerland)

Reinhard Hütter, The Catholic University of America

Bruce Marshall, Southern Methodist University

Emmanuel Perrier, OP, Dominican Studium, Toulouse

Richard Schenk, OP, University of Freiburg (Germany)

Kevin White, The Catholic University of America

A Thomistic Christocentrism

Recovering the Carmelites of Salamanca on the Logic of the Incarnation

DYLAN SCHRADER

The Catholic University of America Press
Washington, D.C.

Copyright © 2021
The Catholic University of America Press
All rights reserved

Design and composition by Kachergis Book Design

Cataloging-in-Publication Data available
from the Library of Congress
ISBN 978-0-8132-3408-3

In memory of Father Evan Patrick Harkins, my friend

Contents

Acknowledgments	ix
Abbreviations	xi
Introduction	1
1. A Dangerous Question: From Anselm to Scotus	6
2. Daring Replies: Late Medieval and Early Modern Themes	44
3. For the Redeemer's Sake: The Salamanca Theory	59
4. A Defense of Salamanca	118
5. Christ the Apex: Karl Rahner and the Salmanticenses	159
6. Cruciform Center: Hans Urs von Balthasar and the Salmanticenses	206
Conclusion: That Primordial Mercy	238
Bibliography	241
Index	261

Acknowledgments

In the first place, "thanks be to God, who gives us the victory through our Lord Jesus Christ" (1 Cor 15:57).

I wish to express my gratitude to the Most Rev. W. Shawn McKnight, bishop of Jefferson City, and the Most Rev. John R. Gaydos, bishop emeritus of Jefferson City, as well as to the clergy and faithful of the diocese for the opportunity to study sacred theology. I appreciate the support of my family and friends, especially Nick and Tony. I am also particularly grateful for the encouragement of Chad C. Pecknold, Reinhard Hütter, and Thomas Joseph White, OP.

This book is based on my doctoral dissertation for the Catholic University of America. It has also benefited from research I did when preparing the translation and introduction of the disputation *On the Motive of the Incarnation* in the Catholic University of America Press's Early Modern Catholic Sources series.

Abbreviations

AAS	*Acta Apostolicae Sedis*
CCCM	*Corpus Christianorum, continuatio mediaeualis*
CCSL	*Corpus Christianorum, series Latina*
CSEL	*Corpus scriptorum ecclesiasticorum Latinorum*
Defensiones in III Sent.	Jean Capréolus, *Defensiones theologicae divi Thomae in tertio Sententiarum*
In III Sent. (Borgnet)	Albert the Great, *Commentarii in tertium librum Sententiarum*
In III Sent. (Quaracchi)	Bonaventure, *Commentarii in tertium librum Sententiarum*
PG	*Patrologiae cursus completus, series Graeca* (ed. J.-P. Migne)
PL	*Patrologiae cursus completus, series Latina* (ed. J.-P. Migne)
SC	*Sources chrétiennes*
ST	Thomas Aquinas, *Summa theologiae*
Super I ad Tim.	Thomas Aquinas, *Super primam epistolam ad Timotheum lectura*
Super II Sent.	Thomas Aquinas, *Commentum in secundum librum Sententiarum*
Super III Sent.	Thomas Aquinas, *Scriptum super libro tertio Sententiarum*
TI	Karl Rahner, *Theological Investigations*

A Thomistic Christocentrism

Introduction

The Lord is the goal of human history, the point on which the desires of history and civilisation turn, the centre of the human race, the joy of all hearts and the fulfilment of all desires.[1]

With these words, the Second Vatican Council emphasizes the relevance of Jesus Christ for all human beings and for every aspect of human life and heralds Christ as their goal and center. The postconciliar magisterium has continued this trend. For example, Pope St. John Paul II (1920–2005) begins his first encyclical letter with the affirmation that "the Redeemer of man, Jesus Christ, is the centre of the universe and of history."[2] The same is reflected in pastoral practice, as when the bishops of the United States determined that cat-

---

1. Vatican Council II, *Gaudium et spes*, Pastoral Constitution, no. 45, in *Decrees of the Ecumenical Councils*, ed. Norman P. Tanner (London: Sheed and Ward, 1990), 2:1099. Throughout, I preserve the spelling and orthography of quotations unless otherwise noted. See also *Gaudium et spes*, nos. 10 and 22 (Tanner, 2:1074–75, 1081–82).

2. John Paul II, *Redemptor hominis*, Encyclical Letter (March 4, 1979), no. 1, in *AAS* 71 (1979): 257. Translation from the Vatican website. For similar magisterial examples, see John Paul II, *Catechesi tradendae*, Apostolic Exhortation (October 16, 1979), nos. 5–6, in *AAS* 71 (1979): 1280–82; *Sollicitudo rei socialis*, Encyclical Letter (December 30, 1987), no. 31, in *AAS* 80 (1988): 554; *Veritatis splendor*, Encyclical Letter (August 6, 1993), no. 19, in *AAS* 85 (1993): 1148–49; *Tertio millennio adveniente*, Apostolic Letter (November 10, 1994), nos. 1–14, in *AAS* 87 (1995): 5–14; *Evangelium vitae*, Encyclical Letter (March 25, 1995), no. 29, in *AAS* 87 (1995): 433–34; Congregation for the Doctrine of the Faith, *Dominus Iesus*, Declaration (August 6, 2000), nos. 11, 13, and 15, in *AAS* 92 (2000): 751–52, 754–55, 755–56; Benedict XVI, *Deus caritas est*, Encyclical Letter (December 25, 2005), no. 1, in *AAS* 98 (2006): 217–18; *Spe salvi*, Encyclical Letter (November 30, 2007), nos. 6 and 47, in *AAS* 99 (2007): 990–91, 1023–24; and Francis, *Evangelii gaudium*, Apostolic Exhortation (November 24, 2013), nos. 264–67, in *AAS* 105 (2013): 1125–27.

echetical curricula should be schematized principally by reference to Christ, including components such as "The Revelation of Jesus Christ in Scripture," "Sacraments as Privileged Encounters with Jesus Christ," and morality understood as "Life in Jesus Christ."[3]

On one level, a focus on Christ is part and parcel of Christianity. To this extent, it is obvious that orthodox Christian belief will emphasize the universal relevance of Jesus Christ, at least for salvation. "There is salvation in no one else, for there is no other name under heaven given among men by which we must be saved" (Acts 4:12).[4] Further, the soteriological import of Christ is universal not only in intension but also in extension if it is really true that God "desires all men to be saved and to come to the knowledge of the truth. For there is one God, and there is one mediator between God and men, the man Christ Jesus" (1 Tm 2:4–5). Moreover, if God orders even natural and otherwise merely human realities to salvation, if "in everything God works for good with those who love him, who are called according to his purpose" (Rom 8:28), then in some sense all created reality is directed to Christ, who accomplishes its return to God. "All are yours; and you are Christ's; and Christ is God's" (1 Cor 3:22b–23). In other words, it is not too big a leap from the basic Christian message of Christ's indispensable relevance for all human beings—as expressed in these and many other passages of Scripture—to the contemporary emphasis on Christ as goal and center of human life and indeed of all created things.

It is not so obvious precisely how Christ's universal relevance as goal and center is to be explained theologically. Given *that* Christ features prominently or even eminently in God's plan for the universe, theology wants to understand *how* this is so.

What is the relationship of Christ to God's plan for history, to

---

3. United States Conference of Catholic Bishops, *Doctrinal Elements of a Curriculum Framework for the Development of Catechetical Materials for Young People of High School Age* (Washington, D.C.: USCCB, 2008). In fact, the title of every core component includes "Jesus Christ."

4. English quotations from the Bible are from the Revised Standard Version, unless otherwise noted.

humanity or human nature as such, and to contingent factors like sin? Christocentric theological approaches have become a service to the magisterium inasmuch as the latter continues to put Jesus Christ, the Word made flesh, at the center of teaching and pastoral initiatives such as evangelization and catechesis. Such theologies are also especially valuable for articulating how Christ and the Church relate to all people and for helping avoid the tendency to relativize or minimize Christ.

"Christocentrism" means the centrality of Christ not only in his divinity but also in his humanity.[5] This is the sense in which I use the term in this book. Every kind of Christocentrism depends on the fact of the incarnation. If there were no God-man, he could be neither the goal toward which the universe strives, nor the key to understanding human nature, nor central or foundational in any other sense. No Christ, no Christocentrism. This means it is especially important to consider the incarnation as an event planned by God. Did God have to become man, or was he free not to? If he was free not to, why did he do so? Could God have chosen other reasons for the incarnation than those he actually chose?

This is to say that theology needs a providential approach, which is precisely how Scholastic theology addressed the great question of the rationale or "motive" of the incarnation. Theologians from the time of St. Anselm of Canterbury, OSB (ca. 1033–1109), onward dedicated increasingly lengthy and subtle treatises to the place of Jesus Christ in God's plan for the world. A providential approach, like that of the Scholastics, is goal-oriented. It is not static but dynamic, not circular but linear. Thus, the Scholastics tended to frame the issue not in terms of *centrality* but of *primacy*. For them, the crux of the matter was whether and how Christ could be considered first in God's intention. Did God make the world for Christ? Or, did he send Christ to save the world?

In contemporary theological discussion, the Scholastic debate is

---

5. B. J. Przewozny, "Christocentrism," in *New Catholic Encyclopedia*, ed. Berard L. Marthaler et al., 2nd ed. (Detroit: Gale Publishing, 2003), 3:558.

often simplified or even glossed over by quick reference to the "Scotistic" and "Thomistic" views—that is, the view that God planned the incarnation of Christ logically prior to and thus independently of human sin (Scotistic) and the view that God planned the incarnation essentially as a response to human sin (Thomistic).[6] This over-simplification does not do justice to the mature Scholastic discussion, which has been largely neglected since the Second Vatican Council despite its potential to provide a scripturally based and logically sound support for the postconciliar Christocentric emphasis.

In particular, the seventeenth-century Discalced Carmelites working at the College of *San Elias* at the University of Salamanca (the Salmanticenses) show that there is a faithfully Thomistic way to maintain Christ's primacy in God's providential plan. Stalwart in the key principles of St. Thomas Aquinas, OP (1225–74), particularly the principle that God's free choices only become known to us by revelation and the principle of divine transcendence, the Salmanticenses also assimilate the insights of other theological systems, especially the logical, ordered approach of Bl. John Duns Scotus, OFM (ca. 1266–1308). At the same time, they avoid certain excesses sometimes associated with Baroque Scholasticism. Despite thorough argumentation, their view remains simple in its core distinctions and respectful of the limits of theological knowledge. In short, the Salmanticenses offer an elegant Thomistic Christocentrism, in which God plans from the beginning to pour out mercy on fallen humanity through Christ the redeemer, who is himself the goal of all God's other works.

While greater familiarity with medieval and early modern theology in general would benefit the postconciliar theological enterprise, my aim in this book is to show how a recovery of the Salmanticenses

---

6. Throughout this book, expressions such as "Scotistic view" and "Thomistic view" should not be understood exclusively of the opinions of the eponymous theologians themselves but instead in the way these labels came to be used, i.e., as shorthand for the views just presented. Neither Scotus nor Aquinas, nor their disciples, argue for more than probable opinion on this point, so neither side's view should be taken as an absolute assertion.

can be especially fruitful for postconciliar Christocentrism. Therefore, in the first chapter, I will trace the development of the Scholastic question about the place of Christ in God's providential plan from Anselm through Duns Scotus. This is when the terms of this discussion took shape. The second chapter will give an overview of major developments from the fourteenth through sixteenth centuries. This serves as the proximate introduction to the Salmanticenses, in the polarization of hardline Scotistic and Thomistic camps and attempts to reconcile them. The third chapter will present the theory of the Salmanticenses, which argues that Christ is the first-willed and intended by God, the proximate end of all God's other works *ad extra*, and yet that his coming in the present providential plan is essentially a response to the fall. The fourth chapter will examine and refute key objections to the Salamanca theory. In the fifth and sixth chapters, I will consider two influential postconciliar Christocentric theologies, those of Karl Rahner, SJ (1904–84), and Hans Urs von Balthasar (1905–85).

Rahner sees Christ as the culmination of a universal process of God's self-communication to the world and thus always meant to become incarnate regardless of sin. Balthasar, in contrast, sees the drama of Christ's cross, descent into hell, and resurrection as precisely how God wanted to reveal himself in the world. Both theologians struggle to account for God's freedom to have enacted different providential plans. Thus, in these final chapters, I will show how the Salamanca theory can preserve Rahner's emphasis on Christ's primacy and Balthasar's focus on the cross while also correcting certain problems with their approaches. In this way, I hope to demonstrate the enduring value of Thomistic Christocentrism as articulated by the Salmanticenses.

1

A Dangerous Question
From Anselm to Scotus

St. Anselm of Canterbury set the stage for the discussion that eventually crystallized at the close of the thirteenth century as the Scotist-Thomist debate over the rationale for the incarnation. In Anselm's *Cur Deus homo?*, questions of contingency and necessity permeate the argument for why only the God-man can offer to God the love the human race owes him and so atone for sins. In Anselm's view, God freely creates human beings, who are meant to return to him in loving obedience, but sin has incapacitated the human race. Like a servant fallen into a pit, lapsed humanity cannot pull itself up, and yet only a member of the human race can offer to God the *human* love owed to his divine majesty. It then becomes necessary for one who is both divine and human to satisfy for sins and restore fallen humanity. If the world falls, the incarnation is the only way for God to achieve the purpose for which he made it. For Anselm, the God-man's existence and atonement are an expression of God's sovereignty and the inability of creatures to thwart divine providence.[1]

---

1. Anselm, *Cur Deus homo?* II, chap. 6, in *S. Anselmi Cantuariensis archiepiscopi opera omnia*, ed. Franciscus Salesius Schmitt (Rome, 1940), 2:101. For a more detailed treatment of the thinkers covered in this chapter, see Justus H. Hunter, *If Adam Had Not Sinned: The Reason for the Incarnation from Anselm to Scotus* (Washington, D.C.: The Catholic University of America Press, 2020).

Anselm's attempt to explain *why* and *how* God's providence has connected the elements of God's freedom, creation, the reparation of fallen humanity, the God-man, and the God-man's obedient suffering and death naturally led into the further question of *whether* these elements must be so connected. Scholastics soon realized the theological stakes and came cautiously but earnestly to speculate about just how separable the pieces of God's providential plan might be. Is the world's greatest good really a response to evil, or is Christ himself so important that God would even have sent him into an empty universe?

In this chapter, I will highlight the most important themes in key Scholastic thinkers between Anselm and Aquinas as they tackled the risky issue of the incarnation's fundamental reason and its relationship to humanity's fall. Then, I will present with greater detail the thought of Aquinas and Duns Scotus, who became emblematic of the two opposing views about whether Christ would have come absent sin.

MAJOR DEVELOPMENTS FROM ANSELM TO AQUINAS

It is probably Rupert of Deutz, OSB (ca. 1075–1129), who gave currency to the question of whether the incarnation would have occurred absent sin.[2] In *De gloria et honore Filii hominis super Matthaeum*, composed between 1125 and 1127, he engages with the issue of predestination.[3] In the last book of this work, Rupert is particularly concerned with solving the dilemma of whether God willed evil or

---

2. Jean-François Bonnefoy, "La question hypothétique: Ultrum [*sic*] si Adam non peccasset [...] au XIIIe siècle," *Revista española de teología* 14 (1954): 331; Edward Christiaan van Driel, *Incarnation Anyway: Arguments for Supralapsarian Christology* (Oxford: Oxford University Press, 2008), 171; and Daniel P. Horan, "How Original Was Scotus on the Incarnation? Reconsidering the History of the Absolute Predestination of Christ in Light of Robert Grosseteste," *The Heythrop Journal* 52, no. 3 (May 2011): 374–75.

3. John H. Van Engen, *Rupert of Deutz*, Publications of the UCLA Center for Medieval and Renaissance Studies (Los Angeles: University of California Press, 1983), 352–55.

was not powerful enough to prevent evil. This is where he raises the question of the incarnation apart from sin as a formal hypothetical:

> Here we may well inquire as to the first part of the verse whether this Son of God, to whom this passage refers, would become man or not, even if sin, on account of which we all die, had not occurred in the meantime. As to the fact that he would not become a mortal man, given that he would not assume a mortal body, unless sin, on account of which we also have all become mortal, had occurred, no one doubts. Only a heathen is ignorant of this. We are inquiring of the passage whether it was going to happen and was in some way necessary for the human race that God become man, the head and king of all, as he now is. And what response should we give to this?[4]

Rupert replies in terms of the effective predestination of the elect. Since Adam and Eve would have begotten children had the state of innocence continued, the number of the elect does not depend on sin. But if the number of the elect does not depend on sin, neither does the incarnation of Christ, who is the first among the elect. God's effective plan for salvation is unchangeable.[5] Thus, sin did not cause the incarnation but only its passible, redemptive mode. In fact, as first of the elect, Christ is the end of all God's other works: "And what cause was there for which God created everything, if not this Son of man?"[6] Not only does God intend the God-man from the beginning; he also intends everything else for his sake.

---

4. "Hic primum illud quaerere libet utrum iste Filius Dei, de quo hic sermo est, etiam si peccatum, propter quod omnes morimur, non intercessisset, homo fieret, an non. Nam de eo quod mortalis homo non fieret, quod mortale corpus non assumeret, nisi peccatum accidisset, propter quod et nos omnes facti sumus mortales, nulli dubium est, nulli nisi infideli incognitum est. Illud quaerimus utrum hoc futurum, et humano generi aliquo modo necessarium erat, ut Deus homo fieret caput et rex omnium, ut nunc est, et quid de hoc respondebitur?" Rupert of Deutz, *De gloria et honore Filii hominis super Matthaeum* XIII, ed. Hrabanus Haacke, CCCM 29 (Turnhout: Brepols, 1979), 415.684–92. All translations are my own unless otherwise indicated. When I have translated a text or when the original is hard to find, I provide the original text in the notes.

5. Rupert of Deutz, *De gloria et honore* XIII (CCCM 29:415.705–416.752). See also Rupert of Deutz, *In Iohannis Evangelium* I (CCCM 9:13–14), an earlier work of Rupert's, finished around 1116 (ed. Hrabanus Haacke, CCCM 9 [Turnhout: Brepols, 1969]). The concern for divine immutability is constant throughout his career.

6. "Et quae causa est, propter quam Deus omnia creauit, nisi iste Filius hominis?" Rupert of Deutz, *De gloria et honore* XIII (CCCM 29:410.491). See also his *De glorificatione Trinitatis et processione Spiritus sancti* III, chaps. 20–21 (PL 169:72–73).

Robert Grosseteste (ca. 1168–1253) also considers the possibility of the incarnation absent sin. In *De cessatione legalium*, written between 1231 and 1235,[7] he observes:

But as to whether God would be man even if man were not fallen, there are not any out of the sacred expositors who make a determination in their books that I have examined up to now, unless my memory deceives me. But they seem more to suggest that if man were not fallen, there would not be the God-man and thus that God has only become man to restore man who was lost. Yet there seem to be effective arguments for showing simply that God would be man even if man had never been fallen.[8]

This passage may indicate that Robert was not familiar with earlier writings on the subject, or the "sacred expositors" he mentions may include only the Fathers and not Robert's immediate predecessors.[9]

Robert gives four arguments for why God would have become man even if humanity had not fallen.[10] First, God is utmost power, wisdom, and goodness; therefore, he gives the universe as much good as it is capable of. Second, sin has not made the universe or human beings more capable of receiving the goodness of the incarnation; therefore, God would have fulfilled this capacity even absent sin. Third, how could the lack of essence, which sin is, be the cause of such a great good as the ability to be assumed into personal union? Fourth, the ability to be assumed into personal union is either an essence or a non-essence (such as a privation). Since it is not

---

7. Dominic J. Unger, "Robert Grosseteste Bishop of Lincoln (1235–1253) on the Reasons for the Incarnation," *Franciscan Studies* 16, no. 1/2 (1956): 2; and Robert Grosseteste, introduction to *De cessatione legalium*, ed. Richard C. Dales and Edward B. King, Auctores Britannici medii aevi 7 (London: Oxford University Press, 1986), xiv–xv.

8. "Verumtamen, an Deus esset homo etiam si non esset lapsus homo non determinant aliqui de sacris expositoribus in libris suis quos ego adhuc inspexerim, nisi fallat me memoria mea. Sed magis videntur insinuare quod si non esset lapsus homo, non esset Deus homo; et ideo solum Deus factus sit homo ut hominem perditum repararet. Videntur tamen esse raciones efficaces ad ostendendum simpliciter quod Deus esset homo etiam si numquam lapsus fuisset homo." Grosseteste, *De cessatione legalium* III.1.2 (Auctores Britannici, 7:119.12–18).

9. Unger believes Robert to have drawn on the work of Rupert and possibly Honorius of Autun. "Grosseteste on the Reasons for the Incarnation," 26.

10. Grosseteste, *De cessatione legalium* III.1.3–9 (Auctores Britannici, 7:120–23).

a non-essence, it must be an essence. But a lack of essence (sin) cannot be the cause of an essence (the ability to be assumed into personal union). Therefore, human nature must always have been capable of personal union. Thus, Robert concludes, "the universe could not *not* receive this good from the utmost good."[11]

The common thread to Robert's argumentation is that God, being the supreme good, must give the creature as much goodness as it can receive. He even suggests that God would be less good than he is if he did not do this.[12] However, Robert does clarify that God does not have to give every possible good to every individual creature. Instead, what really matters is that God fills out all the possible kinds of creaturely perfection.[13] The incarnation, he argues, has introduced into the universe the man who can be worshiped. It has made human flesh, of itself merely something created, glorious and worthy of adoration. Like the otherwise bare and plain wood of a torch, Christ's humanity has been lit up with blazing splendor.[14] If God would not have left out the smallest species of worm from his creation absent sin, why would he leave out the God-man? On this basis, Robert's reasoning seeks to demonstrate that sin has not made human nature any more *capable* of being assumed into personal union, and he thinks that it follows thereby that God would have decreed the incarnation even if there had been no sin.

After his arguments from the capacity of human nature, Robert offers several more lines of reasoning for the incarnation apart from sin.[15] First, Christ would still have to have been the head of the

11. "Non potuit universitas non recipere hoc bonum a summo bono." Grosseteste, *De cessatione legalium* III.1.7 (Auctores Britannici, 7:121.17–18).

12. See Grosseteste, *De cessatione legalium* III.1.3 (Auctores Britannici, 7:120.5–7). See also Hunter, *If Adam Had Not Sinned*, 80.

13. Grosseteste, *De cessatione legalium* III.1.9 (Auctores Britannici, 7:122.18–123.7).

14. Grosseteste, *De cessatione legalium* III.1.8 (Auctores Britannici, 7:121.19–122.17).

15. Grosseteste, *De cessatione legalium* III.1.10–30 (Auctores Britannici, 7:123–33). Given that in some places Robert's discussions are more dialectical and extended, it is possible to enumerate them differently. Unger, for example, outlines ten basic arguments, whereas James McEvoy lists five. I present the main lines of argumentation as briefly as possible, with a view to the motifs that later theologians will pick up. Unger, "Grosseteste on the Reasons for the Incarnation," 27–34; McEvoy, "The Absolute Predestination

Church. Second, even if man did not need satisfaction for sin through the God-man, he still would have needed the God-man in order to be just. This consideration, however, leads Robert into an extended discussion of the relation of the God-man to satisfaction and justification.[16] If God would have given sinless man justice apart from the God-man, then why is the God-man needed for justification after sin? What does Christ's passion add if God can justify directly? There are further considerations from the fact that humanity receives adoptive filiation in Christ and from the fact that Christ and the Church make up "one Christ" (*unus Christus*).[17] Third, Adam knew the nature of matrimony before the fall, but matrimony is a sign of Christ's union with the Church. In fact, matrimony's indissolubility derives from its being a sign of the union of natures in Christ and of the union of Christ and the Church. Fourth, a passage in *De spiritu et anima* (attributed to Augustine) says that human beatitude requires the vision of God in both the mind and the senses, which requires seeing Christ's humanity.[18] Fifth, the whole universe is one, but this requires a single principle of unification. This principle of unification must be greater than all other creatures, and this can only be the God-man, whose constitution also spans the entire hierarchy of being from divinity down to the four elements. Sixth, likewise, the completion of the universe further entails linking God, the principle, to man, the last created.[19] Seventh, this completion extends to human generation, which forms a kind of circle in the incarnation. For a woman (Eve) took her flesh from a man alone (Adam), and in the incarnation, a

---

of Christ in the Theology of Robert Grosseteste," in *"Sapientiae Doctrina": Mélanges de théologie et de littérature médiévales offerts à Dom Hildebrand Bascour O.S.B.*, Recherches de théologie ancienne et médiévale, numéro spécial 1 (Leuven: Imprimerie Orientaliste, 1980), 213–17; and McEvoy, *Robert Grosseteste*, Great Medieval Thinkers (Oxford: Oxford University Press, 2000), 128. Cf. Horan, "How Original Was Scotus on the Incarnation?," 379; and Hunter, *If Adam Had Not Sinned*, 77–79. Grosseteste repeats the same arguments in briefer form in a sermon entitled *Exiit edictum*, which has been edited by Unger in "Grosseteste on the Reasons for the Incarnation," 18–23.

16. Grosseteste, *De cessatione legalium* III.1.12–15 (Auctores Britannici, 7:123–25).
17. Grosseteste, *De cessatione legalium* III.1.16–19 (Auctores Britannici, 7:125–27).
18. Pseudo-Augustine, *De spiritu et anima*, chap. 9 (PL 40:785).
19. Cf. Irenaeus of Lyon, *Adversus haereses* IV, chap. 20, no. 4 (SC 100:634).

man (Christ) has taken flesh from a woman alone (Mary). Further, Jesus is descended from Adam through Mary, but Adam was also made through Jesus, which adds another form of circularity.

Robert concludes his argumentation with a disclaimer:

> By these reasonings and others like them, it seems possible to construe God's being man even though man had never sinned. But as to whether it is true, I know that I am ignorant, and I lament my ignorance in this matter to no small extent. For, as we have said above, I do not recall having seen anything determined on this issue by our authors. And I do not wish nor do I dare to assert anything in such a difficult question without an express authority, since a reasoning with the veneer of truth can quickly deceive what little talent and knowledge I have. But if it were true, that is, that God would have been man even if man were not fallen, then all creation would appropriately be directed to that man, who is the head of the Church.[20]

Thus, it is clear that Robert sees his effort as speculative and provisional. His arguments, he thinks, have the ring of truth, but as a good theologian, he is also well aware of the danger of wishful thinking. A difficult question like this cannot be settled simply by intuition but requires an express authority.

Alexander of Hales, OFM (ca. 1185–1245), was the first Franciscan to hold a chair at the University of Paris. He helped set the tone for Franciscan theology, including the rationale for the incarnation.[21] Alexander does not ask whether the incarnation would have

---

20. "Hiis et huiusmodi raciocinacionibus videtur posse astrui Deum esse hominem licet numquam peccasset homo. Quod tamen an verum sit me ignorare scio, et meam in hac parte ignorantiam non mediocriter doleo. Nichil enim, ut supradiximus, a nostris auctoribus super hoc determinatum me vidisse recolo. Nec sine expressa auctoritate aliquid in tam ardua questione asserere volo vel audeo, quia parvitatem ingenii mei et scientie mee cito potest fallere verisimilis ratiocinacio. Si hoc tamen verum esset quod Deus scilicet fuisset homo licet non esset lapsus homo, congruenter omnis creatura intenderet illum hominem, qui est capud ecclesie." Grosseteste, *De cessatione legalium* III.2.1 (Auctores Britannici, 7:133.20–29).

21. Christopher M. Cullen, "Alexander of Hales," in *A Companion to Philosophy in the Middle Ages*, ed. Jorge J. E. Gracia and Timothy B. Noone, Blackwell Companions to Philosophy (Oxford: Blackwell, 2003), 104; and Walter H. Principe, *Alexander of Hales' Theology of the Hypostatic Union*, vol. 2 of *The Theology of the Hypostatic Union in the Early Thirteenth Century*, Pontifical Institute of Mediaeval Studies 12 (Toronto: Pontifical Institute of Mediaeval Studies, 1967), 86.

occurred absent sin but instead investigates what sort of benefit the incarnation could possibly have apart from the human need of redemption. Alexander does not make a definitive claim, but he does give some reasons for thinking of the God-man as valuable and fitting in himself.

The *Summa fratris Alexandri* poses the question this way: "Consequently, we can ask about the fittingness of the incarnation if nature had not been fallen through sin, namely, whether there would be a reason or fittingness for the incarnation."[22] There are four initial arguments for the fittingness of the incarnation apart from sin.[23] First, goodness is diffusive of itself. Second, the beatitude of the whole human being entails both the intellect and the senses. Thus, human blessedness requires the vision of God both as intellectual object and as sensible object. Third, there are three persons in one substance (the Trinity), and there are three persons in three substances (e.g., three human beings), and so it is fitting for there to be the other extreme of three substances in one person (body, soul, and divinity in Christ). Fourth, if it is a perfection for one nature to be in more than one person, it is a perfection for one person to have more than one nature.

In Alexander's response to this question he affirms, "Without prejudice, we should grant that even if human nature had not been fallen, there is still a fittingness for the incarnation."[24] He bases this

22. "Consequens est quaerere de convenientia incarnationis, si non fuisset natura lapsa per peccatum, utrum scilicet esset ratio vel convenientia ad incarnationem." Alexander of Hales, *Summa fratris* III, pars 1, inquisitio unica *de Verbo incarnato*, tract. 1, q. 2, tit. 2, no. 23, in *Doctoris irrefragabilis Alexandri de Hales Ordinis Minorum Summa theologica seu sic ab origine dicta "Summa fratris Alexandri"* [...], (Ad Claras Aquas [Quaracchi]: Ex typographia Collegii S. Bonaventurae, 1948), 4:41. The first three books were completed before Alexander's death in 1245, so it is possible that in addition to being the initial source of the work, he also oversaw the editing of the relevant section. See Cullen, "Alexander of Hales," 105.

23. Alexander of Hales, *Summa fratris* III, pars 1, inquisitio unica *de Verbo incarnato*, tract. 1, q. 2, tit. 2, no. 23, a–d (Quaracchi, 4:41–42). See also Alexander of Hales, *Quaestio disputata XV*, disp. 2, m. 4, nos. 45–49, in *Quaestiones disputatae "antequam esset frater,"* Bibliotheca Franciscana scholastica medii aevi 19 (Ad Claras Aquas [Quaracchi]: Ex typographia Collegii S. Bonaventurae, 1960), 207–9.

24. "Sine praeiudicio concedendum est quod, etiamsi non fuisset humana natura

on the fact that Lucifer fell through envy of the incarnation, which means that it was planned prior to sin, and that complete human beatitude requires seeing God with the eyes of the body, citing *De spiritu et anima*. In his earlier commentary on the *Sentences*, probably from around 1220 to 1227, Alexander notes that while God was able to assume angelic nature, angelic nature was not assumed because it had no need of restoration: "And granted that there would be present a fittingness between angelic and divine nature, this is not enough. Rather, some need is required in the assumed that can be restored by union."[25] This resonates with the tone of the *Summa fratris*, which limits itself to fittingness and does not settle whether the incarnation actually would have occurred absent sin. Alexander distinguishes between what God could do and what he actually does. The mere fact that God might accomplish some great good by acting in a certain way does not entail that he has actually acted or would actually act in that way.

Guerric of Saint-Quentin, OP (d. 1245), also emphasizes God's transcendence. Although the God-man gives the universe its highest perfection, God is not bound by the very fact of creation to become incarnate.[26] Actually, the fact that God became incarnate for humanity's sake serves to make human beings grateful to God and draw them closer to him. Scripture passages (such as Rom 1:4) and

---

lapsa, adhuc est convenientia ad incarnationem." Alexander of Hales, *Summa fratris* III, pars 1, inquisitio unica *de Verbo incarnato*, tract. 1, q. 2, tit. 2, no. 23, co. (Quaracchi, 4:42). See Bernard of Clairvaux, Sermon 1 on Advent, nos. 2–4, in *S. Bernardi opera*, ed. J. Leclercq and H. Rochais (Rome: Editiones Cistercienses, 1966), 4:162–64; and Pseudo-Augustine, *De spiritu et anima*, chap. 9 (PL 40:785).

25. "Et licet esset ibi convenientia inter angelicam et divinam [naturam], non tamen hoc sufficit; sed aliqua indigentia [requiritur] in assumpto, quae possit reparari per unionem." Alexander of Hales, *Glossa in tertium librum Sententiarum secundum codicem L*, d. 2, no. 13, a. 1, in *Glossa in quattuor libros Sententiarum Petri Lombardi, nunc demum reperta atque primum edita, studio et cura PP. Collegii S. Bonaventurae*, Bibliotheca Franciscana scholastica medii aevi 14 (Ad Claras Aquas [Quaracchi]: Ex typographia Collegii S. Bonaventurae, 1954), 3:26.

26. Guerric of Saint-Quentin, *Quodlibet* 7, a. 1, sol., nos. 10–11, in *Quaestiones de quolibet*, ed. Walter H. Principe and Jonathan Black, Studies and Texts 143 (Toronto: Pontifical Institute of Mediaeval Studies, 2002), 312–13. Justus Hunter comments on the manuscript variants of Guerric's discussion in *If Adam Had Not Sinned*, 121–24.

other authoritative statements about Christ's predestination can be understood as presupposing the context of the fallen world: "God foresaw the disease and so also foresaw the medicine."[27]

Guerric's student, St. Albert the Great, OP (ca. 1200–80), is even more cautious. He addresses the rationale for the incarnation in his commentary on the third book of the *Sentences*, which originates from after 1240, when he was sent to complete theological studies at the University of Paris.[28] Following the text of Peter Lombard (ca. 1096–1160), Albert raises the question in terms of the love that the incarnation has elicited. If humanity had not sinned, would God have incited man to love as great as the love that the redemptive incarnation has brought about?[29] Albert offers four arguments against the incarnation absent sin.[30] First, there is a liturgical sequence containing the line "O exceedingly blessed fault, whereby nature has been redeemed!" Second, there is the famous *felix culpa* of the *Exsultet*, which Albert notes is sung in "some churches." Third, in reference to the verse "We know that in everything God works for good with those who love him, who are called according to his purpose" (Rom 8:28), a gloss explains that this includes their sins. Fourth, if there had been no need for a physician, liberator, or redeemer, to what purpose would the incarnation have been and how would it have aroused such great charity?

---

27. "Deus praevidit morbum, ideo praevidit et medicinam." Guerric of Saint-Quentin, *Quodlibet* 7, a. 1, no. 23 (Studies and Texts, 143:317). On this point, see Hunter, *If Adam Had Not Sinned*, 126–27.

28. Mechthild Dreyer, "Albertus Magnus," in *A Companion to Philosophy in the Middle Ages*, 92. The relevant article from Albert's *Sentences* commentary is *Commentarii in tertium librum Sententiarum*, d. 20, B, a. 4, in *B. Alberti Magni, Ratisbonensis episcopi, Ordinis praedicatorum, opera omnia*, ed. Steph. Caes. Aug. Borgnet (Paris: Apud Ludovicum Vivès, 1894), 28:360–62. The Cologne critical edition of this work is still in preparation.

29. We gather this from the beginning of the first objection: "Secundum hoc enim si homo non peccasset, videtur quod non tantum ad amorem suum nos provocasset." Albert the Great, *In III Sent.*, d. 20, B, a. 4 (Borgnet, 28:360).

30. Albert the Great, *In III Sent.*, d. 20, B, a. 4, obj. 1–4 (Borgnet, 28:360–61). The sequence Albert mentions is one for the Nativity: *Eia recolamus*, in Francis Andrew March, *Latin Hymns with English Notes for Use in Schools and Colleges*, Douglass Series of Christian Greek and Latin Writers 1 (New York: Harper, 1874), 89.

To the contrary, Albert offers six arguments, clearly drawing on Robert and Alexander.[31] First, goodness is diffusive of itself. Second, Anselm says that there are four ways for God to produce a human being: from a man and a woman (natural generation); from neither a man nor a woman (Adam); from a man but not a woman (Eve); and, to complete the possibilities, from a woman but not a man, which means the virginal conception and birth of Christ. Third, angelic nature is not capable of being united to divinity, so if human nature has this capacity, it should be fulfilled. Fourth, human nature should have been even more capable of union without sin, seeing as it would be more like God. Fifth, the perfection of the universe consists in circularity according to Aristotle, so the first principle should be joined to the last creature. Sixth, God's love is so great that he would unite the creature to himself.

Albert's own response is modest:

In this question the solution is uncertain. But so far as I can give an opinion, I believe that the Son of God would have become man even if there had never been sin, though he would not have become an angel, since an angel is not by nature capable of being united like man, as we showed above. Even so, I say nothing about this by way of assertion. Rather, I believe that what I have said more harmonizes with the piety of faith.[32]

Albert's reasoning for why angelic nature is not capable of assumption by a divine person draws not only on the fact that the angels do not have the possibility of an inherited state of sin but also on his view that the individual angelic nature is not separable from personal distinction.[33] Thus, an individual angelic nature could not

---

31. Albert the Great, *In III Sent.*, d. 20, B, a. 4, s.c. 1–6 (Borgnet, 28:361). He refers to Aristotle, *On the Heavens*, 2.4.286b10–30; Irenaeus of Lyon, *Adversus haereses* IV, chap. 20, no. 4 (SC 100:634); and Anselm, *Cur Deus homo?* II, chap. 8 (Schmitt, 2:104).

32. "Dicendum, quod in hac quaestione solutio incerta est. Sed quantum possum opinari, credo quod Filius Dei factus fuisset homo, etiamsi numquam fuisset peccatum: nec tamen factus fuisset Angelus, quia Angelus non est unibilis ex natura sicut homo, ut supra ostendimus: tamen nihil de hoc asserendo dico: sed credo hoc quod dixi, magis concordare pietati fidei." Albert the Great, *In III Sent.*, d. 20, B, a. 4, co. (Borgnet, 28:361).

33. Albert the Great, *In III Sent.*, d. 2, A, a. 2 (Borgnet, 28:23–24).

in any way exist without thereby being an angelic person. Therefore, Albert rules out the assumption of angelic nature as a metaphysical impossibility, not just a soteriological one.

When Albert addresses the arguments for and against, he explains that goodness diffuses itself according to capacity. Human nature is not capable of meriting union and would be complete even without the highest grace, since God does not have to do the best possible.

In his later *Quaestio de conceptione Christi*, Albert again raises the hypothetical question. There he states that divine revelation, which would be the only way to settle the matter, does not give a definite answer. When explaining his opinion that the incarnation would have occurred apart from sin, Albert distinguishes between God's coming into *the* world and God's coming into *this* world.[34] The reason for the former is God's love for humanity and human nature's capacity for personal union. The reason for the latter is this fallen world's need for redemption through Christ's passion and death. This distinction between the fact of the incarnation and its concrete modality will become increasingly important.[35]

As Donald Goergen, OP, notes, on this matter "uncertainty is Albert's most fundamental assertion."[36] Albert wishes to maintain God's freedom to become incarnate or not, as well as to distinguish incarnation from redemption, despite the fact that these are historically inseparable. Along these lines, there are two important principles in Albert that set him apart from previous theologians. First, Albert stresses that the incarnation does not fulfill a natural capacity. In other words, Albert attends more in this matter to the *kind* of capacity in question (natural or obediential) than does someone like

---

34. "Alia est causa veniendi in mundum et alia veniendi in hunc mundum." Albert the Great, *Quaestio de conceptione Christi*, a. 4, in *Alberti Magni opera omnia*, ed. Henryk Anzulewicz and Wilhelm Kübel (Münster: Aschendorff, 1993), 25.2:263.

35. See Hunter, *If Adam Had Not Sinned*, 135–36.

36. Donald Goergen, "Albert the Great and Thomas Aquinas on the Motive of the Incarnation," *The Thomist* 44 (1980): 527.

Robert Grosseteste. Second, Albert is also thereby equipped to assert clearly that God does *not* need to do the best possible or to fulfill every kind of capacity in the creature.

St. Bonaventure, OFM (ca. 1217–74), put his commentary on the *Sentences* into writing around 1252.[37] His commentary on the third book, dealing with the incarnation, was probably the last written. Having affirmed that the incarnation was appropriate (*congruum*) for God, Bonaventure poses the question: "What was the chief reason for the incarnation?" (*Quae fuerit incarnationis ratio praecipua*).[38] He offers five initial arguments that the chief reason for the incarnation was the redemption of the human race as well as nine arguments against this view.[39] Besides repeating arguments drawn from previous theologians, such as Robert and Alexander, Bonaventure is concerned about the incarnation's being a good produced only *occasionaliter*. After all, it seems unfitting for Christ, being supremely noble, to be willed only for the lesser good of human redemption. In fact, if sin is what afforded Christ as man the grace of union, he would even have to be glad that Adam sinned.

In his own response, Bonaventure cites two opinions, which he says are held by various masters.[40] Some, he says, distinguish between the substance of the incarnation and the defects of passibility

---

37. Marianne Schlosser, "Bonaventure: Life and Works," in *A Companion to Bonaventure*, ed. Jay M. Hammond, J. A. Wayne Hellmann, and Jared Goff, Brill's Companions to the Christian Tradition (Leiden: Brill, 2014), 13.

38. Bonaventure, *In III Sent.*, d. 1, a. 2, q. 2, in *Doctoris seraphici S. Bonaventurae S. R. E. episcopi cardinalis opera omnia* [...] (Ad Claras Aquas [Quaracchi]: Ex typographia Collegii S. Bonaventurae, 1887), 3:21–28.

39. Bonaventure, *In III Sent.*, d. 1, a. 2, q. 2, args. 1–5 (Quaracchi, 3:21–22), where he invokes Gal 4:4–5a; Heb 2:10; Augustine, *Enarrationes in psalmos*, psalm 68, serm. 1, no. 5 (CCSL 39:906); Augustine, *In Iohannis euangelium tractatus*, tract. 49, no. 5 (CCSL 36:422); and the *Glossa ordinaria* on Heb 2:16, in *Bibliorum sacrarum cum glossa ordinaria* (Venice, 1603), 6:818–19. See also Bonaventure, *In III Sent.*, d. 1, a. 2, q. 2, s.c. 1–9 (Quaracchi, 3:22–23), where he invokes Rom 5:20b; Augustine, *In Iohannis euangelium tractatus*, tract. 66, no. 2 (CCSL 36:494); Augustine, *De libero arbitrio* III, chap. 5, no. 13 (CCSL 29:282–83); Pseudo-Augustine, *De spiritu et anima*, chap. 9 (PL 40:785); *Glossa ordinaria* on Heb 2:16, in *Biblia sacra cum glossa ordinaria* (Venice, 1603), 6:819; and Anselm, *Cur Deus homo?* II, chap. 8 (Schmitt, 2:104).

40. Bonaventure, *In III Sent.*, d. 1, a. 2, q. 2, co. (Quaracchi, 3:23–25).

and mortality. They argue that the mortality of Christ's humanity is principally for redemption but that the assumption of humanity itself is principally because of the dignity of the work, perfecting the universe in the orders of nature, grace, and glory. Further, the incarnation fulfills the greatest appetite or openness in human nature. These theologians also hold that when Scripture and the saints seem to hold the incarnation as principally redemptive, they are speaking of the incarnation considered in its entirety, including the aspects of passibility and mortality.

Others, says Bonaventure, hold that redemption was the chief reason for the incarnation, even though there are many other benefits connected with it. They argue that the super-abundant outpouring of goodness in the incarnation corresponds to the great need for correction introduced by sin, that God would not have sought his sheep in this way unless it had been lost (cf. Lk 15:4).

Having laid out these two opinions, Bonaventure remarks: "Now which of these manners of speaking is more true, he knows who deigned to become incarnate for us. Which of them, too, is to be preferred to the other is difficult to see, given that both manners of speaking are Catholic and are maintained by Catholics. Both manners of speaking, too, rouse the soul to devotion with respect to different considerations."[41] Bonaventure goes on to explain that the first opinion—that the incarnation was principally for the perfection of the universe and circumstantially for redemption—harmonizes more with reason, whereas the second—that the incarnation was essentially redemptive—harmonizes more with the piety of faith.[42] This, he says, is because Scripture and the saints always seem to speak of the Son of God's descent as being for the purpose

---

41. "Quis autem horum modorum dicendi verior sit, novit ille qui pro nobis incarnari dignatus est. Quis etiam horum alteri praeponendus sit, difficile est videre, pro eo quod uterque modus catholicus est et a viris catholicis sustinetur. Uterque etiam modus excitat animam ad devotionem secundum diversas considerationes." Bonaventure, *In III Sent.*, d. 1, a. 2, q. 2, co. (Quaracchi, 3:24).

42. Thus, Albert and Bonaventure both appeal to the "piety of faith" (*pietas fidei*), though to opposite effect.

of freeing humanity from sin, and we must not say anything apart from Scripture. Further, the second opinion honors God more, since it holds that the mystery of the incarnation is above and beyond the perfection of the universe, whether in nature, grace, or glory. Moreover, the second opinion is right to argue that a truly great reason, such as satisfaction for sin, was needed to warrant the incarnation. Finally, the second opinion also enkindles greater faith-filled affection, since it asserts that God became incarnate to take away his people's sins rather than to complete the works he had begun. Bonaventure thus prefers the second opinion, that the chief reason for the incarnation was the redemption of the human race, "even though it does not seem as sophisticated [*subtilis*] as the preceding one."[43]

Bonaventure concludes his treatment by stating: "But all this has been said without prejudice, for it is not my intention to restrict God's goodness but to extol the surplus of his charity toward fallen man, that our affections may be roused to love him when we focus on the abundance of his exceeding love."[44] In this way, the Seraphic Doctor's caution is clear as well as his attention to the *sensus fidelium*. The theologian's task is not only to inquire from the point of view of faith but from the perspective of faith informed by charity.

It is also important to note that Bonaventure's preference for the opinion that the incarnation was essentially a response to sin does not lessen his emphasis on Christ's primacy as the one who both perfects and heals creation. This is evident from his *Breviloquium* (ca. 1257), as even its structure belies. At its chiastic center lies part 4, treating of the Word incarnate, who leads creation back to God, overcoming the twofold distance of limited creaturely being and the alienation of sin.[45] The same comes across in the *Collatio-*

---

43. "Etsi non videatur esse ita subtilis, sicut praecedens." Bonaventure, *In III Sent.*, d. 1, a. 2, q. 2, co. (Quaracchi, 3:25).

44. "Haec autem omnia absque praeiudicio dicta sunt: non enim volo bonitatem Dei coarctare, sed nimietatem caritatis suae erga *hominem lapsum* commendare, ut affectus nostri excitentur ad amandum ipsum, dum attendimus nimiae dilectionis eius excessum." Bonaventure, *In III Sent.*, d. 1, a. 2, q. 2 (Quaracchi, 3:28).

45. On the structure of the work from the perspective of Christology, see Joshua Benson, "The Christology of the *Breviloquium*," in *A Companion to Bonaventure*, 251–57.

nes in hexaëmeron, a series of lectures Bonaventure gave at the end of his life and never completed.[46] In these, Bonaventure considers the Word incarnate as the hermeneutic key for Scripture, which he says is mainly about the work of restoration.[47]

Bonaventure's approach to the motive of the incarnation is important for at least two reasons. First, he consistently frames the question not by the use of a hypothetical such as "Would God have been incarnate if there had been no sin?" but instead by inquiry into the mystery's "chief reason" (*ratio praecipua*).[48] Second, he thereby avoids an adversarial either-or approach. He sees the Word incarnate as the mediator who simultaneously redeems and perfects. The *exitus* is twofold: the procession of creatures from God and their fall into sin. The corresponding *reditus* that Christ accomplishes is, therefore, also twofold in his work of perfecting and restoring.

Further, Bonaventure's own preference for a *felix culpa* theology of the incarnation grows out of his embrace of three key principles. First, he insists that the God-man perfects the universe in a way that is over and above its natural perfection or even the perfections of grace and glory. Second, he is committed to the non-necessity of the incarnation and, therefore, relies on authority as the determining factor in deciding the chief reason for the mystery. Third, Bonaventure is sensitive to the fact that even if an absolutely decreed incarnation seems more straightforward and logical, the piety of faith focuses on the mystery as essentially a response to human sin.

Having highlighted developments from Anselm to Bonaventure, I will now turn to Thomas Aquinas and John Duns Scotus. Because they defined the terms of the discussion and its two main sides for the centuries that followed, I will present their views in greater detail.

---

46. Schlosser, "Bonaventure: Life and Works," 52–55.
47. Bonaventure, *Collationes in hexaëmeron: Redactio A*, Principium, chap. 3, nos. 10–12, in *Collationes in hexaëmeron et Bonaventuriana quaedam selecta*, Bibliotheca Franciscana scholastica medii aevi 8 (Ad Claras Aquas [Quaracchi]: Ex typographia Collegii S. Bonaventurae, 1934), 38.
48. Cf. Francesco Saverio Pancheri, *The Universal Primacy of Christ*, trans. Juniper B. Carol (Front Royal, Va.: Christendom Publications, 1984), 20, 24.

THOMAS AQUINAS

Thomas Aquinas addresses the rationale for Christ's incarnation directly in three places: his commentary on the third book of the *Sentences*, his commentary on 1 Timothy, and the *Tertia pars* of the *Summa theologiae*. His reasoning and theological argumentation remain fundamentally the same throughout these works, which span from the beginning to the end of his career, but his conviction that the incarnation was most likely conditioned on sin does grow stronger.[49]

Commentary on the *Sentences*

Aquinas lectured on the *Sentences* of Peter Lombard in Paris around 1252–55, the written form of his commentary on the four books appearing by 1256.[50] In this commentary, he asks "whether, if man had not sinned, God would have been incarnate."[51] Drawing partly on Robert and Alexander, Aquinas then proceeds to put forth seven arguments for why God would have become incarnate even if there had been no sin.[52] First, the perfection of God's work requires that what is last be joined to the principle in a kind of complete circle.[53]

---

49. Cf. Goergen, "On the Motive of the Incarnation," 530–36.

50. Jean-Pierre Torrell, *Saint Thomas Aquinas*, trans. Robert Royal, rev. ed., vol. 1, *The Person and His Work* (Washington, D.C.: The Catholic University of America Press, 2005), 39–45, 328, 424–25.

51. "Utrum si homo non peccasset, Deus incarnatus fuisset." Thomas Aquinas, *Super III Sent.*, d. 1, q. 1, a. 3, in *S. Thomae Aquinatis, doctoris communis ecclesiae, Scriptum super Sententiis magistri Petri Lombardi*, ed. Maria Fabianus Moos, new ed. (Paris: Sumptibus P. Lethielleux, 1933), 3:19. Even if the title was added by the editor, it is derived directly from the introduction to the article: "Ad tertium sic proceditur. Videtur quod si homo non peccasset Deus incarnatus fuisset."

52. *Super III Sent.*, d. 1, q. 1, a. 3, obj. 1–7, n. 52 (Moos, 3:19–21). In these objections, Aquinas invokes Dt 32:4; Rom 1:20; Pseudo-Augustine, *De spiritu et anima*, chap. 9 (PL 40:785); *Glossa ordinaria* on Mt 3:15, in *Bibliorum sacrarum cum glossa ordinaria* (Venice, 1603), 5:77; and Bernard of Clairvaux, Sermon 1 on Advent, nos. 2–4 (Leclercq and Rochais, 4:162–64).

53. Aquinas gives no explicit reference, but he is evidently combining here two notions we have already seen in the argumentation of Robert Grosseteste. Cf. Aristotle, *On the Heavens*, 2.4.286b10–30; and Irenaeus of Lyon, *Adversus haereses* IV, chap. 20, no. 4 (SC 100:634).

Second, the incarnation is an expression of God's most perfect humility. Third, the infinite power, wisdom, and goodness of God should be expressed visibly through an infinite effect. Fourth, God does not deny a good of which the creature is capable, and humanity was capable of being assumed by God prior to sin. Fifth, we should not believe that man has gained such an advantage from sin. Sixth, *De spiritu et anima* asserts that man's total beatitude requires seeing the humanity of Christ. Seventh, as St. Bernard of Clairvaux, O. Cist. (1090–1153), says, the devil tempted man because he foresaw the incarnation, and so the incarnation must have been determined to occur prior to human sin.

Aquinas puts forth four arguments to the contrary.[54] First, he argues from an authority of Augustine on the verse "For the Son of man came to seek and to save the lost" (Lk 19:10); second, from a gloss of Augustine on the verse "Christ Jesus came into the world to save sinners" (1 Tm 1:15); third, from the verse "he himself likewise partook of the same nature, that through death he might destroy him who has the power of death" (Heb 2:14), seeing as death came through sin; fourth, from the line "Being born has been no good to us had there not been the good of being redeemed" of the *Exsultet*.[55]

Aquinas's own response is:

> We should say that the truth of this question can be known by him alone who was born and "was offered because he willed it" (Is 53:7).[56] For what depends on the divine will alone is unknown to us except to the extent that it becomes known to us through the authorities of the saints, to whom God has revealed his will.

> And because in the canon of Scripture and the statements of the saints giving exposition on it, this is the only reason assigned for the incarnation, that is, the redemption of man from the slavery of sin, some say with prob-

---

54. *Super III Sent.*, d. 1, q. 1, a. 3, s.c. 1–4, nos. 53–56 (Moos, 3:21–22). Aquinas cites Mt 18:11; Rom 5:12; Heb 2:14; 1 Tm 1:15; Augustine, Sermon 8 *de verbis Apostoli*, Sermon 174 (PL 38:940) and Sermon 9 *de verbis Apostoli*, Sermon 175 (PL 38:945); and the *Exsultet*.
55. "Nihil nobis nasci profuit, nisi redimi profuisset."
56. As it reads in the Vulgate.

ability that if man had not sinned, the Son of God would not have been man. We also have this expressly from the words of Pope Leo, "For if man, made after the image and likeness of God, had remained in his honor, the creator of the world would not become a creature, nor would the everlasting become subject to temporality, nor would the Son of God equal to God the Father assume the form of a slave." (*Sermon on the Trinity*). Again, Augustine has: "For to what purpose would you bear for sinners the one who knows no sin, if there had not been anyone who had sinned? Or why would you become the mother of the savior if there were no need of salvation?" (*Prayer to the Blessed Virgin*). Again, on the passage "He will save his people" (Mt 1:21), Augustine says, "If man had not sinned, the virgin would not have borne."

But others say that since through the incarnation of the Son of God not only liberation from sin but also the exaltation of human nature and the consummation of the whole universe has been accomplished, even without there being sin, there would have been the incarnation for these reasons. And this, too, can be maintained with probability.[57]

---

57. "Dicendum quod hujus quaestionis veritatem solus ille scire potest qui natus et *oblatus est quia voluit*. (Is. 53, 7.) Ea enim quae ex sola voluntate divina pendent, nobis ignota sunt, nisi inquantum innotescunt per auctoritates sanctorum quibus Deus suam voluntatem revelavit.

"Et quia in canone Scripturae et in dictis sactorum expositorum, haec sola causa assignatur incarnationis, redemptio scilicet hominis a servitute peccati; ideo quidam probabiliter dicunt, quod si homo non peccasset, Filius Dei homo non fuisset. Quod etiam ex verbis Leonis Papae in *Sermone de Trinitate*, expresse habetur. *Si enim*, inquit, *homo ad imaginem et similitudinem Dei factus, in suo honore mansisset, Creator mundi creatura non fieret, aut sempiternus temporalitatem subiret, aut aequalis Deo Patri Dei Filius formam servi assumeret*. Item Augustinus in oratione ad beatam Virginem: *Ut quid enim nescium peccati pro peccatoribus pareres, si deesset qui peccasset? Aut quid mater fieres Salvatoris, si nulla esset indigentia salutis?* Item super illud Mat., I: *Ipse enim salvum faciet populum suum*, Augustinus: *Si homo non peccasset, Virgo non peperisset.*

"Alii vero dicunt quod, cum per incarnationem Filii Dei non solum liberatio a peccato, sed etiam humanae naturae exaltatio et totius universi consummatio facta sit, etiam peccato non existente, propter has causas incarnatio fuisset. Et hoc etiam probabiliter sustineri potest." *Super III Sent.*, d. 1, q. 1, a. 3, nn. 57–58 (Moos, 3:22).

The quotation from Leo is actually from his Tractate 77 on Pentecost (CCSL 138A:488). The prayer attributed to Augustine is edited as *Oratio ad Beatam Mariam Virginem*, in *Bibliotheca Casinensis seu codicum manuscriptorum qui in tabulario Casinensi asservantur series*, ed. Monks of the Order of Saint Benedict (Monte Casino: Ex typographia Casinensi, 1875), 2:329. I can find no source for the other quotation Aquinas attributes to Augustine.

The response articulates a key of Aquinas's theological method, one that he will hold to throughout his career: what depends on the free will of God alone is unknown to us unless God reveals it. The incarnation is a preeminent example of this, and so, despite its tremendous fittingness, we cannot demonstrate the fact of the incarnation by aprioristic arguments but instead only come to knowledge of it by revelation.[58] Because the incarnation is truly non-necessary, no analysis of the created order and no knowledge of God's being and attributes will prove that God has willed or would will the incarnation. Thus, it is on the basis of Scripture and the expositions of the saints that Aquinas holds it as more probable that the incarnation would not have occurred if there had been no sin. However, as we just saw, he also identifies the contrary opinion as probable.

At this point, we should note that in the objections and the response, Aquinas mixes two ways of framing his inquiry: what God would have done *if Adam had not sinned*, and what God would have done *if there had been no sin*. The reason Aquinas uses these interchangeably is that he also holds that the incarnation is more principally a response to original sin, not actual sins.[59] Later theologians, including the Salmanticenses, will distinguish these inquiries.

Aquinas's replies to the objections elucidate his own sense of the non-necessity of the incarnation, a view he shares with Bonaventure.[60] To the first, he says that while the perfection of the universe does indeed consist in the joining of the last to the first principle, this need not be a personal union. To the second, he distinguishes

---

58. In point of fact, Aquinas thinks that in the state of original justice Adam did have faith in the future incarnation without knowing that the incarnation would be essentially a response to his own fall. *ST* II-II, q. 2, a. 7, co. (Leonine, 8:34); and III, q. 1, a. 3, ad 5 (Leonine, 11:14). All citations to Aquinas's *Summa theologiae* are taken from vols. 4–12 of *Opera omnia iussu impensaque Leonis XIII. P. M. edita* (Rome: Ex Typographia Polyglotta S. C. de Propaganda Fide, 1888–1906).

59. *Super III Sent.*, d. 1, q. 1, a. 2, ad 6, nos. 43–46 (Moos, 3:17–18); and *ST* III, q. 1, a. 4 (Leonine, 11:17).

60. *Super III Sent.*, d. 1, q. 1, a. 3, ad 1–7, nos. 59–65 (Moos, 3:22–24). Aquinas refers to Rom 5:20b and the *felix culpa* of the *Exsultet*. His first, third, fourth, and sixth replies in this article present arguments we have already encountered in Bonaventure.

that while humility is a perfect virtue in man, there need not be humility, properly speaking, in God, seeing as God truly is the highest and is independent. To the third, Aquinas says that God's infinite power, wisdom, and goodness can be arrived at from the consideration of even the least created thing: any finite effect reveals the infinite first cause. To the fourth, following Albert, he distinguishes natural potency from obediential potency. The latter need never be fulfilled, since the creature's natural perfection relies on its natural powers not being in vain, but it does not require that God do whatever he is capable of realizing in the creature above the natural order. To the fifth, Aquinas argues that "where sin increased, grace abounded all the more" (Rom 5:20) and cites the *felix culpa* of the *Exsultet* as evidence of the principle that nothing prevents God from bringing a greater good out of evil. To the sixth, he points out that the essence of beatitude is the vision of the divinity, whereas the bodily vision of Christ's humanity is an accidental aspect of beatitude. Finally, to the seventh, Aquinas says that even if the devil did foresee the incarnation, he may not have foreseen all its circumstances, just as he did not foresee his own fall. Foreknowledge of the event does not make the event unconditional.

In this way, Aquinas's sense of the super-gratuity of the incarnation as a gift becomes clear. The personal union of God and man in the Word incarnate is not the missing piece of the puzzle of creation whose outline can be clearly discerned in advance. Instead, it is a communication of God to the creature over and above any prior expectation. Further, there is nothing unfitting in the greater good's being conditioned on evil, so that the incarnation is both a greater blessing and essentially a response to human sin. Nevertheless, Aquinas goes on to give a reply on behalf of the opinion that the incarnation would have occurred absent sin.[61] The authorities, he says, could perhaps be explained as referring to the incarnation in passible flesh and not to the incarnation *simpliciter*.

---

61. *Super III Sent.*, d. 1, q. 1, a. 3, ad s.c., no. 66 (Moos, 3:24).

Commentary on 1 Timothy

Aquinas's commentary on 1 Timothy comes down to us in the form of a *reportatio* by Reginald of Piperno, OP (ca. 1230–90). It may derive from Aquinas's teaching in Rome from 1265–68, but this is not certain.[62] In his lecture on the passage "Christ Jesus came into the world to save sinners" (1 Tm 1:15b), Aquinas has occasion to ask: "If there had not been any sinners, does that mean he would not have been incarnate?"[63] Aquinas answers that most likely Christ would not have become incarnate in that event and, and he cites a passage from Augustine to this effect.[64]

Aquinas's full response is:

> I answer: This is clear enough from the words of the saints. But this question does not enjoy great authority, since God ordained what would happen with reference to the affairs that were going to happen. And we do not know what he would have ordained if he had not foreknown sin. Nevertheless, the authorities seem expressly to sound as if he would not have been incarnate if man had not sinned, and I myself lean more to this side.[65]

Once again we see Aquinas's caution and reliance on revelation for knowledge of God's free choices. The basis for his own opinion is still the "words of the saints," not *a priori* arguments. In contrast to his commentary on the *Sentences*, here Aquinas does not give any arguments for the contrary opinion, alluding to it only implicitly by his admission that what he is putting forward is only what "seems" to be the case and is the opinion to which he himself inclines.

---

62. Torrell, *Saint Thomas Aquinas*, 1:255, 340. Cf. Rafael Cai, introduction to *S. Thomae Aquinatis, doctoris angelici, super epistolas s. Pauli lectura*, 8th rev. ed. (Rome: Marietti, 1953), 1:vi–vii.

63. "Si nullus fuisset peccator, numquid incarnatus non fuisset?" *Super I ad Tim.*, chap. 1, l. 4, no. 40 (Cai, 2:219).

64. Sermon 9 *de verbis Apostoli*, Sermon 175 (PL 38:945).

65. "Respondeo. Dicendum est quod ex verbis sanctorum satis hoc patet. Sed haec quaestio non est magnae auctoritatis, quia Deus ordinavit fienda secundum quod res fiendae erant. Et nescimus quid ordinasset, si non praescivisset peccatum; nihilominus tamen auctoritates videntur expresse sonare quod non fuisset incarnatus, si non peccasset homo, in quam partem ego magis declino." *Super I ad Tim.*, chap. 1, l. 4, no. 40 (Cai, 2:219).

The *Tertia pars* of the *Summa theologiae*

In contrast to his commentary on the *Sentences* and his commentary on 1 Timothy, which were fruits of his class lectures, Aquinas's *Summa theologiae* was conceived of and executed from the beginning as a written work, an aid to the "beginners" (*incipientes*) famously referenced in its prologue. Aquinas probably began the *Tertia pars* in Paris in 1271 or 1272 and wrote the bulk of it in Naples in 1273.[66]

Aquinas introduces the *Tertia pars* in these words:

> Because our savior, the Lord Jesus Christ, "saving his people from their sins," as the angel bears witness, has shown us in himself the way of truth through which we can arrive at the blessedness of immortal life by rising, it is necessary that after the consideration of the last end of human life and of the virtues and vices, in order to consummate the whole business of theology, our consideration of the savior of all himself and of his benefits bestowed on the human race should follow.[67]

Already in these words, Aquinas presents the consideration of Christ the redeemer as the completion of the theological task. Thus, it is not surprising that he begins consideration of the incarnate redeemer by asking whether the incarnation was fitting (*ST* III, q. 1, a. 1), whether it was necessary (*ST* III, q. 1, a. 2), and then whether it would have occurred if man had not sinned (*ST* III, q. 1, a. 3).

Aquinas lays out five objections arguing that God would have become incarnate apart from sin.[68] First, Augustine says that the incarnation was for many other reasons, and where the cause remains the effect remains. Second, God's omnipotence should be manifested through an infinite effect, specifically the joining of God and man

---

66. Torrell, *Saint Thomas Aquinas*, 1:261, 329, 333.

67. "Quia Salvator noster Dominus Iesus Christus, teste Angelo, *populum suum salvum faciens a peccatis eorum*, viam veritatis nobis in seipso demonstravit, per quam ad beatitudinem immortalis vitae resurgendo pervenire possimus, necesse est ut, ad consummationem totius theologici negotii, post considerationem ultimi finis humanae vitae et virtutum ac vitiorum, de ipso omnium Salvatore ac beneficiis eius humano generi praestitis nostra consideratio subsequatur." *ST* III, prol. (Leonine, 11:5).

68. *ST* III, q. 1, a. 3, obj. 1–5 (Leonine, 11:13–14). In the objections, he appeals to Gen 2:23; Rom 1:4; Eph 1:9–10; Augustine, *De Trinitate* XIII, chap. 17 (CCSL 50A:412); and Augustine, *De nuptiis et concupiscentia* I, chap. 21 (CSEL 42:236).

(the last creature) for the perfection of the universe. Third, sin has not made human nature more capable of grace, and so human nature would have been capable of the grace of union without sin, and God does not deny a good of which the creature is capable. Fourth, God's predestination is eternal, and thus the predestination of the man Christ would have to be fulfilled even without sin. Fifth, the first man knew the mystery of the incarnation by revelation, but he could not have foreknown his own fall. As contrary arguments, Aquinas offers authorities already cited in his previous works.[69]

Thus, we see a reprisal of the arguments Aquinas noted in his commentary on the *Sentences*, though in slightly stronger and more condensed form. The new elements of greatest importance are the introduction of an authority from Augustine in the first objection; the combination of the argument from the manifestation of God's infinity and the argument from the perfection of the universe by the joining of the last to the first in the second objection; and the introduction of the argument from the predestination of Christ as man in the fourth objection. We also note that the argument in the fifth objection now centers on Adam's own knowledge of the future incarnation and not the devil's.

Aquinas's response in the body of the article is:

I answer: People have various opinions concerning this. For some say that even if man had not sinned, the Son of God would have been incarnate. But others assert the contrary. Their assertion seems more to warrant our assent. For what proceeds from the will of God alone above everything due to the creature can only become known to us insofar as it is handed down in sacred Scripture, through which the divine will becomes known. Hence, since in every place in sacred Scripture the reason for the incarnation is assigned on the basis of the first man's sin, it is more fittingly said that the work of the incarnation was ordained by God as a remedy for sin such that, if sin did not exist, there would not have been the incarnation. In any case, God's power is not limited to this. For, even if sin did not exist, God would have been able to become incarnate.[70]

---

69. Augustine, Sermon 29 *de verbis Domini*, Sermon 105 (PL 38:618–25) and Sermon 8 *de verbis Apostoli*, Sermon 174 (PL 38:940).

70. "Respondeo dicendum quod aliqui circa hoc diversimode opinantur. Quidam

This reply develops Aquinas's previous thought in several key ways. First, while acknowledging the existence of the contrary opinion and not asserting his own as absolute (*assentiendum videtur*), Aquinas does not give the contrary opinion as much probability or weight as he did in his commentary on the *Sentences*. Second, he refers only to the authority of Scripture and not to the statements of the saints. This may reflect his attention to the fact that in theological argumentation the Scriptures alone establish necessity, while the authorities of the saints are proper but only establish probability.[71] Third, Aquinas qualifies what depends on God's will alone as "above everything due to the creature," anticipating his reply to the third objection. Fourth, Aquinas begins to distinguish more clearly and explicitly two levels of contingency in the event of the incarnation.

This last point requires further explanation. Aquinas is addressing a question that is hypothetical in form: "Would God have been incarnate if man had not sinned?" At first glance, this may lead us to think that Aquinas is dealing with a purely unreal course of history, one without human sin. This is true as far as it goes, but it is not the whole picture. In point of fact, Aquinas is aware of two levels of contingency that need to be addressed: one within the present course of history and one underlying it.[72]

---

enim dicunt quod, etiam si homo non peccasset, Dei Filius fuisset incarnatus. Alii vero contrarium asserunt. Quorum assertioni magis assentiendum videtur. Ea enim quae ex sola Dei voluntate proveniunt, supra omne debitum creaturae, nobis innotescere non possunt nisi quatenus in sacra Scriptura traduntur, per quam divina voluntas innotescit. Unde, cum in sacra Scriptura ubique incarnationis ratio ex peccato primi hominis assignetur, convenientius dicitur incarnationis opus ordinatum esse a Deo in remedium peccati, ita quod, peccato non existente, incarnatio non fuisset. Quamvis potentia Dei ad hoc non limitetur: potuisset enim, etiam peccato non existente, Deus incarnari." *ST* III, q. 1, a. 3, co. (Leonine, 11:14).

71. *ST* I, q. 1, a. 8, ad 2 (Leonine, 4:22).

72. See Bonnefoy, "La question hypothétique," 340; and Reginald Garrigou-Lagrange, "De motivo Incarnationis: Examen recentium objectionum contra doctrinam S. Thomae III^a, q. 1, a. 3," in *Acta Pont. Academiae Romanae S. Thomae Aquinatis et Religionis Catholicae*, Nova series 10 (Rome: Academia Romana S. Thomae Aquinatis, 1945), 9–10. It later becomes customary to clarify the inquiry as "by virtue of the present decree" (*ex vi praesentis decreti*) or "by virtue of another decree" (*ex vi alterius decreti*). Theologians we

Sin, like all human acts, is a fundamentally contingent event. It does not proceed from the free will necessarily but freely. Thus, the sin that Adam committed was contingent in the actual course of history. This is an example of the contingency contained *within* the present state of affairs. In this article of the *Summa*, this is what Aquinas is primarily addressing. In the present state of affairs, did the incarnation that has actually occurred depend on the sin of Adam as on its necessary condition, so that if the latter had not occurred the former would also not have occurred?

There is, however, another level of contingency, one with which Aquinas is not immediately concerned in terms of the incarnation's connection to sin. This is the contingency underlying the entire present course of history, the course that includes creation, the permission of sin, God's foreknowledge of actual sin, and the redemptive incarnation. Contingency undergirds all of these events taken together because God could have chosen to realize another complete set of events or not to create anything at all. This is what Aquinas alludes to when he concludes his response by affirming God's absolute power to have acted otherwise (*potuisset*). And in his commentary on 1 Timothy, Aquinas says, "And we do not know what he would have ordained if he had not foreknown sin" (*Et nescimus quid ordinasset, si non praescivisset peccatum*). In contrast, when Aquinas inquires within the present order as actually decreed and foreseen, his explanation is that "God ordained what would happen with reference to the affairs that were going to happen" (*Deus ordinavit fienda secundum quod res fiendae erant*).

An example may clarify the point. Suppose a man travels to Rome on business. While in the city, he also does some sightseeing, visits an old friend who lives there, and goes shopping. We can ask two distinct questions of the traveler. The first is about his actual trip: would he have gone to Rome apart from the business? This is the direct inquiry into whether business was the *sine qua non* for

---

will consider in subsequent chapters, including the Salmanticenses, even devote separate inquiries to these.

the trip. However, we can also ask whether, if he had not had any business in Rome, he would have made plans for a trip to go there for some other reason. This second inquiry is not about the plan of the traveler's actual trip but instead about what other sort of trip he might have planned.

Similarly, Aquinas's question about whether God would have become incarnate absent sin is not about merely possible incarnations in merely possible orders of history. Antecedently, God *could have* created a universe in which the statement "Christ's coming does not depend on Adam's sin" would be true. What interests Aquinas is whether it is true in our present universe. The hypothetical form of the inquiry is particularly effective for getting at the question of contingency, but it also requires careful reading lest we think that Aquinas is addressing purely unreal events. Further indications that Aquinas is investigating the actual event by means of the hypothetical question are that in the *Summa* he refers to the remediation of sin as the *ratio* for the incarnation and that in his commentary on the *Sentences* he calls it the *causa* of the incarnation. Aquinas's attention is on humanity's need for redemption as an element of God's providential plan for the present order.

I turn, then, to Aquinas's responses to the objections in the *Summa*.[73] To the first, he says that all the other reasons (*causae*) assigned for the incarnation pertain to the remediation of sin. To the second, he replies that the infinity of divine power is belied in the production of any creature, given that it is from nothing. To the third, he distinguishes natural from obediential potency and adds that nothing prevents God's giving humanity a greater gift after sin than before. To the fourth, he argues that predestination presupposes the foreseeing of what is going to be (*futurorum*). Thus, the predestination of Christ as man presupposes foresight of human sin. To the fifth,

---

73. *ST* III, q. 1, a. 3, ad 1–5 (Leonine, 11:14). Aquinas appeals to Rom 5:20b; Augustine, *In Iohannis euangelium tractatus*, tract. 2, nos. 15–16 (CCSL 36:19); and the *felix culpa* of the *Exsultet*.

Aquinas explains that God can reveal the effect to someone without revealing the cause. Thus, Adam could know that the incarnation would occur without knowing that he himself was going to sin.

The reply to the fourth objection deserves one further comment. Here, Aquinas discusses the predestination of Christ as an individual man. Aquinas holds that the term of this predestination is primarily natural filiation from God through the grace of union.[74] This is to say that God predestined Christ, considered in his humanity, to be his natural Son. Aquinas explains in this reply that this predestination presupposes God's foreknowledge of human sin. In other words, God's destining the man Christ to natural divine sonship includes the consideration of sin. This question of the relationship between Christ's predestination and humanity's fall, considered in terms of conceptual priority, will become the whole starting point for John Duns Scotus, to whom we are about to turn.

Conclusion to Aquinas

As we have seen from his commentary on the *Sentences*, his commentary on 1 Timothy, and the *Summa theologiae*, Aquinas holds as more probable and worthy of assent the opinion that the incarnation is essentially redemptive, that it is a greater good than man had prior to sin, and yet that it is conditioned on sin. He also mentions this in passing in the *De veritate*, where he comments on "the end of the incarnation, which has principally occurred for the liberation of human beings from sin."[75]

Aquinas's governing principle throughout is his distinction of fittingness from necessity and the corresponding methodological reliance on scriptural authority. The incarnation is a perfection over and

---

74. *ST* III, q. 24, a. 1 (Leonine, 11:269–70).
75. "Quantum ad finem incarnationis, quae quidem principaliter facta est propter hominum liberationem a peccato." Thomas Aquinas, *Quaestiones disputatae de veritate*, q. 29, a. 4, ad 5, no. 5, in *Opera omnia iussu impensaque Leonis XIII. P. M. edita* (Rome: Editori di San Tommaso, 1970–76), 22:860. He had alluded to the existence of various opinions on this matter in the reply to the third objection of this same article.

above what the universe requires or even what human redemption requires, and so God is free to decree it as he wills. Theology, then, only has access to that decision through what God reveals about it.

JOHN DUNS SCOTUS

The difficulty in establishing the authentic thought of John Duns Scotus through his extant texts is well known. "The works of Scotus have suffered more than those of any other Scholastic thinker from confused transmission and damaging misattributions."[76] From his time at Oxford, we have Scotus's *Lectura* on the *Sentences* of Peter Lombard, his own notes of his earlier lectures. Scotus later reworked these into his fuller *Ordinatio* on the *Sentences*. From his time at the University of Paris, beginning in 1302, we have Scotus's *Reportatio* on the *Sentences*. The chronological relationship between the *Ordinatio* and the Paris *Reportatio* remains uncertain.[77]

Lectura

In his *Lectura* on the third book of *Sentences*, Scotus asks whether Christ was predestined to be the Son of God. This was a standard inquiry for theologians of this time period, and here we should remark briefly on why this was the case. Theologians of the high Middle Ages were following a pattern set by Augustine and taken up by Peter Lombard when they asked whether Christ was predestined to be the Son of God.[78] Augustine and Lombard, however, were dealing with the interpretation of a single scriptural passage: "[God's

---

76. Stephen D. Dumont, "John Duns Scotus," in *A Companion to Philosophy in the Middle Ages*, 354.

77. Scotus's *Ordinatio* may represent the later stage of this thought, but it is also possible that he began work on it prior to leaving Oxford for Paris. Dumont, "John Duns Scotus," 354.

78. See Augustine, *De praedestinatione sanctorum*, chap. 15 (PL 44:981–83); and Peter Lombard, *Liber tertius Sententiarum*, throughout Distinctions 7 and 10, in *Magistri Petri Lombardi Parisiensis episcopi Sententiae in IV libris distinctae*, Spicilegium Bonaventurianum 5 (Grottaferrata [Rome]: Editiones Collegii S. Bonaventurae ad Claras Aquas, 1981), 2:59–66, 72–77.

Son,] who was predestinated the Son of God in power, according to the spirit of sanctification, by the resurrection of our Lord Jesus Christ from the dead" (Rom 1:4 [Douay]). In point of fact, however, the word at issue in the verse cited is universally attested to be ὁρισθέντος ("declared" or "designated") and not προορισθέντος ("predestined") in the Greek New Testament.[79] In the Old Latin versions, however, as well as in the Vulgate, the verse reads: "*qui praedestinatus est Filius Dei in virtute secundum Spiritum sanctificationis ex resurrectione mortuorum Iesu Christi Domini Nostri.*"[80] The difficulty that the Scholastic theologians had to deal with was how the Son of God could be predestined to be the Son of God.

This question gives Scotus the opportunity to work out whether Christ as a person was predestined or whether his human nature was predestined and, further, whether he was first predestined to hypostatic union or to glory. Scotus answers that Christ's humanity (not his person) was first predestined to great glory and second to hypostatic union, since the hypostatic union is what brings about such great glory.[81] In this way, he conceives of the hypostatic union as a means for the glorification of Christ's humanity, and the end is logically prior to the means in intention.

This is the context in which Scotus asks whether Christ's predestination hinged on the human race's need of redemption. As Daniel Horan, OFM, explains, "Scotus does not begin his effort, nor is he

79. See the critical apparatus for Romans 1:4 in Eberhard Nestle, Barbara Aland, Kurt Aland, Johannes Karavidopoulos, Carlo M. Martini, and Bruce M. Metzger, eds., *Novum Testamentum Graece et Latine*, 4th ed. (Stuttgart: Deutsche Bibelgesellschaft, 2002).

80. Robert Weber and Roger Gryson, eds., *Biblia sacra Vulgata*, 5th ed. (Stuttgart: Deutsche Bibelgesellschaft, 2007). The *Nova Vulgata*, in contrast, reads: "qui constitutus est Filius Dei in virtute secundum Spiritum sanctificationis ex resurrectione mortuorum, Iesu Christo Domino nostro." Aquinas adverts to the discrepancy, remarking that "all the Latin books" have *qui praedestinatus*, in his *Super epistolam ad Romanos lectura*, chap. 1, l. 3, no. 50 (Cai, 1:11).

81. John Duns Scotus, *Lectura in tertium librum Sententiarum*, d. 7, q. 3, n. 77, in *Doctoris subtilis et Mariani B. Ioannis Duns Scoti Ordinis Fratrum Minorum opera omnia* [...] *studio et cura Commissionis Scotisticae ad fidem codicum edita* (Vatican City: Typis Vaticanis, 2003), 20:214.

primarily concerned, with an alternate or hypothetical order. Rather, Scotus's approach begins with the Incarnation as factual premise."[82] From this starting point, Scotus reasons as follows:

> It seems to me that we should say that the predestination of none of the elect has had an occasionary cause. And if the least of the elect was not predestined on account of the fall and restoration of someone, much less did the predestination of Christ, who is the head of the elect, have an occasionary cause such as the fall of the human race. Rather, if the human race had not so fallen, he still would have been predestined with a nature united to the Word.[83]

This is to say that in God's "decision-making process," election, especially the election of Christ, comes before sin is taken into account.

Parsing out the logical steps of this process is key to Scotus's method. Thus, in Distinction 19 of the *Lectura*, Scotus inquires about Christ's merit, and on this occasion, he summarizes the order of conceptual stages in God's knowing and willing as follows:

> First, God willed glory for the determinate number of the elect, such that the first thing he willed for the elect was final joining to himself as to the last end of beatitude. Second, he ordained final grace in the second *instans naturae*,[84] without which he arranged not to give beatitude. In the third *instans*, he foresaw that they would fall in Adam. In the fourth *instans*, he foresaw the remedy that he most of all arranged to take place through Christ's passion, which could please him on behalf of all—on whose behalf the first man was displeasing—more than [the first man] displeased

---

82. Horan, "How Original Was Scotus on the Incarnation?," 385. See also Enrique del Sagrado Corazón, "Juan Duns Escoto en la doctrina de los Salmanticenses sobre el motivo de la Encarnación," in *De doctrina Ioannis Duns Scoti: Acta Congressus Scotistici internationalis Oxonii et Edimburgi 11–17 sept. 1966 celebrati*, Studia Scholastico-Scotistica 4 (Rome: Ercolano, 1968), 498.

83. "Videtur mihi dicendum quod nullius electi praedestinatio habuit causam occasionariam; et si minimus electus non fuit praedestinatus propter lapsum ac reparationem alicuius, multo fortius nec praedestinatio Christi, qui est caput electorum habuit causam occasionariam, ut lapsum generis humani; immo si genus humanum non fuisset ita lapsum, adhuc fuisset praedestinatus et natura unita Verbo." Scotus, *Lectura* III, d. 7, q. 3, no. 76 (Vatican, 20:213).

84. I will explain *instans naturae* further in the next chapter. Suffice it to say for the present that it means a nonchronological, conceptual moment.

him. Hence Christ was first foreseen as a comprehensor and then as a wayfarer.[85]

In this way, Scotus insists that "Christ's soul was predestined from eternity to the greatest glory, not because others had been foreseen to fall, but to enjoy God."[86] God wills "with an orderly willing" (*ordinata volitione*), which means willing the end prior to the means, and this implies that his willing the glory of the elect, particularly Christ, is conceptually prior to his willing Christ's passion as the means to that glory.[87]

Ordinatio

In his *Ordinatio* on the third book of the *Sentences*, Scotus considers the relation of God's willing Christ to his knowledge of human sin again by looking at Christ's predestination.[88] He phrases the inquiry

---

85. "Primo voluit Deus gloriam determinato numero electorum, ita quod primum quod voluit electis fuit ultimata coniunctio ad se ut ad finem ultimum beatificum; secundo, ordinavit gratiam finalem, in secundo instanti naturae, sine qua disposuit non dare beatitudinem; et in tertio instanti praevidit lapsuros in Adam; in quarto vero instanti praevidit remedium, quod potissime disposuit fieri per passionem Christi, quae plus pro omnibus potuit placare—pro quibus displicuit primus homo—quam ipse displicuit. Unde Christus prius praevisus est ut comprehensor, et postea ut viator." Scotus, *Lectura* III, d. 19, q. 1, no. 21 (Vatican, 21:32–33). Different schemata—to similar effect as far as the primacy of Christ is concerned—can be found also in John Duns Scotus, *Reportata Parisiensia: Liber tertius* [henceforth *Reportatio Parisiensis* III], d. 7, q. 4, no. 5, in *Joannis Duns Scoti doctoris subtilis, Ordinis Minorum, opera omnia* […], new ed. (Paris: Apud Ludovicum Vivès, 1894), 23:303; and *Quaestiones in tertium librum Sententiarum*, d. 19, q. 1, no. 6 (Vivès, 14:714). See also *Quaestiones in tertium librum Sententiarum*, d. 32, q. 1, no. 6 (Vivès, 15:432–33).

86. "Anima Christi praedestinata fuit ab aeterno ad maximam gloriam, non quia alii praevisi erant cadere, sed ut frueretur Deo." Scotus, *Lectura* III, d. 19, q. 1, no. 20 (Vatican, 21:32).

87. Scotus, *Lectura* III, d. 19, q. 1, no. 20 (Vatican, 21:32). There is a resonance in Scotus's argument with Bonaventure, *In III Sent.*, d. 1, a. 2, q. 2, s.c. 5 (Quaracchi, 3:22–23), where the Seraphic Doctor raises the objection against his opinion that Christ's coming should not be an occasioned good and that because Christ is a greater good than human redemption, he should be willed more principally than human redemption.

88. John Duns Scotus, *Ordinatio* III, d. 7, q. 3, nos. 55–72, in *Doctoris subtilis et Mariani B. Ioannis Duns Scoti Ordinis Fratrum Minorum opera omnia* […] *studio et cura Commissionis Scotisticae ad fidem codicum edita* (Vatican City: Typis Vaticanis, 2006–2007), 9:284–91.

in these terms: "Whether this predestination necessarily has the fall of human nature as its prerequisite?—which is what many authorities seem to say, sounding as if the Son of God never would have been incarnate if man had not fallen."[89] Scotus answers:

> Without prejudice, it can be said that since anyone's predestination to glory naturally precedes, on the part of the object, the foreknowledge of anyone's sin or damnation, according to the opinion last stated in Distinction 41 of Book 1, all the more is this true of the predestination of that soul that was predestined to utmost glory. For generally, one who wills in an orderly way seems first to will what is closer to the end, and thus, just as [God] wills glory to someone prior to grace, so also among the predestined—to whom he wills glory—he seems in an orderly way to will first glory to the one whom he wills to be close to the end and thus to this soul.[90]

Election always precedes consideration of sin—and most of all in the case of Christ. If God predestines Peter to glory prior to foreseeing Peter's merits or demerits, then he also predestines Christ prior to consideration of humanity's fall. This sets Scotus against Aquinas, who, as we saw, says expressly that God's predestining Christ takes sin into account. As for the "many authorities" who seem to say that Christ's predestination had the fall of humanity as its necessary condition, Scotus says that they can be interpreted as meaning that Christ would not have come *as redeemer* if there had been no sin.[91]

Scotus then goes on to give several arguments as to why redemption does not seem to be the single necessary condition for the in-

---

89. "Utrum ista praedestinatio praeexigat necessario lapsum naturae humanae,—quod videntur sonare multae auctoritates, quae sonant Filium Dei numquam fuisse incarnatum si homo non cecidisset." Scotus, *Ordinatio* III, d. 7, q. 3, no. 60 (Vatican, 9:286).

90. "Sine praeiudicio potest dici quod cum praedestinatio cuiuscumque ad gloriam praecedat ex parte obiecti naturaliter praescientiam peccati vel damnationis cuiuscumque, secundum opinionem ultimam dictam distinctionem 41 I libri, multo magis est hoc verum de praedestinatione illius animae quae praedestinabatur ad summam gloriam: universaliter enim, ordinate volens prius videtur velle hoc quod est fini propinquius, et ita, sicut prius vult gloriam alicui quam gratiam, ita etiam inter praedestinatos—quibus vult gloriam—ordinate prius videtur velle gloriam illi quem vult esse proximum fini, et ita huic animae." Scotus, *Ordinatio* III, d. 7, q. 3, no. 61 (Vatican, 9:287).

91. Scotus, *Ordinatio* III, d. 7, q. 3, no. 62 (Vatican, 9:287–88).

carnation.⁹² First, the glory of Christ's soul is a greater good than the redemption of the whole human race. Second, it is not plausible for such a great good to be occasioned by a lesser good. Third, if the incarnation were contingent on sin, then God would have predestined Adam to as great a good as Christ, which is implausible. Fourth, it would even follow that in predestining Adam to glory, God foresaw Adam's sin prior to predestining Christ to glory, but we should not say that God predestines one man to glory only because another is going to fall. Scotus warns here against the danger in rejoicing over another's fall.⁹³

I noted above that Aquinas uses the hypothetical form of inquiry to get at whether the actual incarnation is essentially redemptive or not. To this extent, Scotus and Aquinas have the same concern: to investigate the intelligibility of the historical incarnation. Yet their approaches clearly differ. In part, Scotus is more ambitious than Aquinas in assigning parameters for how God could freely will the incarnation. This is not to say that Scotus believes the fact of the incarnation could be arrived at deductively but simply to say that, for him, given that the incarnation has indeed occurred, we can reasonably reach some conclusions about the kind of motivation that God must have had for it. Thus, as Richard Cross puts it, "Scotus argues that natural reason will allow us to gain some insight into what God's decision-making process must look like."⁹⁴ This is why Scotus's arguments hinge on his understanding of God as one who wills in an orderly way (*ordinate volens*).⁹⁵ Still, we must not forget that Scotus

92. Scotus, *Ordinatio* III, d. 7, q. 3, nos. 63–67 (Vatican, 9:288–89).

93. He says, "Et nullus est praedestinatus tantum quia alius praevisus est casurus, ut ita nullum oporteat gaudere de lapsu alterius." Scotus, *Ordinatio* III, d. 7, q. 3, no. 67 (Vatican, 9:289). Juniper B. Carol, OFM (1911–90), points out that Scotus is not arguing here that anyone *would have to* take pleasure in another's fall but is merely pointing out that there would be a danger in rejoicing over another's sin if the predestination of one depended on the fall of another. Juniper B. Carol, *Why Jesus Christ? Thomistic, Scotistic and Conciliatory Perspectives* (Manassas, Va.: Trinity Communications, 1986), 251–52.

94. Richard Cross, *Duns Scotus*, Great Medieval Thinkers (Oxford: Oxford University Press, 1999), 128.

95. On the foundational character of order for Scotus, see also Pancheri, *Universal Primacy of Christ*, 42–44.

prefaces his own opinion with the disclaimer *sine praeiuducio*, meaning that he does not wish to rule out the contrary opinion altogether.

Paris Reportatio

There is not yet a critical edition of Scotus's Paris *Reportatio* on the third book of the *Sentences*. With this caveat, I will give an overview of the text available in the Wadding edition.[96] Here, as before, Scotus's treatment of Christ's predestination leads him to ask about its relationship to other predestinations.[97]

He begins by relating the opinion that "man's fall is the necessary reason for this predestination."[98] Rejecting that God first saw that Adam was going to fall and then saw Christ's humanity as going to be assumed and then glorified, Scotus says: "Yet I say that the fall was not the cause of Christ's predestination. And, in fact, if neither the angels nor man had fallen, Christ would still have been predestined in this way, even if no one other than Christ alone had been going to be created."[99] This text differs from the *Ordinatio* in its articulation of Christ's primacy as a primacy of independence: Christ is not just the first of the elect; he would have been predestined even apart from them and from the rest of creation. In proof of this forceful claim, Scotus offers three arguments that we also saw in his *Ordinatio*. First, God wills in an orderly way (*ordinate volens*) and so wills the end prior to the means and what is closer to the end prior to what is farther from it. Thus, he wills Christ's soul prior to all other created goods. Second, God predestines the elect prior to the reprobation of the wicked, so that the fall of one is not the cause of

---

96. This is the text of the so called *Reportatio Parisiensis* III-A. The B, C, and D variants of the *Reportatio Parisiensis* on the third book of the *Sentences* have not yet been edited.

97. Scotus, *Reportatio Parisiensis* III-A, d. 7, q. 4, no. 4 (Vivès, 23:303).

98. "Dicitur quod lapsus hominis est ratio necessaria hujus praedestinationis." Scotus, *Reportatio Parisiensis* III-A, d. 7, q. 4, no. 4 (Vivès, 23:303).

99. "Dico tamen quod lapsus non fuit causa praedestinationis Christi, imo si nec fuisset Angelus lapsus, nec homo, adhuc fuisset Christus sic praedestinatus, imo, et si non fuissent creandi alii quam solus Christus." Scotus, *Reportatio Parisiensis* III-A, d. 7, q. 4, no. 4 (Vivès, 23:303).

another's election. Thus, Christ was predestined prior to God's foreseeing the fall. Third, if the fall were the cause of Christ's predestination, it would follow that God's utmost work is only occasioned, for Christ's glory is greater than the whole work of redemption. This seems "quite unreasonable."[100]

Scotus again explains the authorities that seem to contradict him as meaning that Christ would not have come as redeemer in passible flesh.[101] And, in Distinction 19 of the Paris *Reportatio*, treating of Christ's merit, we find the same sequence of conceptual stages as we saw in the *Lectura* and with the same argumentation: God wills the end (Christ's glory) prior to the means (his passion).[102] Again, Scotus takes priority to imply independence, so that God willed Christ's glory regardless of whether the passion would have been the means to it. Subsequent theologians will challenge this presumption.

Conclusion to Scotus

Scotus influences the discussion about the rationale for the incarnation in at least two key ways. First, he couches everything in terms of logical priority and posteriority (the *ordinate volens* principle). Second, his methodology therefore relies on articulating sequential conceptual stages in God's knowledge and will. Theologians who come after Scotus usually adopt this method and enumerate sequences of such stages as a way to describe God's plan. This leads them, in turn, to see the hypothetical question of whether Christ would have come apart from sin as practically equivalent to the question of whether God decreed Christ *before* taking sin into account or *after* taking sin into account. For theologians after Scotus, discussing the rationale for the incarnation means discussing the ordinal position of Christ in a logical sequence.

---

100. "Valde irrationabile." Scotus, *Reportatio Parisiensis* III-A, d. 7, q. 4, no. 4 (Vivès, 23:303).
101. Scotus, *Reportatio Parisiensis* III-A, d. 7, q. 4, no. 5 (Vivès, 23:303).
102. Scotus, *Reportatio Parisiensis* III-A, d. 19, q. 1, no. 7 (Vivès, 23:404).

CONCLUSION

This chapter has shown how key theologians from Anselm to Scotus explored the reason for Christ's incarnation. Rupert of Deutz, Robert Grosseteste, Guerric of Saint-Quentin, Albert the Great, and Thomas Aquinas raise a hypothetical question: "Would God have become incarnate if there had been no sin?"). In contrast, Alexander of Hales asks: "Would there still have been a fittingness or benefit to a nonredemptive incarnation?" Bonaventure, in turn, puts the inquiry in terms of the "chief reason" (*ratio praecipua*) for the mystery. Scotus looks at the logical relationship of Christ's predestination to God's other works.

On the most basic level these approaches amount to the same inquiry. For example, Aquinas also refers to the *ratio* or *causa* of the incarnation, and Bonaventure also speaks in hypothetical terms in the course of his treatment. Still, the emphasis given by the way the question is framed does color the issue. Bonaventure's *ratio praecipua* approach focuses on the concrete event of the incarnation while seeking to appreciate the relation of its various facets to one another, whereas the hypothetical approach of Albert and Aquinas sharpens the distinct aspects of the mystery and allows for a clearer response as to their relative importance and separability. Alexander's approach is more generic and really only establishes that a nonredemptive incarnation would not be unfitting and would not be useless. Scotus approaches the issue from the perspective of Christ's predestination, applying his principle that God must will in an orderly way (*ordinate volens*). This leads to a logical sequence of stages describing the conceptual interplay between God's knowledge and will. The result is that Scotus translates the hypothetical form of the inquiry "Would God have become incarnate if there had been no sin?" into the question of whether in the concrete order God predestined Christ logically prior to foreseeing human sin. Earlier theologians, including Aquinas,[103] dealt somewhat with the relationship of

---

103. Aquinas deals with the logical priority of divine foreknowledge vis-à-vis Christ's

Christ's predestination and human sin from the perspective of logical priority and posteriority, but Scotus makes logical order foundational.

For Aquinas, God's decision to send Christ seems to be essentially a response to sin according to Scripture. For Scotus, God predestines Christ prior to any other considerations and then, once sin becomes a factor, specifies that Christ will be redeemer through his passion. In this way, the hypothetical question (Aquinas) and the question of logical order (Scotus) come together: either God wills Christ prior to considering sin, or he does not. If he does, then Christ's coming does not depend on sin, and if he does not, then it does. With the issue cast in these terms, the polarization of the Thomistic and Scotistic schools was sure to follow.

---

predestination in *ST* III, q. 1, a. 3, ad 4 (Leonine, 11:14). This should be read in conjunction with *ST* III, q. 24, a. 4 (Leonine, 11:274), where Aquinas explains how Christ's predestination is the cause of ours.

2

Daring Replies

Late Medieval and Early Modern Themes

From the fourteenth century onward, the Thomistic and Scotistic schools engaged each other directly. By this time, the missteps of the preceding era (e.g., arguments based on numerology, such as those of Robert Grosseteste and Alexander of Hales) had been purged and the terms of the discussion clarified. The number and length of writings on the rationale for the incarnation grew tremendously. The Thomistic and Scotistic schools refined their arguments and marshalled scriptural and patristic authorities like never before.

Debate over the Immaculate Conception also contributed to the discussion over the relation of Christ's coming to human redemption. Generally speaking, those maintaining that the Blessed Virgin Mary was free from any debt of contracting original sin tended to be Scotistic, whereas others tended to hold that the event of the incarnation depended on sin.[1] Growing magisterial support for the Im-

---

1. Trent Pomplun, "Baroque Catholic Theologies of Christ and Mary," in *The Oxford Handbook of Early Modern Theology, 1600–1800* (Oxford: Oxford University Press, 2016), 114–15. For a catalog of various positions, see Juniper B. Carol, *A History of the Controversy over the "debitum peccati,"* Franciscan Institute Publications, Theology Series 9 (St. Bonaventure, N.Y.: Franciscan Institute, 1978).

maculate Conception and the growing force of the best arguments on both sides led some thinkers to adopt more synthetic positions in an effort to preserve the best insights of each camp.

The Salmanticenses exemplify this trend. While they reject a complete reconciliation of the Thomistic and Scotistic views, they do articulate the Scotistic emphasis on Christ's primacy within a Thomistic framework. The developments of the fourteenth through sixteenth centuries, particularly in the work of theologians like Cajetan, Godoy, Gonet, and even Molina, are what equip them to do this. In this chapter I will first explain three methodological issues that become crucial in this era: *signa rationis*, the notion of the incarnation's "motive," and the notion of the "present decree" versus "another decree." Then I will highlight key developments from the time of Scotus up to the Salmanticenses.

SIGNA RATIONIS

Fourteenth- through sixteenth-century works on the rationale of the incarnation cannot be understood without grasping *signa rationis*. As we saw in the preceding chapter, Scotus approaches Christ's predestination from the perspective of logical ordering. This leads him to view the question of why Christ became incarnate as the question of where to locate Christ in the sequence of conceptual stages in God's decision-making. Does God decree Christ *prior* to consideration of Adam's sin or *posterior* to it?

The conceptual stages or moments used to assign an order of priority and posteriority within a single, simultaneous reality are called in Latin *signa* (or *instantia*) *rationis*.[2] When applied to theology, *signa rationis* indicate successive conceptual stages in the divine know-

---

2. At times, Scotus uses *instans naturae* (not *rationis*) in his discussion of divine providence, but it seems evident that he means only to emphasize the atemporal character of the moments he enumerates, not to posit that they are really distinct in God himself. See, for example, Scotus, *Lectura* III, d. 19, q. 1, no. 21 (Vatican, 21:32–33). Scotus was the first to make such widespread use of this apparatus, and so the terminology was not yet fully standardized.

ing and willing. All the theologians we will look at agree that God is perfectly simple and that the divine knowledge and will are thus singular, really identical, and nondiscursive. At the same time, they also recognize the human need to affirm that God knows or wills certain objects *before* others. For example, theologians holding that God's effective choice of the elect is *ante praevisa merita* mean by this that God's consideration of a person's actual merits does not give rise to his choice of the person for heaven. Election causes merits, not vice versa. Here, the nonreciprocal entailment serves as the basis for the use of the word "before": God's choice of the person is prior to his consideration of the person's merits as actual, since the latter depends utterly on the former.

As far as the terminology goes, *instans*, meaning "instant" or "moment" is plain enough. *Signum*, on the other hand, requires some explanation. *Signum* as a synonym of *instans* arises ultimately from Aristotle's *Physics*. Addressing a difficulty raised by Zeno, Aristotle writes:

> It is also plain that unless we hold that the point of time that divides earlier from later always belongs only to the later so far as the thing is concerned, we shall be involved in the consequence that the same thing at the same moment is and is not, and that a thing is not at the moment when it has become. It is true that the point is common to both times, the earlier as well as the later, and that, while numerically one and the same, it is not so in definition, being the end of the one and the beginning of the other.[3]

The early Latin translation of *Physics*, ascribed to James of Venice (d. ca. 1147), expresses the phrase "the point of time that divides earlier from later" (τοῦ χρόνου τὸ διαιροῦν σημεῖον τὸ πρότερον καὶ ὕστερον) as *temporis dividens signum prius et posterius* and renders "in definition" (λόγῳ) as *ratione*.[4] In other words, the Greek σημεῖον,

---

3. Aristotle, *Physics*, 8.8.263b9–15, in *The Complete Works of Aristotle: The Revised Oxford Translation*, ed. Jonathan Barnes, Bollingen Series 71.2 (Princeton, N.J.: Princeton University Press, 1984), 1:440. The Greek text is *Aristotelis Physica*, ed. W. D. Ross, Scriptorum classicorum bibliotheca Oxoniensis (Oxford: Clarendon Press, 1950, reprinted 2009). The Latin edition is *Physica (translatio vetus)*, ed. Fernand Bossier and Jozef Brams, Aristoteles Latinus 7.1 (Leiden: Brill, 1990), 325.

4. *Physica (translatio vetus)* 8.8.263b.

which in this context does not mean "sign" but instead refers to a "mark" or "point" of time, was translated literalistically as *signum* in the Latin text available to thirteenth-century theologians.[5]

Neither Aquinas nor Bonaventure applies *signa rationis* to divine acts. Henry of Ghent uses *signa* to identify conceptual moments in the Trinitarian processions on the model of human generation.[6] But Scotus is the theologian usually associated with *signa rationis*, and for good reason, since he applies this methodology quite broadly, for example, to the Trinitarian processions,[7] to actual grace,[8] to human decision-making,[9] and, as we saw in the last chapter, to divine providence and predestination.

The introduction of *signa rationis* as a theological tool drew criticism even in the fourteenth century, for example, from Hervaeus Natalis, OP (d. 1323);[10] Peter Auriol, OFM (d. 1322);[11] and William of Ockham, OFM (d. 1347).[12] Nevertheless, this method came

---

5. When Aquinas is referring directly to the Aristotelian text, he uses *signum*, whereas in other contexts he prefers *instans*, *punctum*, or *nunc*. See, for example, *Super II Sent.*, d. 3, q. 2, a. 1, ad 5, in *S. Thomae Aquinatis, Ordinis praedicatorum, doctoris communis ecclesiae, Scriptum super Sententiis magistri Petri Lombardi episcopi Parisiensis*, ed. Mandonnet, new ed. (Paris: Sumptibus P. Lethielleux, 1929), 2:111–12; *Super III Sent.*, d. 3, q. 5, a. 2, ad 4 (Moos, 3:147–48); *ST* I, q. 25, a. 2, arg. 3 (Leonine, 4:292); *ST* I, q. 46, a. 1, ad 7 (Leonine, 4:480); *ST* I, q. 105, a. 2, arg. 3 (Leonine, 5:472); *ST* III, q. 75, a. 7, ad 1 (Leonine, 12:175); *Quaestio disputata de caritate*, a. 12, ad 14, in *Quaestiones disputatae*, ed. P. Bazzi et al., 10th ed. (Rome: Marietti, 1965), 2:788. In *De veritate*, Aquinas first quotes *Physics* 8 as "aliquid in movendo utitur uno signo ut duobus." However, when repeating the principle in his own argument, he substitutes *instans* for *signum*. Later in *De veritate*, he quotes the same passage from Aristotle as "aliquod mobile utitur uno puncto ut duobus." *De veritate*, q. 28, a. 2, ad 10 (Leonine, 22:824); and q. 29, a. 8, arg. 6 (Leonine, 22:868).

6. Henry of Ghent, *Summae quaestionum ordinarium*, a. 59, q. 2, in *Summae quaestionum ordinariarum theologi recepto praeconio solennis Henrici a Gandavo* (Paris: Venumdatur in aedibus Iodoci Badii Ascensii, 1520), 2:137–44.

7. Scotus, *Ordinatio* I, d. 6, q. 1, no. 15 (Vatican, 4:95).

8. Scotus, *Ordinatio* II, dd. 34–37, q. 5, no. 102 (Vatican, 8:412).

9. Scotus, *Lectura* III, d. 36, q. 1, no. 60, (Vatican, 21:328–29).

10. Hervaeus Natalis, *De esse et essentia*, par. 2, chap. 4, ad 3, no. 227, in *De quattuor materiis sive Determinationes contra magistrum Henricum de Gandavo*, ed. L. M. de Rijk, Studia artistarum 35 (Turnhout: Brepols, 2013), 2:96.

11. Peter Auriol, *Scriptum super primum Sententiarum*, d. 8, q. 3, a. 3, C, no. 91, in *Scriptum super primum Sententiarum*, ed. Eligius M. Buytaert, Franciscan Institute Publications, Text Series 3 (St. Bonaventure, N.Y.: Franciscan Institute, 1956), 2:1000.

12. William of Ockham, *Scriptum in librum primum Sententiarum: Ordinatio*,

to permeate the theological discussion of the rationale for the incarnation among both Scotists and Thomists. For now, I will defer addressing the criticisms of *signa rationis*.

THE "MOTIVE" OF THE INCARNATION

When Scholastic theologians speak of the "motive" of the incarnation, what do they mean? In common parlance, a motive is what moves the will, eliciting a certain act from the agent. For this reason, some object to applying the word "motive" to God.[13] Nevertheless, the Scholastics who use "motive" apply it to God only by analogy. By "motive" they mean the reason or rationale for the incarnation on the part of the objects of God's will.[14] Similarly, we saw in the preceding chapter that Bonaventure and Aquinas speak of the incarnation's *ratio* or *causa*, though both theologians hold that nothing moves God. The incarnation's motive is the end to which God directed the incarnation. This end is only an end, a final cause, with respect to creaturely effects like human nature's being assumed by a divine person; it is not something that really moves God from potency to act.

THE "PRESENT DECREE"

In the preceding chapter, we saw that some theologians, such as Albert and Aquinas, inquire about the incarnation's rationale by using a hypothetical formula: would Christ have come if Adam had not sinned? It is of the utmost importance to grasp that, for the mature Scholastic discussion, this inquiry is not about purely unreal circumstances. In other words, the hypothetical inquiry is equivalent

---

d. 1, q. 5, in *Guillelmi de Ockham opera philosophica et theologica* [...], Opera theologica 1 (St. Bonaventure, N.Y.: Institutum Franciscanum, 1967), 1:471–85; and d. 9, q. 3 (Opera theologica, 3:294–317).

13. See Bonnefoy's response in Garrigou-Lagrange, "De motivo Incarnationis," 24–30.

14. See Garrigou-Lagrange, "De motivo Incarnationis," 34–35.

to the question of whether Adam's sin is a *sine qua non* condition for the coming of Christ that has really taken place.

As Reginald Garrigou-Lagrange, OP (1877–1964), explains, when we look at a building and ask whether it would stand if a certain column were absent, we are asking whether the column that is actually present is load-bearing or not.[15] It would be a purely unreal hypothetical to ask whether the building's architect would have chosen something other than the column if he had designed a different building. So, too, when we look at the event of Christ's incarnation, the hypothetical inquiry is asking whether the incarnation that has taken place and the God-man who now exists have an essential dependence on the fact of Adam's sin. As the discussion develops, theologians begin to distinguish the hypothetical "by virtue of the present decree" (the real order of history) from "by virtue of another decree" (an unreal but possible order of history) to clarify this. Therefore, despite what we may think at first glance, by the end of the thirteenth century the Scholastic discussion over the motive of the incarnation, often taken up in hypothetical form, is about the real world and its concrete history, not a mere speculation.

MAJOR DEVELOPMENTS FROM SCOTUS TO THE SALMANTICENSES

One early challenge to Scotus's position was the problem of the incarnation's modality: would the Word assume passible or impassible flesh? Since passibility is a consequence of sin, if God predestined Christ prior to taking sin into account, as Scotus claims, either Christ would have been impassible or else God must have changed his mind. Since the latter is impossible and the former did not occur, it remains that God predestined Christ as passible, which entails that Christ's predestination is a response to sin.

Scotists typically responded by accepting that Scotus himself

---

15. Garrigou-Lagrange, "De motivo Incarnationis," 39.

does implicitly distinguish the incarnation's *substance* (the fact of its occurrence) from its *modality* (its concrete circumstances) but that this does not lead to multiple divine decrees, as the Thomists charged.[16] The Scotistic point is that the single, effective divine decree that is actually carried out in the world includes Christ's suffering for the salvation of sinners, but that there is still a conceptual moment within this decree where the glory of the God-man as such belongs more to God's intention than does Christ's passion. After all, Christ's suffering is not lovable in itself but only because it redeems humanity and leads to Christ's own glorification.

Another point of development concerns Scotus's *ordinate volens* principle, the argument that God wills in an orderly way and so wills the end first, then what is closer to the end, and finally what is farther from it. The Scotist Juan de Rada, OFM Obs. (ca. 1545–1608), distinguishes two senses in which *ordinate volens* can be applied.[17] If "closer to the end" means what is more directly connected with the end in the process of attaining it, then it is true that one who wills in an orderly way wills what is closer to the end prior to what is farther from it. However, if "closer to the end" only means that which bears greater resemblance to the end, then this is not necessarily the

---

16. See, e.g., Peter of Aquila, *Quaestiones in quatuor Sententiarum libros* III, d. 2, q. 1, in *Petri Aquilani cognomento Scotelli ex Ord. min. in doctrina Ioan. Duns Scoti spectatissimi quaestiones in quatuor Sententiarum libros, ad ejusdem doctrinam multum conferentes*, ed. M. Constantius a Sarnano (Venice: Apud Hieronymum Zenarius, 1584), 327–28; Juan de Rada, *Controversiae theologicae* III, contr. 5, a. 3, concl. 3, in *Controversiae theologicae inter S. Thomam et Scotum super quatuor libros Sententiarum* (Cologne: Apud Ioannem Crithium sub signo Galli, 1620), 3:162–63; Bartolomeo Mastri, *Disputationes theologicae in tertium librum Sententiarum*, disp. 4, q. 1, a. 5, no. 72, in *R. P. F. Bartholomaei Mastri de Meldula Ordinis Minorum conventualium S. Francisci theologi disputationes theologicae in tertium librum Sententiarum*, latest ed. (Venice: Apud Paulum Balleonium, 1698), 219; Claude Frassen, *De divini Verbi Incarnatione*, tract. 1, disp. 1, a. 3, sect. 3, q. 1, in *Scotus academicus seu universa Doctoris subtilis theologica dogmata*, new ed. (Rome: Ex typographia Sallustiana, 1901), 7:276; and Juan de Campoverde, *Tractatus de Incarnatione Verbi divini*, disp. 9, chap. 1, no. 2, in *Tractatus de Incarnatione Verbi divini divisus in tres tomos* (Alcalá de Henares: Apud Iulianum Franciscum Garcia Briones, typographum Universitatis Complutensis, 1712), 2:133. For a discussion of Christ's passibility according to the Scotistic view, see Trent Pomplun, "The Immaculate World: Predestination and Passibility in Contemporary Scotism," *Modern Theology* 30, no. 4 (2014): 525–51.

17. Rada, *Controversiae theologicae* III, contr. 5, a. 3, obs. 3 (Ioannes Crithius, 3:158).

case. The Scotistic view still holds, in Rada's opinion, because resemblance to God is an essential element in the glorification of God and thus the two senses of "closer to the end" overlap in the case of Christ.

Confronted with the developing logical sophistication of Scotism and its emphasis on Christ as the goal of God's other works, Thomists began to distinguish senses of final cause. For example, the Prince of Thomist Theologians, Jean Capréolus, OP (ca. 1380–1444), taught that the incarnation is meant to bring about redemption but that it also glorifies Christ.[18] Thus it has two ends, each of which enjoys priority from its own perspective.[19] Still, Capréolus only speaks of Christ as an end in the sense that glory does, in fact, accrue to him as a result of having redeemed humanity (order of execution) but does not expressly affirm that Christ is also an end in God's providential plan (order of intention).[20]

Francesco Silvestri de Ferrara, OP (ca. 1474–1528), continued this development. He maintains the Thomistic view that God only predestined Christ with sin taken into account. However, among the objects of God's will, he says, there is a way that Christ's soul is prior to human salvation from the perspective of formal cause (since it is more perfect than salvation) and final cause (since it receives glory as a result of human salvation).[21] Thus, "the incarnation of Christ

18. "Nam dupliciter aliquid potest dici finis alicujus, puta A esse finis ipsius B. Primo modo, quia B ordinatur ad acquisitionem vel conservationem ipsius A.... Secundo modo, A potest dici finis B, quia ex ipso B provenit aliqua utilitas vel aliquod bonum ipsi A, vel ipsum A tendit in ipsum B sicut in illud cujus similitudinem et participationem desiderat." Jean Capréolus, *Defensiones in III Sent.*, dist. 1, q. 1, a. 3, ad 3, in *Johannis Capreoli Tholosani Ordinis praedicatorum, Thomistarum princeps defensiones theologiae divi Thomae Aquinatis*, ed. Ceslas Paban and Thomas Pègues (Tours: Sumptibus Alfred Cattier, 1904), 5:7.

19. "Sua praedestinatio et nostra invicem se praecedunt." Capréolus, *Defensiones in III Sent.*, dist. 1, q. 1, a. 3, ad 3 (Paban and Pègues, 5:7).

20. "Praedestinatio Christi uno modo potest dici finis nostrae praedestinationis ex parte effectus temporalis." Capréolus, *Defensiones in III Sent.*, dist. 1, q. 1, a. 3, ad 3 (Paban and Pègues, 5:7).

21. Francesco Silvestri de Ferrara, *Commentary on the* Summa contra Gentiles IV, chap. 55, no. 18.3, in *Opera omnia iussu impensaque Leonis XIII. P. M. edita* (Rome: Ex Typographia Polyglotta S. C. de Propaganda Fide, 1930), 15:188.

is ordered to the salvation of the human race, whereas human salvation, as caused by Christ, is ordered to Christ's glory and exaltation."[22]

Tommaso de Vio Cajetan, OP (1469–1534), applied an even finer set of distinctions in his arguments against Scotus. What is more "willable" (*volibile*), explains Cajetan, is not necessarily more willed (*volitum*). For example, the salvation of all people is more willable than the salvation of only some, but it is not actually effectively willed by God.[23] Further, being willed *more* does not have to mean being willed *prior*. Thus Christ's supreme dignity does not prove that God willed him prior to everything else. Moreover, says Cajetan, being willed prior does not have to mean being willed independently. An end that can be willed independently may also be willed in conjunction with certain means directed to that end. Thus, even if Christ's glory is a final cause of the incarnation, we have it from Scripture that God has actually willed the incarnation only in conjunction with the need for redemption as a material cause. The two causal perspectives are complementary, not independent.

Cajetan's explanation of how sin (from the perspective of material cause) logically precedes the decree to send Christ relies on distinguishing three ontological levels: nature, grace, and the hypostatic union.[24] Nature is the foundation for grace, while nature and grace together underlie the hypostatic union. Like a three-storied building, the higher levels presuppose the lower. Since human beings can sin from their natural capacity, sin belongs to the level of nature, and it is also opposed to grace. Therefore sin and the loss of grace must be accounted for prior to God's decreeing the incarnation. Just as a

---

22. "Dicimus ipsam Christi Incarnationem esse ordinatam ad humani generis salutem; humanam autem salutem, ut causatam per Christum, esse ad Christi gloriam et exaltationem ordinatam." De Ferrara, *Commentary on the* Summa contra Gentiles IV, chap. 55, no. 19 (Leonine, 15:1:88).

23. Tommaso de Vio Cajetan, *Commentary on the* Summa theologiae III, q. 1, a. 3, no. 9, in *Opera omnia iussu impensaque Leonis XIII. P. M. edita* (Rome: Ex Typographia Polyglotta S. C. de Propaganda Fide, 1903), 11:16. Cajetan grants, of course, that God wills all people to be saved by his antecedent will.

24. Cajetan, *Commentary on* Summa theologiae III, q. 1, a. 3, no. 6 (Leonine, 11:15–16).

building is constructed from the bottom up, the lower ontological levels must be put in place before the higher.

Cajetan's three-level theory of providence and predestination and his application of complementary causal perspectives became a commonplace in the discussion. Even if subsequent theologians adopt some of his distinctions, they are not slow to point out flaws in the great commentator's reasoning. One criticism is that Cajetan mixes up the order of execution with the order of intention. A building may be *constructed* from the bottom up, but it does not follow that it must be *intended* from the bottom up. For example, an architect may form the idea and intention for a grand spire prior to designing the structure beneath it. Another objection is that not *everything* on a higher level depends upon *everything* on a lower level. In fact, there are cases where something on a lower level depends upon a higher level, such as the sins of those who killed Christ and the Christian martyrs, which presuppose the fact of the incarnation.

Gabriel Vásquez, SJ (1549–1604), maintained hardline fidelity to the Angelic Doctor, rejecting any attempt to integrate the Scotistic emphasis on Christ's primacy in God's intention into Thomism. Scripture says that Christ became incarnate to redeem us, not that he became incarnate for his own sake, and so it is baffling that a Thomist would consider the Scotistic theory salvageable.[25] Thus, insists Vásquez, the incarnation's goal was redemption, and its beneficiary was the fallen human race—not Christ himself.[26]

Vásquez identifies four *signa rationis*.[27] First, God decreed the

---

[25] "Ego quidem valde miror, hos Recentiores Theologos argumento Scoti convictos, tam facile ei concessisse, Christum praefinitum fuisse a Deo prius in genere causae finalis ante praevisionem peccati originalis, simulque sententiam sancti Thomae in hoc articulo defendere voluisse." Gabriel Vásquez, *In III Thomae*, q. 1, a. 3, disp. 11, chap. 4, no. 50, in *Commentariorum, ac disputationum in tertiam partem S. Thomae, tomus primus* (Alcalá de Henares: Apud viduam Iusti Sanchez Crespo, 1609), 1:163. See also *In III Thomae*, q. 1, a. 3, disp. 11, chap. 5, no. 56 (Sanchez Crespo, 1:165).

[26] "Finis cuius gratia, incarnationis Dei, fuit redemptio, et salus nostra, non contra, finis autem cui, fuit homo lapsus, non Christus, aut Verbum." Vásquez, *In III Thomae*, q. 1, a. 3, disp. 11, chap. 6, no. 64 (Sanchez Crespo, 1:166).

[27] Vásquez, *In III Thomae*, q. 1, a. 3, disp. 11, chap. 6, nos. 61–62 (Sanchez Crespo, 1:166).

creation of humanity in a state of grace in such a way that, if human beings cooperated, they would merit glory. Second, God permitted sin. Third, foreseeing humanity's sin, God remained firm in his original will for mankind's holiness and chose the best means to secure this, which was perfect satisfaction by the human race, even though God could have remedied sin without satisfaction. Fourth, God decided to send the Son in mortal flesh to obtain salvation and impart grace by his merits.

John of St. Thomas, OP (1589–1644), concedes that Christ is the goal of God's other works but emphasizes that being the goal cannot exclude either Christ's status as redeemer or other qualities that Christ has in the real order of things.[28] According to John, Vásquez is incorrect in asserting simply that the incarnation's goal is redemption because redemption is not something separate from the incarnation. What God has willed is not so much the incarnation for redemption but the redemptive incarnation.[29] God wills the incarnation as redemptive because he first willed a distinct providential order with its own ends that did not include Christ, but this order was destroyed (with God's permission) through human sin.[30]

At the same time, strict Scotists, such as Francesco Licheto, OFM (1465–1520), explain and defend the Subtle Doctor. Licheto wants to show why Scotus is correct in saying that God first predestined Christ's humanity to a certain degree of glory and then chose the hypostatic union as the means to reaching that level of glory. Once this argument is in place, Licheto follows Scotus in situating the question of the incarnation's relationship to sin within the discussion of Christ's predestination. He uses the example of a king who wishes to elevate someone to royal dignity. The king is right to

---

28. John of St. Thomas, *Cursus theologicus* III, q. 1, disp. 3, a. 2, nos. 17–26, in *Admodum reverendi et eximii patris Joannis a S. Thoma Ordinis praedicatorum, doctoris theologi in Complutensi academia professoris primarii, supremi fidei censoris cursus theologicus in Summam theologicam D. Thomae*, new ed. (Paris: Ludovicus Vivès, 1886), 8:100–2.

29. John of St. Thomas, *Cursus theologicus* III, q. 1, disp. 3, a. 2, no. 60 (Vivès, 8:110); and q. 1, disp. 3, a. 3, nos. 13–14 (Vivès, 8:114).

30. John of St. Thomas, *Cursus theologicus* III, q. 1, disp. 3, a. 2, nos. 48–63 (Vivès, 8:108–11).

choose a relative (e.g., his son) for this honor, but it would be unreasonable for the king to bestow such honor on his son only on the condition that a servant of his commits some crime.[31]

Luis de Molina, SJ (1536–1600), also locates the question of the incarnation's motive within his treatment of Christ's predestination.[32] However Molina's concern is to eliminate *signa rationis* as far as possible.[33] Instead of multiplying conceptual stages, it is better to state that God first knows all future contingents (whether natural, gratuitous, or hypostatic) and then, out of all possibilities, freely wills the entire actual order of affairs by a single decree.[34] Since God freely wills the end together with its means, conditions, and circumstances (not before them), Scotus's *ordinate volens* principle does not apply.

Francisco Suárez, SJ (1548–1617), applies Molina's theory of middle knowledge (*scientia media*) in a grand attempt to reconcile the Thomistic and Scotistic views. Convinced that the core of each position is correct in what it affirms and that the two schools are talking past one another, Suárez spends many pages carefully parsing out the conceptual steps in God's decision-making process and how they relate to events as they play out in the world.

The first element of Suárez's theory is that God (like any agent) can act for two complete motives simultaneously.[35] The second el-

31. Francesco Licheto, *Commentary on Scotus's* Quaestiones in tertium librum Sententiarum, d. 7, q. 3, no. 11, in *Joannis Duns Scoti doctoris subtilis, Ordinis Minorum, opera omnia editio nova juxta editionem Waddingi XII tomos continentem a patribus Franciscanis de Observantia accurate recognita* (Paris: Apud Ludovicum Vivès, 1894), 14:356.

32. Luis de Molina, *Commentaria in primam divi Thomae partem*, q. 23, aa. 4–5, disp. 1, memb. 7–8, in *Ludovici Molinae e Societate Iesu S. theologiae doctoris, et professoris commentaria, in primam D. Thomae partem* (London: Sumptibus Ludovici Prost haeredis Roville, 1622), 1:308–15.

33. "Sane exterminanda omnino videntur instantia Scoti, et aliorum ... quae certe instantia adeo obscuram reddunt quaestionem hanc, ut vix, aut ne vix quidem, intelligi queat." *Commentaria in primam divi Thomae partem*, q. 23, aa. 4–5, disp. 1, memb. 7 (Prost, 1:311).

34. *Commentaria in primam divi Thomae partem*, q. 23, aa. 4–5, disp. 1, memb. 7 (Prost, 1:310–11).

35. Francisco Suárez, *In III Thomae*, q. 1, a. 4, disp. 5, sect. 4, no. 6, in *R. P. Francisci Suarez e Societate Jesu opera omnia*, new ed. (Paris: Apud Ludovicum Vivès, 1878), 17:240.

ement is middle knowledge, which for Suárez is God's knowledge, prior to his exercise of free will, of the truth or falsity of all propositions that are conditioned by the free choices of creatures. Putting these two elements together, Suárez argues that God wills the incarnation primarily for its own sheer excellence and wills that it would be accomplished in the best way. Then, foreseeing through middle knowledge that humanity would fall into sin in the circumstances in that God did, in fact, choose to realize, God also foresees that a redemptive incarnation would be the best way. Thus, when he actually wills the incarnation to occur, God wills it both for its sheer excellence and as a response to human sin.

Suárez explains that "if Adam had not sinned" can be understood in two senses.[36] Either it means that God would not have foreseen that Adam would sin in the real circumstances in which Adam was actually placed, or it means that God would have foreseen his sin and then chosen to place him in other circumstances in which he would not sin. In the first sense, God's providential decree would be identical to the present one. In the second sense, it would be different.[37] In the first sense, it is true that Christ would have come even if Adam had not sinned, whereas in the second sense it is true that Christ would not have come unless Adam sinned.[38] In this way, Suárez believes he has harmonized the Scotistic and Thomistic views.[39]

36. Suárez, *In III Thomae*, q. 1, a. 4, disp. 5, sect. 5, no. 7 (Vivès, 17:255).
37. In the Molinist-Suaresian view, God's middle knowledge is not the cause of Adam's choice but merely God's certainty of how Adam would choose in any given circumstances. Whether Adam will sin or not lies in Adam's free will alone. Therefore, if Adam had not been going to sin, God would have instead always foreknown that Adam would not sin. But this difference in Adam's choice would not result from any changes in God's interventions in the world and so would not alter the present decree. Alternatively, if God arranges circumstances differently in order to avoid Adam's sinning, then a decree different from the present one does arise.
38. Suárez, *In III Thomae*, q. 1, a. 4, disp. 5, sect. 5, no. 16 (Vivès, 17:260–61).
39. Francesco Saverio Pancheri, OFM Conv. (1920–86), and Juniper B. Carol assert that later in his career Suárez changed his mind and came to hold the strictly Scotistic position. They base this on his tract *De angelis*, published in 1620. However, in the relevant passage, *De angelis* VII, chap. 13, no. 9 (Vivès, 2:883–84), Suárez is not rejecting his own theory but instead that of theologians—like Godoy and Gonet—who hold that God permitted sin for the sake of Christ the redeemer. Nor is Suárez endorsing the Scotistic

A different way of integrating insights from the two camps emerged in the work of Pedro de Godoy, OP (d. 1677), and Jean-Baptiste Gonet, OP (1615–81). Under the influence of the Scotist Luis de León, OESA (1527–91), professor at Salamanca and teacher of St. John of the Cross, these Thomists looked for a way to affirm the primacy of Christ in God's intention. They settled on the view that God intended Christ to be the proximate end of all other works *precisely as redeemer*.[40] For them, the redeemer is what God first intends while redeemed humanity is his beneficiary. This idea also influenced Antonio de la Madre de Dios, one of the Salmanticenses and author of the section in their *Cursus theologicus* on Christ's predestination, who argues that God made the whole universe out of love for Christ as the first-born of the elect.[41]

---

viewpoint when he says, "absolute censeo, quod licet non fuisset Adam peccaturus, unio Verbi in humana natura fieret, licet officium redemptoris non assumeret." Rather, context makes it clear that what Suárez is asserting is that the need for redemption is not the only factor that makes human nature more likely to be assumed than angelic nature, so that even apart from sin any hypostatic union would still occur in human nature *as opposed to angelic nature*. This is also why Suárez says that he has never held the rejected opinion, not that he formerly held it.

40. Pedro de Godoy, *Disputationes theologicae in tertiam partem*, q. 1, tract. 1, disp. 8, §10, no. 228, in *Illustrissimi, ac reverendissimi D. D. F. Petri de Godoy Ordinis praedicatorum: Salmanticensis academiae in sacra theologia magistri: Eiusdemque universitatis quondam cancellarii: Diu vespertina, et primaria cathedra moderatoris: Concionatoris regii: Et nunc episcopi Oxomensis disputationes theologicae in tertiam partem divi Thomae* (Venice: Apud Ioannem Iacobum Hertz, 1686), 1:155–56; and Jean-Baptiste Gonet, *Clypeus theologiae Thomisticae* III, tract. 1, disp. 5, a. 1, §6, nos. 52–53, in *Clypeus theologiae Thomisticae contra novos eius impugnatores* (Paris: Apud Ludovicum Vivès, 1876), 5:483.

41. Salmanticenses, *Cursus theologicus*, tract. 5, disp. 5, dub. 1, §3, no. 20, in *Cursus theologicus Collegii Salmanticensis Fr. Discalceatorum B. Mariae de Monte Carmeli* [...] *Summam theologicam angelici doctoris D. Thomae complectens*, new corrected ed. (Paris: Apud Victorem Palmé, 1876), 2:351. On Luis's influence, see Enrique del Sagrado Corazón, "Juan Duns Escoto en la doctrina de los Salmanticenses," 510–15. On the influence of Godoy and Gonet, see Robert B. Pfisterer, "El motivo de la Encarnación según los Salmanticenses" (PhD diss., Universidad Pontificia de Salamanca, 1950), 225–28; and Otho Merl, *Theologia Salmanticensis: Untersuchung über Entstehung, Lehrrichtung und Quellen des theologischen Kurses der spanischen Karmeliten* (Regensburg: J. Habbel, 1947), 157–58. Gonet's own high estimation of the Salamanca project is evidenced by his dedicating his *Clypeus theologiae Thomisticae* to St. Theresa in honor of the Carmelites. See *Clypeus theologiae Thomisticae* (Vivès, 1:i–vii).

CONCLUSION

The Scholastics following Aquinas and Scotus devoted thousands of pages to the motive of the incarnation. To establish the thrust of revealed truth, they mined the Bible and the Fathers for authoritative statements on the reason for Christ's coming. To sharpen rational precision, they distinguished causal perspectives, delineated ontological orders and logical dependencies, and clarified how these apply to divine providence. While the Thomist and Scotist schools polarized, they also drew on each other's arguments. Thomists adopted the Scotistic use of *signa rationis*, and Scotists nuanced the Subtle Doctor's *ordinate volens* principle in light of divine sovereignty. Theologians such as Suárez took this a step further and endeavored to harmonize the two positions. Others, like Godoy and Gonet, simply sought to articulate the Scotistic emphasis on Christ's primacy within a Thomistic framework. In this, they set the stage for the Salmanticenses.

3

For the Redeemer's Sake
The Salamanca Theory

Against the background of the first two chapters, which traced how the discussion of the incarnation's motive took shape between Anselm and Scotus and then developed through the fourteenth through sixteenth centuries, it is now possible to present the view of the Salmanticenses. The main source for their view is the immense *Cursus theologicus*, a theological counterpart to the *Artium cursus* of the college of Discalced Carmelites in Alcalá de Henares, near Madrid. Both works were at first intended for students of their order.[1]

The composition of the *Cursus theologicus* lasted from around 1625 to 1710.[2] Antonio de la Madre de Dios, OCD (1583–1637), began the work. He outlined its scope and wrote the first tractates until poor health forced him to turn the work over to a promising student of his, Domingo de Santa Teresa, OCD (1604–59).[3] Domingo,

---

1. Enrique del Sagrado Corazón, "El colegio de San Elías y los *Salmanticenses*," in *Trayectoria histórica e instituciones vinculadas*, vol. 1 of *Historia de la Universidad de Salamanca*, ed. Luis Enrique Rodríguez-San Pedro Bezares, Acta Salmanticensia: Historia de la Universidad 61 (Salamanca: Ediciones Universidad de Salamanca, 2002), 696–99.

2. See del Sagrado Corazón, "El colegio de San Elías y los *Salmanticenses*," 699–703.

3. Enrique del Sagrado Corazón, *Los Salmanticenses: su vida y su obra. Ensayo histórico y proceso inquisitorial de su doctrina sobre la Inmaculada*, Pontificia Universidad Eclesiastica de Salamanca (Madrid: Editorial de Espiritualidad, 1955), 45.

in turn, labored on the *Cursus* until his death, when he was succeeded by Juan de la Anunciación, OCD (1633–1701), who contributed substantially to it before his election as general of the order in 1694.[4] Antonio de San Juan Bautista, OCD (1641–99), and Ildefonso de los Angeles, OCD (1663–1737), assisted Juan and became the last authors of the *Cursus*, which received permission to be printed as a whole in 1710.[5] Robert B. Pfisterer, OFM, characterizes the completed *Cursus theologicus* as "the work that best synthesizes and shows the perfection of this theological movement [of Spanish theology].... No commentary on St. Thomas surpasses it in amplitude, detailedness, zeal for exact interpretation of the master's mind, familiarity with preceding and contemporary theological currents."[6] Indeed, despite being the work of several authors over the better part of a century, the *Cursus* shows remarkable unity due to its careful planning and the shared theological commitments of the authors.[7]

Within the *Cursus*, the disputation *De motivo Incarnationis*, the work of Juan de la Anunciación, was first published in 1687 in Lyon.[8] Juniper B. Carol, OFM (1911–90), calls this disputation on the motive of the incarnation "undoubtedly one of the most satisfactory, influential and lengthy treatments of our subject ever written from the Thomistic viewpoint."[9] In its most recent edition, *De motivo*

---

4. Del Sagrado Corazón, *Los Salmanticenses*, 62.
5. Del Sagrado Corazón, *Los Salmanticenses*, 69–73.
6. "La obra que mejor sinteteza y muestra la perfección de este movimiento teológico es el *Cursus* de los Salmanticenses. Ningún comentario sobre santo Tomás le sobrepuja en amplitud, en abundancia de detalles, en celo por la interpretación exacta de la menta del Maestro, en conocimiento de las corrientes teológicas que les precedieron y les fueron contemporáneas." Pfisterer, "El motivo de la Encarnación según los Salmanticenses," xi.
7. Pfisterer, "El motivo de la Encarnación según los Salmanticenses," 128–29; and del Sagrado Corazón, "Juan Duns Escoto en la doctrina de los Salmanticenses," 463. The Salmanticenses pride themselves on being devoted followers of St. Thomas, as the encomium to the Angelic Doctor and commendation of Thomism at the beginning of the *Cursus* show. Salmanticenses, *Cursus theologicus* (Palmé, 1:iii–xx). On the Salmanticenses' commitment to Thomism, see also del Sagrado Corazón, *Los Salmanticenses*, 126–29.
8. Del Sagrado Corazón, "El colegio de San Elías y los *Salmanticenses*," 702.
9. Carol, *Why Jesus Christ?*, 70.

Incarnationis comprises seventy folio pages.[10] The disputation is divided into four doubts. First, would God have assumed flesh by virtue of the present decree if man had not sinned? Second, would he have assumed flesh by virtue of a different decree if man had not sinned? Third, would Christ have come if there were original sin but no actual sins? Fourth, would Christ have come if there were actual sins but no original sin?

The Salmanticenses' precision comes across in the fact that they formulate the first and second doubts distinctly. The first doubt inquires about whether the incarnation that has actually occurred in the present course of history had sin as its necessary condition. The second doubt asks about a purely hypothetical state of affairs. In some other order of history, if God had not foreseen sin, would he have decreed another incarnation by virtue of another decree? The third and fourth doubts are more straightforward, seeking to clarify precisely what *kind* of sin is meant in the assertion that Christ would not have come if humanity had not sinned.

Before entering directly into their argumentation concerning the first doubt, the Salmanticenses lay out upfront certain matters in order to avoid needless repetition and confusion. First of all, God's own glory is the chief end of all his works. The entire discussion of the end or motive of the incarnation is within the ambit of the work itself. The "motive" of the incarnation does not mean something outside God that moves his will. Instead, it means the "specific motive on the part of the work."[11] Further, God was able to decree the incarnation for many ends—for example, for its intrinsic excellence or the perfection of the universe. These are all possible to God. How-

---

10. Salmanticenses, *Cursus theologicus*, tract. 21, *De Incarnatione*, disp. 2, *De motivo Incarnationis* [henceforth *De motivo Incarnationis*] (Palmé, 13:263–332). All English translations of the Salmanticenses' *De motivo Incarnationis* are from the Salmanticenses (Discalced Carmelites of Salamanca), *On the Motive of the Incarnation*, trans. Dylan Schrader, Early Modern Catholic Sources 1 (Washington, D.C.: The Catholic University of America Press, 2019). However, I have left some terms, such as *finis cuius gratia* and *finis cui*, in Latin for consistency.

11. "Speciale motivum ex parte operis." *De motivo Incarnationis* (Palmé, 13:263).

ever, the present query is not about mere possibility but about why God has actually decreed the incarnation.

PRELIMINARY CONSIDERATIONS

Before inquiring whether God decreed the incarnation with a dependence on sin, the Salmanticenses want to establish that God was *able* to decree it in this way. Unless the incarnation with sin as a *sine qua non* condition is logically contradictory, God can decree it as such. And unless it can be proved that this condition introduces a logical impossibility, we must hold that it is logically possible and thus within God's power.

For this reason, drawing on Scotus, the Salmanticenses propose and reject three arguments that it is logically impossible for the incarnation to be contingent on sin.[12] First, if the incarnation were dependent on sin, it would be an occasioned good. Second, if God willed the incarnation to depend on sin, he would have to will sin itself. Third, if God decreed the incarnation as a response to sin, then Christ, as man, would have to rejoice at the presence of sin and be grateful to humanity for having sinned.

Against these objections, the Salmanticenses argue that God was able to decree the incarnation with a dependence on sin.[13] In response to the first, they distinguish two senses of "occasioned": one meaning apart from the agent's intention or by chance, and the other meaning conditioned on some occurrence or on the occasion of something else. The incarnation could not be occasioned in the first sense, seeing as it could hardly occur apart from God's intention, but there is nothing logically contradictory in its being occasioned in the second sense. Since this is not logically contradictory, it was possible for God to decree the incarnation in this way.

In response to the second objection, they explain that for the incarnation to be effectively decreed as a remedy, either God foresees

---

12. *De motivo Incarnationis*, dub. 1, §1, no. 2 (Palmé, 13:264–65).
13. *De motivo Incarnationis*, dub. 1, §1, no. 3 (Palmé, 13:265–66).

sin prior to the efficacious decree or else the efficacious decree includes the permission of sin. Neither of these amounts to God's positively willing sin. In support of this, the Salmanticenses offer the example of God's decreeing an act of penitence, an act that of its nature presupposes sin, without thereby willing the sin. In any case, God actually has decreed the incarnation in passible flesh for the forgiveness of sins, but this does not mean that God willed sin.

In response to the third objection, the Salmanticenses explain that Christ's soul would not rejoice at sin or be grateful for it, seeing as sin is not the kind of thing that of itself calls for the incarnation. In fact, humanity's sinfulness is all the more reason for God *not* to decree the incarnation. Instead, God's abundant mercy is why he decrees the incarnation in response to sin, and it is this mercy that prompts Christ's joy and gratitude.[14] Similarly, Matthias would not have been an apostle if Judas had not fallen, but Matthias was grateful to God for the gift of apostleship, not to Judas for having sinned.

Having settled these objections purporting to show the logical impossibility of God's decreeing the incarnation with a dependence on sin, the Salmanticenses move on to the question of whether God has actually decreed the mystery with this dependence. As I see it, there are two principal keys to grasping the Salmanticenses' theory. The first is the distinction between two species of final cause: *finis cuius gratia* and *finis cui*. The second is the necessity and sufficiency of precisely two conceptual stages (*signa rationis*) to describe God's providential "decision-making process" for the incarnation. I will present both of these keys before explaining the Salamanca theory and its argumentation.

Finis cuius gratia and *finis cui*

The first key to the Salmanticenses' theory is the distinction between species of final cause: *finis cuius gratia* (the "end for-the-sake-of-which") and *finis cui* (the "end to-which"). The former is that which

---

14. In this reply, the Salmanticenses build on Bonaventure, *In III Sent.*, d. 1, a. 2, q. 2, ad 6 (Quaracchi, 3:27).

motivates the agent to act, while the latter is the one whom the agent wills to benefit from the action. The distinction arises ultimately from Aristotle, who writes in *On the Soul*: "The phrase 'for the sake of which' is ambiguous; it may mean either the end to achieve which, or the being in whose interest, the act is done."[15]

Now, there is potential for confusion because authors differ in their conception of this distinction and their terminology. Writers generally agree in calling the thing desired the *finis qui* (the "end which"). However, some contrast the *finis qui* with the person to whom the benefit is willed, calling the latter either the *finis cuius gratia* or the *finis cui*.[16] Such writers treat *finis cuius gratia* and *finis cui* as synonymous. For them, the distinction is between the *finis qui* on the one hand and the *finis cuius gratia* or *finis cui* on the other.[17]

This is not the case for the Salmanticenses, who articulate the distinction this way: "The [*finis*] *cuius gratia* is what we call that good which is desired on its own account and others on its account, whereas the *finis cui* is what we call the subject or person for whom such a good is desired."[18] They also call the *finis cui* the *finis utilitatis* (the "end of benefit"), since it is the subject to whom the benefit accrues. The *finis cuius gratia* and the *finis cui* are not in competition with each other but are complementary aspects of a single total end or motive.[19] Thus, for the Salmanticenses it is not a question of two

---

15. Aristotle, *On the Soul* 2.4.415b1–3 (Barnes, 1:661).

16. For a more recent philosophical manual that identifies the terms finis cuius gratia and finis cui, see Sebastian Reinstadler, *Ontologia*, lib. 3, *De categoriis*, chap. 2, a. 3, sect. 2, §2, no. 2, in *Elementa philosophiae scholasticae*, 7th and 8th ed. reviewed by the author (Freiburg: Herder, 1913), 1:374.

17. To be sure, there are further accepted distinctions, e.g., between a *finis ultimus* and a *finis intermedius*. For a thorough list, see the helpful diagram in Reginald Garrigou-Lagrange, "Le principe de finalité," *Revue Thomiste* 26, no. 3 (1921): 420.

18. "*Cujus gratia* dicitur bonum, illud quod propter se appetitur, et alia propter ipsum: finis vero *cui* vocatur subjectum, vel persona, cui tale bonum appetitur." Salmanticenses, *Cursus theologicus*, tract. 8, *De ultimo fine*, q. 1, proem., no. 4 (Palmé, 5:3).

19. Salmanticenses, *Cursus theologicus*, tract. 8, q. 1, proem., no. 4 (Palmé, 5:3). For an example of a more recent writer taking this approach, see Carlo Boyer, *Introductio metaphysica*, q. 4, a. 1, §1, no. 1, in *Cursus philosophiae ad usum seminariorum* (Bilbao: Desclée de Brouwer, 1962), 1:356. See also Nunzio Signoriello, *Lexicon peripateticum philosophico-theologicum in quo scholasticorum distinctiones et effata praecipua explicantur*,

ends, strictly speaking, but of two components of a single end as willed by the agent.[20] For example, when the physician wills health as the *finis cuius gratia,* that state of health can only exist in a patient, who is the *finis cui.*[21] Although the components can be considered distinctly, they cannot be willed separately in practice. The *finis cuius gratia* and the *finis cui* are thus intimately linked since they come together to constitute the total end willed by the agent.

Further, there is nothing disordered about ordering the more perfect to the less perfect as its *finis cui.* In fact, as John of St. Thomas notes, we should expect the *finis cui* to be inferior to the *finis cuius gratia.*[22] The Salmanticenses cite several examples to this effect.[23] First, a king provides for the well-being of a peasant, and in this way the peasant is the *finis cui* of the king's providence.[24] Second, the motion of the heavens is the cause of generation in lower bodies, and in this way lower bodies are the *finis cui* of the heavens. Third, God appoints certain angels to minister to human beings, and in this way a human being becomes the *finis cui* of an angel. In all three cases, the nobler is fittingly ordered to the less noble.

Because the *finis cuius gratia* is willed on its own account and because other things are willed on its account, it shares more basically in the characteristic of finality within the total end. This means that the *finis cuius gratia* can be designated as the end *simpliciter,* despite

---

2nd expanded ed. (Naples: Apud officinam Bibliothecae Catholicae scriptorum, 1872), s.v. "finis quo—finis cuius—finis cui," 123.

20. As Pfisterer and Enrico di Santa Teresa rightly note. Pfisterer, "El motivo de la Encarnación según los Salmanticenses," 7; and di Santa Teresa, "Il carattere del 'Cristocentrismo, nella tesi dei Salmanticesi sul motive dell'Incarnazione," *Vita Carmelitana* 3 (1942): 51n8.

21. Salmanticenses, *Cursus theologicus,* tract. 8, q. 1, proem., no. 4 (Palmé, 5:3).

22. John of St. Thomas, *Cursus philosophicus Thomisticus,* vol. 2, pars 1, q. 13, a. 1, in *Admodum reverendi et eximii patris Joannis a S. Thoma Ordinis praedicatorum, doctoris theologi in Complutensi academia professoris primarii, supremi fidei censoris cursus philosophicus Thomisticus secundum exactam, veram et genuinam Aristotelis et doctoris angelici mentem,* new ed. (Paris: Ludovicus Vivès, 1883), 2:242.

23. *De motivo Incarnationis,* dub. 1, §1, no. 1 (Palmé, 13:264).

24. The Salmanticenses do not give a citation here, but this example is from Aquinas, *Super II Sent.,* d. 15, q. 1, a. 1, ad 6 (Mandonnet, 2:369–70).

the fact that it is only ever willed in conjunction with a *finis cui*.[25] This is why we can say "health is the end of giving medicine" without further qualification, since the patient who enjoys the resulting health is understood.

A further subtlety of the distinction between *finis cuius gratia* and *finis cui* arises in conjunction with the distinction between intention and execution. From the perspective of the order of execution, what the agent's work achieves is called the *finis effectus* (the "end effected") because it results from the agent's action.[26] In contrast, the *finis cuius gratia* is called the *finis causa* (the "end as cause").[27] Now, at times the *finis effectus* is materially identical with the *finis causa*, as when a craftsman labors out of the desire for a certain artifact (first in intention) and the artifact itself results from his labor (last in execution).[28] Here, the artifact both motivates the agent's action and results from it. Thus, it is a cause from the perspective of intention and an effect from the perspective of execution. However, in other cases the *finis effectus* and the *finis causa* are not materially identical. For example, a craftsman may work to produce an artifact in order to make a profit. In this case, the artifact is only a means to the profit, which is the true end.[29]

The Salmanticenses generally refer to redeemed humanity as both the *finis cui* and the *finis effectus* of the incarnation. This is understandable, since redemption for humanity is what the redemptive

---

25. *De motivo Incarnationis*, dub. 1, §5, no. 30 (Palmé, 13:292).

26. This is to say that in the taxonomy of final cause, the *finis effectus* is on the side of the *finis operis*, not the *finis operantis*. In other words, when we speak of *finis effectus* in the strict sense, we are speaking of the result or end-state toward which the work naturally tends. For example, health is naturally produced by exercise and is thus the *finis effectus* of exercise. Now, when the agent intends health and so chooses exercise as a means to produce health, then on the part of the *finis operantis*, health will also be the *finis cuius gratia* and thus a *finis causa*. See R. P. Phillips, *Modern Thomistic Philosophy: An Explanation for Students* (Westminster, Md.: The Newman Bookshop, 1935), 2:246.

27. See John of St. Thomas, *Cursus philosophicus*, vol. 2, pars 1, q. 13, a. 1 (Vivès, 2:242).

28. Josef Gredt, *Elementa philosophiae Aristotelico-Thomisticae*, 13th ed. reviewed and expanded by Eucharius Zenzen, vol. 2 (Barcelona: Herder, 1961), no. 770.

29. Gredt, *Elementa philosophiae Aristotelico-Thomisticae*, vol. 2, no. 770.

incarnation accomplishes.[30] Similarly, we might say that health results from medicine, and so "the healed patient" is both the *finis cui* and the *finis effectus* of giving medicine. Again, the *finis effectus* can be limited strictly to the order of execution, where it means the result that the work tends to produce considered as a mere outcome and without reference to whether anyone intends that outcome.

The most precise distinction the Salmanticenses make in their disputation *De motivo Incarnationis* is that God willed "the remediation from sin to be the *finis cui* of Christ's Incarnation, [and] the remedy for sin its *finis effectus*."[31] In other words, the incarnation brings about remediation from sin (*finis effectus*), and it is the human race to whom this remediation is intended as a benefit (*finis cui*). Typically, however, the Salmanticenses treat *finis cui* and *finis effectus* as functionally equivalent.[32] The practical equivalence is natural enough in the present matter, since if God wills humanity in need of redemption to be the *finis cui* of the incarnation, then the incarnation so decreed will of its nature produce redemption (*finis effectus*). It is precisely because the redemption that the incarnation produces can only be the redemption *of someone* that the *finis effectus* and the *finis cui* overlap.

For the Salmanticenses, the *finis effectus* of the incarnation and the *finis causa* are not materially identical—that is, they are not the same object considered in two ways. Instead, Christ himself is the *finis cuius gratia* and thus the *finis causa*.[33] In contrast, redeemed hu-

30. Cf. Gonet, who remarks that what some call *finis cui* others call *finis effectus*, in *Clypeus theologiae Thomisticae* III, tract. 1, disp. 5, a. 1, §6, no. 53 (Vivès, 5:483); and John of St. Thomas, who explains, "Omnia autem motiva ad aliquid eligendum, vel habent rationem finis causae, vel rationem finis effectus. Vocatur finis causae, ille cujus gratia aliquid sit, sive finis proximus, sive ultimus: finis effectus, ille qui consequitur, et ad quem utilis est positio talis rei; et iste finis etiam motivus esse potest." John of St. Thomas, *Cursus theologicus* III, q. 1, disp. 3, a. 1, no. 18 (Vivès, 8:95).
31. "Hominum remedium a peccato esse finem *cui* Incarnationis Christi, et remedium peccati finem ejus effectum." *De motivo Incarnationis*, dub. 1, §2, no. 11 (Palmé, 13:273).
32. As they do in *De motivo Incarnationis*, dub. 1, §1, no. 5 (Palmé, 13:268); dub. 1, §1 no. 7 (Palmé, 13:269); dub. 1, §6, no. 34 (Palmé, 13:296); dub. 1, §6, no. 36, (Palmé, 13:298); and dub. 1, §8, no. 42 (Palmé, 13:305).
33. In *De motivo Incarnationis*, the Salmanticenses never use the term *finis causa*, but

manity is the subject the benefit of the incarnation is directed toward (*finis cui*), and human redemption is what results from the incarnation in the order of execution (*finis effectus*). Therefore, the Salmanticenses do not hold that redemption is the primary and principal final cause of the incarnation.[34]

This does not mean that redeemed humanity, as the *finis cui*, has no share in the incarnation's finality.[35] Nor does it mean that redemption is not a *sine qua non* condition for the incarnation. After all, an agent can decide to pursue the *finis cuius gratia* precisely with an order to a given *finis cui* and not otherwise. For example, a physician can will the health of one patient while not willing the health of another. In this way, a particular *finis cui* becomes an intrinsic part of the agent's total motive, one without which the agent would not act. Again, this is because *finis cuius gratia* and *finis cui* are not two ends but two aspects of the single end as the agent concretely intends it.[36]

Though nuanced, this consideration is necessary, since *finis cuius gratia* and *finis cui* cannot be strictly isolated, even conceptually, as long as we are considering a concrete action. For example, the fact that the God-man is the *finis cuius gratia* of the decree of the incarnation and redeemed humanity the *finis cui*, according to the Salmanticenses, does not exclude that the God-man himself also falls under

---

that Christ is the *finis causa* is implied by way of contrast with what they say about redeemed humanity as the *finis effectus*.

34. When the Salmanticenses contrast the terms *finis effectus* and *finis cuius gratia*, they characterize the *finis effectus* as "minus principalis et secundarius." They give the example of the corporeal glory that Christ merited, which was a result of his actions but not the primary intention motivating them. See Salmanticenses, *Cursus theologicus*, tract. 19, *De charitate theologica*, dub. 2, §3, no. 27 (Palmé, 12:23).

35. Only when we focus on the *finis effectus* precisely as such (i.e., only within the order of execution) do we exclude the aspect of final causality, since in this case we limit our perspective solely to the object considered as resulting from the agent's action. Cf. Gredt, *Elementa philosophiae Aristotelico-Thomisticae*, vol. 2, no. 770.

36. "Omnia haec fuerunt volita a Deo per illam intentionem ut constituerint unum finem adaequatum, coalescentem ex ratione *cujus gratia*, et ex ratione *cui*, cum mutua eorum inter se dependentia in diversis generibus." *De motivo Incarnationis*, dub. 1, §6, no. 34 (Palmé, 13:296–97).

the *finis cui*, since glory redounds to him as redeemer.[37] Conversely, it is also true that the *finis cui* in a way enters into the composition of the *finis cuius gratia*.

A further distinction is needed to grasp this point with precision. In the Salmanticenses' view, the end is divided into the *finis cuius gratia* and the *finis cui*. Of these two elements, the *finis cuius gratia* is the more dominant. However, the *finis cuius gratia* is itself divided into the *finis qui* (the "end which") and the *finis quo* (the "end whereby").[38] "The first is the thing itself or the object we desire to acquire. The second is the acquiring and attainment of such a thing."[39]

Table 3-1 summarizes the kinds of final cause discussed by the Salmanticenses in the course of their argument. In concrete acts, there can be overlap among these kinds of final cause. Sometimes, the *finis cui* enters into the composition of the *finis qui* (the objective aspect of the *finis cuius gratia*). For example, when looking at predestination to glory, the person is the *finis cui* of the glory willed, the glory itself being the *finis cuius gratia*. Yet the *finis qui* is nothing other than the glorified person. In this way, the *finis cui*, considered from a different angle, partly constitutes the *finis qui* and thus the *finis cuius gratia*.[40]

Similarly, health is the *finis cuius gratia* of the physician's work, while the patient who is to be healed is the *finis cui*. Nevertheless, the *finis qui*, the objective thing that the physician wills, is really the healthy patient. Only what is definite and concrete can be effectively willed. The physician can consider or love "health" in the abstract, but he cannot *intend* health in this way, since such a thing cannot ex-

---

37. *De motivo Incarnationis*, dub. 1, §6, no. 32 (Palmé, 13:295).

38. Salmanticenses, *Cursus theologicus*, tract. 8, q. 1, proem., no. 4 (Palmé, 5:3); and tract. 19, dub. 2, §3, no. 26 (Palmé, 12:23). Confusingly, when Aquinas himself makes this distinction, he calls by the name of *finis cuius* what later theologians, including the Salmanticenses, call *finis qui*. See ST I-II, q. 1, a. 8, co. (Leonine, 6:16); and q. 2, a. 7, co. (Leonine, 6:23).

39. "Primus est ipsa res, vel objectum, quod adipisci desideramus: secundus adeptio, et consecutio talis rei." Salmanticenses, *Cursus theologicus*, tract. 8, q. 1, proem., no. 4 (Palmé, 5:3).

40. *De motivo Incarnationis*, dub. 1, §6, no. 34 (Palmé, 13:297).

Table 3-1. Aspects of Finality in the Salmanticenses

Term	Meaning	Example
Finis cuius gratia	"End for-the-sake-of-which": That which is desired on its own account and on whose account other things are desired. This can be considered as the end *simpliciter*.	Health
Finis cui (*finis utilitatis*)	"End to-which" ("end of benefit"): The subject to whom the agent wills the benefit of the desired good.	The patient
Finis causa	"End as cause": The end considered as what motivates the agent to act. From this perspective, the means are an effect of the end.	Health as the reason for taking medicine
Finis effectus	"End effected": The end considered not as a cause but as the result or outcome of the agent's action. From this perspective, the end is an effect of the means.	Health as the result of taking medicine
Finis qui	"End which": The object desired, a component of the *finis cuius gratia*.	The healthy patient
Finis quo	"End whereby": The attainment of the object desired, a component of the *finis cuius gratia*.	The patient's experience of health

ist and cannot, therefore, be practically pursued.[41] Rather, when the physician intends health, what he really intends is *a concrete state of health in a certain person*.

The same is true of God's choice of the incarnation. God not only

---

41. As Juan de la Anunciación, himself the writer of *De motivo Incarnationis*, notes in his edition of the Carmelites' *Artium cursus*. See Juan de la Anunciación, *Liber II Physicorum*, disp. 14, q. 1, §1, no. 1, in *Collegii Complutensis Fr. Discalceatorum B. M. de Monte Carmeli, artium cursus, ad breviorem formam collectus, et novo ordine, atque faciliori stylo dispositus* (London: Sumptibus Petri Chevalier, 1670), 2:231–32. The Salmanticenses expressly endorse the treatment of final causality found in the *Artium cursus* as their own view in *Cursus theologicus*, tract. 8, q. 1, proem., no. 7 (Palmé, 5:4).

loves the abstract idea of the incarnation but also decrees it with all its determinate circumstances. The concrete finality of God's decree can be analyzed in terms of the complementary components of that finality. This is the first key to the Salamanca theory. But God's decree can also be analyzed from the viewpoint of how what he could choose relates to what he does choose. This leads to the second key.

Two *signa rationis in quo* Are Necessary and Sufficient

The second key principle of the Salmanticenses' theory is the use of precisely two *signa rationis in quo*. In the preceding chapter, I explained the origin and nature of *signa rationis* as a theological instrument for clarifying logical priority and posteriority without real temporal succession. Now I will summarize how the Salmanticenses use this instrument. Complaining of theologians who needlessly multiply *signa* in their explanations of God's knowing and willing,[42] the Salmanticenses settle on precisely two such stages, one prior to the determination of the divine will and one posterior to it.[43] Again, this is a conceptual distinction necessary from a human perspective, not a real distinction in God himself.

The first *signum* is that in which God knows himself and thus all possible things he can do—with all their possible interdependencies and combinations—by his knowledge of simple intelligence. The second *signum* is that in which he has willed to actualize a given historical order and thus sees it with the knowledge of vision.

The Salmanticenses qualify each of these as a *signum* "*in quo*," as opposed to a *signum* "*a quo*."[44] The qualifier *in quo* indicates one-way entailment, whereas the qualifier *a quo* indicates two-way entailment.[45] If A is prior to B *in quo*, this means that B implies A but not

---

42. *De motivo Incarnationis*, dub. 1, §1, no. 5 (Palmé, 13:268).
43. *De motivo Incarnationis*, dub. 1, §1, no. 6 (Palmé, 13:268).
44. *De motivo Incarnationis*, dub. 1, §1, no. 6 (Palmé, 13:268).
45. Cf. Antoine Goudin, *Philosophia juxta inconcussa tutissimaque d. Thomae dogmata*, vol. 1, *Logica* (Pompei: Urbeveteri, 1859), 362. As Thomas Harper notes, the seemingly strange terminology reflects that *in quo* priority is intrinsic to the thing, while *a quo*

vice versa. On the other hand, if A is prior to B *a quo*, then B implies A, and A also implies B. *Signa in quo* are conceptual stages based on relations of priority *in quo*. *Signa a quo* are stages based on relations of priority *a quo*.

For this reason, the qualifier "*in quo*" is often used for straightforward temporal priority and posteriority.[46] In the present discussion, however, temporal priority is not at issue. Instead, the Salmanticenses identify a different kind of priority as the basis for their two *signa in quo*: *prioritas consequentia subsistendi* ("priority in existential entailment").[47] This kind of priority is atemporal, referring instead to a relationship of logical or existential entailment that is nonreciprocal, particularly one conceived of in terms of higher and lower orders. For example, "animal" is prior to "human" *consequentia subsistendi*, seeing as "animal" can exist or can be conceived of without "human," but not vice versa. Similarly, God can know all possible orders of history without willing or seeing any actualized order of history. The latter implies the former, but the converse is not true. Hence, priority *consequentia subsistendi* is a kind of priority *in quo*, meaning that it can serve as the basis for *signa in quo*.

The qualifier "*a quo*," on the other hand, refers to reciprocal causal relationships.[48] In the case of mutual causes, each cause is prior

---

priority is based on a relation of derivation from another. Thomas Harper, *The Metaphysics of the School* (London: Macmillan, 1881), 2:565–66.

46. For an example of typical usage, see Capréolus's treatment of the Immaculate Conception, where he contrasts priority *in quo* (temporal) with reciprocal causal priority (*a quo*). Capréolus, *Defensiones in III Sent.*, d. 5, q. 2, a. 3, ad 12 prob. (Paban and Pègues, 5:83). The Salmanticenses discuss various kinds of priority, including temporal priority *in quo*, in *Cursus theologicus*, tract. 15, disp. 3, dub. 4, §1, no. 71 (Palmé, 10:579). Cf. Gredt, *Elementa philosophiae Aristotelico-Thomisticae*, vol. 1, no. 206.

47. Aristotle identifies this kind of priority in *Categories*, 12.14b9–23. The Latin terminology derives from Boethius's translation: "Videtur autem praeter eos qui dicti sunt alter esse prioris modus; eorum enim quae convertuntur secundum essentiae consequentiam, quod alterius quomodolibet causa est digne prius natura dicitur. Quoniam autem sunt quaedam talia, manifestum est; nam esse hominem convertitur secundum subsistentiae consequentiam ad verum de eo sermonem." Aristotle, *Categoriae vel praedicamenta: Translatio Boethii*, ed. L. Minio-Paluello (Bruges: Desclée de Brouwer, 1961), 38. In other words, the logical "consequence" (entailment) does not run both ways.

48. See, for example, the Salmanticenses' discussion of *signa* in the context of

from its own perspective, so that A is prior to B in one causal order but posterior to B in another. This complementarity avoids a vicious circle.[49] For example, in the order of material cause, matter is prior to form, but in the order of formal cause, form is prior to matter. Because these two perspectives are complementary, there is two-way entailment. Matter cannot be prior to form in such a way as to exist or be conceived of entirely apart from form. Similarly, a material form cannot really exist or be conceived of without reference to matter. Hence, reciprocal causal priority is priority *a quo*, not priority *in quo*.

This applies to *finis cuius gratia* and *finis cui*. For the Salmanticenses, Christ is the *finis cuius gratia* and thus prior from that perspective to all other divine works. This is priority *a quo* because *finis cuius gratia* is complemented by other causal perspectives, particularly *finis cui*. Thus, from the perspective of *finis cui*, humanity in need of redemption is prior *a quo*, and from the perspective of material cause, sin to be destroyed is prior *a quo*. God's knowledge and effective choice extend to all these mutually interrelated causal aspects by a single act.[50] No matter how complex the world and its

---

predestination and the Immaculate Conception in *Cursus theologicus*, tract. 5, disp. 9, dub. 3, §6, nos. 108–10 (Palmé, 2:452–53); tract. 13, disp. 15, dub. 2, §2, nos. 54–58 (Palmé, 8:109–11); and tract. 15, disp. 3, dub. 4, §1, no. 71 (Palmé, 10:578–79). Cf. Dominic Lynch, *Summa philosophiae speculativae* III, q. 6, a. 2, in *Summa philosophiae speculativae iuxta mentem et doctrinam D. Thomae et Aristotelis* (Paris: Sumptibus Antonii Bertier, 1670), 3:566; and Signoriello, *Lexicon peripateticum*, s.v. "prioritas temporis—naturae—originis—cognitionis," 266.

49. The Scholastic maxim (variously paraphrased) is "causae sunt sibi invicem causae (sed in diverso genere)." This means that A can be a cause of B while B is also a cause of A, as long as A is related to B by one kind of causality and B is related to A by another mutually corresponding kind of causality. See Gredt, *Elementa philosophiae Aristotelico-Thomisticae*, vol. 2, no. 749.6. Cf. Complutenses, *Artium cursus, Liber I de generatione et corruptione*, disp. 2, q. 7, §2, no. 69 (Chevalier, 3:62); Gonet, *Clypeus theologiae Thomisticae* III, tract. 1, disp. 5, a. 1, §6, no. 54 (Vivès, 5:483); and Reginald Garrigou-Lagrange, "Motivum Incarnationis fuit motivum misericordiae," *Angelicum* 7, no. 3 (1930): 298–302.

50. On analogy, one might say that we can look within a material substance and identify causal components (matter and form) that will each be prior to the other *a quo* in their own respective orders. However, we can also look at the whole substance and distinguish its possible existence from its actual existence. From this latter perspective,

history become, God can still choose, actualize, and see everything by a single act. And—more to the point—this can be *conceptualized* as a single act.⁵¹

This is why the Salmanticenses characterize the relationship between what God can do and what he does as priority *in quo* rather than priority *a quo*: the entailment is entirely one-way. Knowing what God can do does not allow us to infer what he has done. In other words, the notion of priority *in quo* safeguards God's freedom. God's effects *ad extra* entail God's power, but God's power does not necessarily entail his effects *ad extra*. The free exercise of the divine will is required.

Thus, in one *signum in quo*, God knows all possible combinations of creatures with all their possible interdependencies and relative priorities. Then, out of all these possibilities, in the second *signum in quo*, he decrees and thus actualizes whichever historical order he wills. In this way, two and only two *signa in quo* are required to conceptualize God's providential decree of the present order of history.

THE SALMANTICENSES' POSITION

The Salmanticenses' position relies on combining the two principal keys outlined above. Putting together distinct species of final cause and precisely two *signa in quo* allows the Salmanticenses to harmonize two opinions: that Christ is truly the first intended by God and that Christ would not have come absent sin.

From the beginning of their treatment, the Salmanticenses profess that they are convinced of Christ's primacy in God's intention.

---

the possible existence is prior *in quo* to the actual existence, since the mere possibility of the substance does not entail its actuality. In the present discussion, it is the universe conceived of as a whole that is at issue.

51. We could not, however, conceptualize the situation adequately with only one *signum in quo* (which would not really be a conceptual *stage* at all), since this would not leave us any way to account for God's freedom. We need one *signum in quo* for what God can do and one *signum in quo* for what God has freely chosen to do. I will defend this more fully in the next chapter.

The Salamanca Theory

We must suppose that God intended the Incarnation for its intrinsic excellence in such a way that he decreed Christ as the first willed, to which all other things, even the very permission and remediation of sin, would be ordered as the *finis cuius gratia*, to the point that our predestination and all its effects depend on Christ and suppose him as previously intended and decreed in the genus of final cause.[52]

They note that this opinion is not common among Thomists.[53] Yet they find it eminently scriptural and Thomistic. In support, they quote Colossians 1:15–18:

He is the image of the invisible God, the first-born of all creation; for in him all things were created, in heaven and on earth, visible and invisible, whether thrones or dominions or principalities or authorities—all things were created through him and for him. He is before all things, and in him all things hold together. He is the head of the body, the church; he is the beginning, the first-born from the dead.

They also quote the passages "He has made him the head over all things for the church, which is his body" (Eph 1:22–23a) and "He chose us in him before the foundation of the world, that we should be holy and blameless before him. He destined us in love to be his sons through Jesus Christ, according to the purpose of his will, to the praise of his glorious grace which he freely bestowed on us in the Beloved" (Eph 1:4–6). Christ's priority, they say, is clearly not in the order of execution, the chronological progression of history, and so such passages must refer to priority in God's intention. The fact that God has willed other things for Christ's sake and the fact that Christ's predestination is the cause of the election of others also prove that Christ enjoys priority in God's intention.

However, affirming Christ as the *finis cuius gratia* of God's oth-

---

52. "Supponendum est Deum intendisse Incarnationem ob ejus intrinsecam excellentiam, ita ut decreverit Christum tanquam primo volitum, in quod omnia alia, et ipsius etiam permissio peccati, atque remedium ordinarentur, sicut in finem cujus gratia: adeo ut praedestinatio nostra, et omnes ejus effectus dependeant a Christo, illumque supponant in genere causae finalis prius intentum, et decretum." *De motivo Incarnationis*, dub. 1, §1, no. 4 (Palmé, 13:266).

53. *De motivo Incarnationis*, dub. 1, §1, no. 4 (Palmé, 13:266).

er providential acts creates a special difficulty for the Salmanticenses. If they were willing to concede the Scotistic thesis, there would be no problem. Because they are committed to the Thomistic thesis that Christ would not have come absent sin, they have to show both that the incarnation was essentially redemptive and dependent on sin and that God willed and intended Christ before all else.

As noted above, the Salmanticenses hope to achieve this by combining the two keys to their theory. This is to say that they consider the whole order of history as falling within a single divine decree. Then, they distinguish different causal components of the historical order that give rise to different relative priorities, since each cause is first in its own order. The Salmanticenses summarize the various species of causality that they discern within the single divine decree of the incarnation as follows:

It should be held that God, by a primary intention, decreed Christ not only in substance but also in the circumstance of passible flesh and the aspect of Redeemer from Adam's sin and by the same act simultaneously willed the permission of the aforementioned sin and the redemption of the human race through Christ. This was in such a way that among the aforementioned objects, not of themselves connected, he decreed and established the mutual dependence in different genera of cause whereby Christ would be the *finis cuius gratia* of the passive permission of the aforementioned sin, the redemption of the human race, and of all the divine works pertaining to the order of nature and of grace, that the sin permitted would be the *materia circa quam* of the redemption, and that the human race would be the *finis cui*.[54]

---

54. "Tenendum est Deum primaria intentione decrevisse Christum non solum secundum substantiam, sed etiam secundum circumstantiam carnis passibilis, et in ratione Redemptoris a peccato Adami; et simul eodem actu voluisse permissionem praedicti peccati, et redemptionis generis humani per Christum. Ita quod inter praedicta objecta ex se non connexa hanc mutuam dependentiam in diverso genere causae decreverit, et constituerit, quod Christus esset finis *cujus gratia* permissionis passivae praedicti peccati, et redemptionis generis humani, et omnium operum divinorum pertinentium ad ordinem tam naturae, quam gratiae: et ut peccatum permissum esset materia circa quam redemptionis, et genus humanum esset finis *cui*." *De motivo Incarnationis*, dub. 1, §5, no. 29 (Palmé, 13:291).

In other words, if we take the event of the incarnation as a whole, sin is the matter addressed (*materia circa quam*), redeemed humanity is the beneficiary (*finis cui*), and Christ himself is the good on whose account the others are permitted or willed (*finis cuius gratia*).

Next, because each cause is first in its own order, there can be mutual dependencies with corresponding relative priorities from the perspective of the various causes. All of these fall within the single divine decree and can thus be accounted for by two *signa in quo*.

In that first *signum*, God knew that the universe comprised of angels, men, and the other creatures that have really been made was possible. He knew that the first man, Adam, was possible, who would receive original justice with the stipulation that by not sinning he would preserve it for himself and his children, whereas by sinning he would lose it for himself and his children, constituting himself and them as guilty and liable to eternal damnation. He knew that the Incarnation, or the union of the divine Word to human nature, was possible, from which Christ, the true God-man, would arise, who by the dignity of his person would be able to elicit infinitely satisfactory acts and thereby to make equal satisfaction for any offenses and to merit whatever reward he willed. He knew that Christ, on account of his infinite excellence, was most suited to be established as the end of all creatures, for all things to be made for him, and for men to be chosen or predestined to glory in such a way that all these effects would regard Christ as the end and would depend on him in the genus of final cause. He also knew that the sins that he would permit both in Adam and in his children would be the sufficient matter as whose remedy and satisfaction Christ would be predestined, in such a way that his predestination would be bound to the remediation of sin and the redemption of men, seeing as there is no doubt that this combination and connection falls within the bounds of what is possible. Finally (to omit other things not as pertinent to our present consideration), he knew that between the Incarnation and the remediation of sin or the redemption of men the connection and mutual dependence could be established such that the permission of sin and its remediation would be ordered to Christ as the *finis cuius gratia* and depend on him in the genus of final cause while, conversely, the Incarnation of Christ would be ordered to the salvation of men as the *finis cui*, the *finis effectus*, would regard sin as the matter to be destroyed through his satisfaction, and would depend on these things in the genus both of material cause and also of final cause *cui*.[55]

This, in a nutshell, is the Salmanticenses' doctrine. They can hold Christ as primary in God's intention because he is the *finis cuius gratia*, the proximate end to which all the other divine permissions (including the permission of sin) and works are directed. From the perspective of *finis cuius gratia*, then, Christ is first. At the same time, from the perspective of material cause and *finis cui*, sin itself and humanity to be redeemed are first. Since God decreed all these elements precisely with this interdependence, Christ would not have come absent sin by virtue of the present decree. How, then, do the Salmanticenses argue for their position?

---

55. "Deus in primo illo signo cognovit possibilem esse universum ex Angelis, et hominibus, aliisque creaturis, quae re ipsa factae sunt, coalescentem; cognovit possibilem esse primum hominem Adam, qui justitiam originalem eo pacto acciperet, ut non peccando, pro se, et filiis conservaret; peccando autem, pro se, et filiis amitteret, se, et illos constituendo reos aeternae damnationis. Cognovit possibilem esse Incarnationem, sive unionem Verbi divini ad naturam humanam, ex qua Christus verus Deus homo consurgeret, qui pro suae personae dignitate posset elicere actus infinite satisfactorios, ac subinde satisfacere ad aequalitatem pro quibusvis offensis, et mereri, quodcumque praemium vellet. Cognovit Christum ob infinitam ipsius excellentiam aptissimum esse, qui constitueretur finis omnium creaturarum, et propter quem omnia fierent, et homines eligerentur, sive praedestinarentur ad gloriam; ita ut omnes hi effectus respicerent Christum ut finem, dependerentque ab eo in genere causae finalis. Cognovit etiam peccata, quae tam in Adamo, quam in filiis permitteret, esse materiam sufficientem, in cujus remedium, et satisfactionem praedestinaretur Christus: ita ut ipsius praedestinatio alligaretur peccati remedio, et hominum redemptioni: ea quippe combinatio, atque connexio dubium non est, quod cadat intra latitudinem possibilium. Cognovit denique (ut alia ad praesentem considerationem non adeo pertinentia praetermittamus, [*sic*] posse inter Incarnationem, et peccati remedium, sive hominum redemptionem eam connexionem, et mutuam dependentiam constitui, quod permissio peccati, ejusque remedium ordinarentur in Christum tanquam in finem *cujus gratia*; ab eoque dependerent in genere causae finalis: e contra vero Christi Incarnatio ordinaretur in salutem hominum tanquam finem *cui*, sive effectum, respiceretque peccatum tanquam materiam destruendam per suam satisfactionem, ab illisque dependeret in genere causae tum materialis, tum etiam finalis *cui*." *De motivo Incarnationis*, dub. 1, §1, no. 7 (Palmé, 13:268–69).

The Salamanca Theory 79

THE SALMANTICENSES' ARGUMENTATION

Having summarized the Salmanticenses' position, I will now give an overview of their argumentation. The scope of their first doubt is whether God would assume flesh by virtue of the present decree apart from sin. To this they reply (with probability, not absolute certainty) in the negative, following the opinion of Aquinas.

In support of this, the Salmanticenses first catalogue Thomists and other theologians who agree with them.[56] This is not a proof, but it establishes that the opinion is common. Turning to the question of what proof to offer, the Salmanticenses state, "It is proved by one single yet most weighty foundation of St. Thomas: if the motive or reason for which God has *de facto* decreed the Incarnation ceased, the Word would not assume flesh by virtue of the present decree."[57] And human redemption is the reason Scripture and the Fathers assign for the incarnation. Certainly, if God had not been going to permit sin, then he might have also decreed the incarnation for some strictly nonredemptive motive, but then we would be speaking of a different decree, not the present one. The Salmanticenses' core principle, then, is the rule that God's free actions are made known only through revelation.[58]

For this reason, the Salmanticenses turn to authority to show that God decreed the incarnation as essentially redemptive.[59] The

---

56. *De motivo Incarnationis*, dub. 1, §2, no. 8 (Palmé, 13:269).

57. "Probatur unico, sed gravissimo D Tho. fundamento: nam cessante motivo aut ratione propter quae Deus de facto decreverit Incarnationem, Verbum non assumeret carnem ex vi praesentis decreti." *De motivo Incarnationis*, dub. 1, §2, no. 8 (Palmé, 13:269–70).

58. In the generation following the Salmanticenses, Pablo de la Concepción, OCD (d. 1734), who published a synopsis of their work, remarks of the principle that we must rely on revelation to speak about the motive of the incarnation: "Haec ratio est adeo solida, ut quamvis millies materiam hanc consideres, non poteris aliam fortiorem, immo nec absolute aliam invenire, pro hac probabilissima sententia." Pablo de la Concepción, *Tractatus theologici*, tract. 16, disp. 2, dub. 1, §2, no. 4, in *Tractatus theologici juxta miram D. Thomae et Cursus Salmanticensis ff. Discalceatorum B. Mariae de Monte Carmeli primitivae observantiae doctrinam*, 2nd ed. (Parma: Apud haeredes Pauli Monti, sub signo fidei, 1725), 4:199.

59. *De motivo Incarnationis*, dub. 1, §2, no. 9 (Palmé, 13:270–71). They cite Mk 10:45;

Salmanticenses conclude their catena of authoritative passages with the statement: "Therefore it cannot be denied that, according to sacred Scripture and the common opinion of the Fathers, God intended, chose, and decreed the Incarnation as a remedy for sin and in connection with the redemption and salvation of men."[60]

Having offered authorities in favor of the view that Christ came for redemption, the Salmanticenses then give a series of even stronger authoritative passages stating that Christ would not have come without humanity's need for redemption.[61] On this basis, the Sal-

---

Lk 5:31–32; Jn 1:3–4; Jn 3:16; Gal 4:4–5a; Heb 2:14; 1 Tm 1:15; Ambrose, *De Incarnationis dominicae sacramento*, chap. 6, no. 56 (CSEL 79:252); Athanasius, *Oratio de Incarnatione Verbi*, no. 4 (PG 25:104); Augustine, Sermon 9 *de verbis Apostoli*, Sermon 175 (PL 38:945); Pseudo-Basil, *Homilia in sanctam Christi generationem*, no. 3 (PG 31:1464); Cyril of Alexandria, *Thesaurus de sancta et consubstantiali Trinitate*, assert. 15 (PG 75:292); Cyril of Jerusalem, Catechesis 6, chap. 11, in *S. patris nostri Cyrilli Hierosolymorum Archiepiscopi opera quae supersunt omnia*, ed. Guilielmus Carolus Reischl, (Munich: Sumtibus Librariae Lentnerianae, 1848), 1:171; Epiphanius of Salamis, *Panarion*, haer. 20, no. 1, in *Epiphanius*, ed. Karl Holl, (Berlin: De Gruyter, 2013), 1:227; Gregory of Nazianzus, Oration 30, *Fourth Theological Oration*, no. 2 (SC 250:228); Gregory of Nyssa, *Oratio in diem natalem Christi* (PG 46:1127–50); Hilary of Poitiers, *De Trinitate* II, chap. 24 (CCSL 62:60); Irenaeus of Lyon, *Adversus haereses* III, chap. 19 (SC 211:372–74); Jerome, *Commentarius in Ecclesiasten*, chap. 7, v. 20 (CCSL 72:309); John Chrysostom, *In Matthaeum homilia LXVI al. LXVII* (PG 58:626) and *In Epistolam ad Hebraeos homilia* V, no. 1 (PG 63:47); John Damascene, *De fide orthodoxa* IV, chap. 4 (SC 540:164); John Scottus Eriugena (attributed to Origen), *Homilia in prologum S. Evangelii secundum Joannem* (PL 122:295); Leo the Great, Tractate 77, Sermon on Pentecost (CCSL 138A:488); Tertullian, *De carne Christi*, chap. 4, no. 3 (CCSL 2:878); Theodoret, *Haereticarum fabularum compendium* V, chap. 11 (PG 83:489); Theophylact, *Enarratio in evangelium Joannis*, chap. 3, v. 16 (PG 123:1212); Bernard of Clairvaux, *In laudibus Virginis Mariae*, homily 3: *super "Missus est"*, no. 14, (Leclercq and Rochais, 4:45–46); Guerric of Igny, Sermon 3 on the Nativity, no. 1 (SC 166:186); and the Nicene Creed's "for us men and for our salvation he came down from heaven."

60. "Negari ergo non potest, quod secundum Scripturam sacram, et communem Patrum sententiam Deus intenderit, elegerit, ac decreverit Incarnationem in remedium peccati, et connexive ad hominum redemptionem, et salutem." *De motivo Incarnationis*, dub. 1, §2, no. 9 (Palmé, 13:271).

61. *De motivo Incarnationis*, dub. 1, §2, no. 10 (Palmé, 13:271–72). They cite Ambrose, *Explanatio psalmorum xii*, Explanation of Psalm 39, chap. 20 (CSEL 64:225); Andrew of Crete, *Oratio X in venerabilem pretiosae et vivificae crucis Exaltationem* (PG 97:1020); Athanasius, *Oratio II contra Arianos*, no. 54, in *Athanasius Werke*, ed. Kyriakos Savvidis (Berlin: De Gruyter, 1998), 1.1.2:230; Augustine, *Enarrationes in psalmos*, psalm 36, serm. 2, no. 15 (CCSL 38:357); Augustine, Sermon 8 *de verbis Apostoli*, Sermon 174 (PL 38:940), and Sermon 9 *de verbis Apostoli*, Sermon 175 (PL 38:945); Pseudo-Augustine,

manticenses profess that their opinion is not only the Thomistic one but also the patristic one: "Since, then, our adversaries consider themselves in this matter to be going against St. Thomas, they must also admit that they have the other sacred doctors against them as well."[62]

The Salmanticenses, however, do identify two sticking points in the evidence they have presented so far.[63] First, is Aquinas right to suppose that what depends on God's free will alone is only made known to us in Scripture and the Church's teaching? For example, the Angelic Doctor himself seems to argue for the existence of angels from reason, not from Scripture alone. Second, if the Fathers are affirming that there was *no* other motive for the incarnation than human redemption from sin, aren't they obviously going too far? If not, then the patristic testimony does not constrain us to view the incarnation as essentially redemptive.

In response to the first, the Salmanticenses reaffirm that we can only make determinate assertions about what is above what nature requires (*supra exigentiam naturae*), what depends on God's free will, if God reveals it to us. "To conduct oneself otherwise is not to do theology but to commit divination and to give oneself over to rash discourse."[64] Aquinas's discussion of the angels, they point out, is not an attempt to prove the angels' existence from reason alone but,

---

Hypomnesticon III, in *Text Edited from the Manuscripts*, vol. 2 of *The Pseudo-Augustinian Hypomnesticon Against the Pelagians and Celestinans*, ed. John Edward Chisholm, (Fribourg: The University Press, 1980), 121; Cyril of Alexandria, *De SS. Trinitate dialogi* VII (PG 75:968); Gregory of Nazianzus, Oration 30, *Fourth Theological Oration*, no. 2 (SC 250:228); Gregory the Great, *Expositio in librum primum Regum* IV, no. 10 (CCSL 144:300–1); Irenaeus of Lyon, *Adversus haereses* V, chap. 14 (SC 153:182); Pseudo-John Chrysostom, *In Ascensionem Domini nostri Jesu Christi sermo* II (PG 52:793–94); Leo the Great, Tractate 77, Sermon on Pentecost (CCSL 138A:488); Bernard of Clairvaux, Sermon 1 on the Vigil of the Nativity, no. 2 (Leclercq and Rochais, 4:199); Rupert of Deutz, *De operibus Spiritus Sancti* II, chap. 6 (CCCM 24:1868); and the *felix culpa* of the *Exsultet*.

62. "Cum ergo Adversarii censeant se in hac causa agere contra D. Thomam; opus est ipsis fateri, quod sibi contrarios habeant sacros alios Doctores." *De motivo Incarnationis*, dub. 1, §2, no. 10 (Palmé, 13:272).

63. They discuss these in *De motivo Incarnationis*, dub. 1, §2, no. 11 (Palmé, 13:272–73).

64. "Et aliter se gerere non est Theologizare, sed divinare et temere se discursui committere." *De motivo Incarnationis*, dub. 1, §2, no. 11 (Palmé, 13:272).

presupposing their existence based on Scripture, to argue rationally that they are purely spiritual substances. It is an inquiry into the angelic nature and an argument from fittingness based on the perfection of the universe. When Aquinas wants to show that angels actually exist, he cites Scripture. Further, the Salmanticenses observe, angels are *natural* creatures, even if not perceptible by human beings, whereas the hypostatic union is radically *above nature*. Philosophers may have suspected the existence of angels, but they did not grasp the mystery of the God-man.

In response to the second, the Salmanticenses explain that when the Fathers assign redemption as the only motive for the incarnation, they are speaking not of *possible* motives but of the actual motive reported in Scripture.[65] In this context, when they deny other motives, they are not denying them as possible but as actual. Further, the Fathers are not denying other actual motives *connected* with the redemption of the human race. Aquinas himself explains that "there are many other benefits that have obtained above what human sensibility can apprehend" and yet these are all linked with redemption in some way.[66]

Initial Scotistic Objections and Salamanca Replies

Next, the Salmanticenses give several Scotistic objections to their doctrine along with their own replies.[67] The first objection is that while Scripture and the Fathers do positively assign redemption as the motive of the incarnation, they do not exclude other motives. Thus, we cannot draw a positive conclusion from the authorities' silence.

In response, the Salmanticenses point out that some of the Fathers do indeed deny other motives of the incarnation. In any case,

---

65. *De motivo Incarnationis*, dub. 1, §2, no. 11 (Palmé, 13:273).
66. "Sunt autem et aliae plurimae utilitates quae consecutae sunt, supra comprehensionem sensus humani." *ST* III, q. 1, a. 2, co. (Leonine, 11:10). Cf. *ST* III, q. 1, a. 3, ad 1 (Leonine, 11:14), referred to by the Salmanticenses in *De motivo Incarnationis*, dub. 1, §2, no. 11 (Palmé, 13:273).
67. *De motivo Incarnationis*, dub. 1, §3, nos. 12–14 (Palmé, 13:273–76).

because we have knowledge of what depends on God's free choice only from revelation, the silence of Scripture and the Fathers does rule out motives unconnected with redemption.[68] In matters of great doctrinal importance, silence is equivalent to express negation. Thus, when Scripture says God created the world, we are to conclude that he created no other world. Or when only the Father, the Son, and the Holy Spirit are spoken of as divine, we are to believe that there are no other divine persons. So, too, because Scripture speaks everywhere about redemption as the reason for the coming of Christ, we must hold that there is not some other motive independent of this.

The second Scotistic objection is that Scripture and the Fathers treat of the incarnation not in itself but in its modality of passible flesh. The Salmanticenses deal with this objection at length, saying that it represents the mind of Scotus himself.[69] Thus, God efficaciously willed the incarnation prior to foreseeing sin for the intrinsic goodness of the mystery. Then, because he foresaw sin, he decreed it with the circumstance of passibility for the redemption of the human race. Because Scripture and the Fathers are dealing with the incarnation as it has actually occurred, when they state that the incarnation would not have occurred absent the need for redemption, what they mean is that the incarnation *in passible flesh* would not have occurred.

In reply, the Salmanticenses observe, first of all, that this objection does not challenge the Thomistic principle that God's free acts are known through revelation. If Scripture and the Fathers are dealing only with the incarnation in its passible modality, not the incarnation as such, then this is *all the more reason* to refuse to affirm that the incarnation would have occurred in a different mode. "Having left revelation aside," ask the Salmanticenses, "from what source

---

68. *De motivo Incarnationis*, dub. 1, §3, no. 12 (Palmé, 13:274).

69. "Continet propriam mentem, et fundamentum Scoti." *De motivo Incarnationis*, dub. 1, §3, no. 13 (Palmé, 13:274). Cf. Scotus, *Ordinatio* III, d. 7, q. 3, no. 62 (Vatican, 9:287–88); and *Reportatio Parisiensis* III-A, d. 7, q. 4, no. 5 (Vivès, 23:303).

do Scotus and his disciples draw this determinate and thoroughly probed knowledge of the divine determination?"[70] Arguments from fittingness do not have enough probative force to show that God has willed or would have willed the substance of the incarnation without its redemptive mode.

Further, the Salmanticenses argue, if this Scotistic objection is correct, then all the scriptural passages testifying that Christ came to save sinners would actually be *false*, as would the Creed's "for us men and for our salvation." The Creed does not say just that Christ became *mortal* to redeem humanity but that he "came down from heaven and became man" to redeem humanity. *A fortiori* does the Scotistic objection contradict the Fathers who deny that Christ would have come if humanity had not needed redemption.

However, the Salmanticenses put forth a possible Scotistic counterargument with a supporting example.[71] When an event can happen in two ways and is not going to happen in one of those ways, the event's occurrence can be denied. For example, Christ denied that he would go up to Jerusalem for the Passover feast (Jn 7:8), and yet he did go up. The reason is that he was able to go up in either of two ways: publicly or privately. Christ had decided not to go up publicly, and so he was justified in denying that he would go up (without further qualification). So, too, the counterargument runs, even if Scripture and the Fathers seem to deny the incarnation in absolute terms, they are really only rejecting one of the ways it might have occurred (in passible flesh apart from the need for redemption).

The Salmanticenses reject the counterargument's interpretation of the Lord's words in John 7:8. An absolute negation negates every mode.[72] Thus, the proposition "this object has no heat in it" is only

---

70. "Unde enim, seclusa revelatione, hauriunt Scotus, et discipuli hanc determinatam, et exploratam divinae determinationis notitiam?" *De motivo Incarnationis*, dub. 1, §3, no. 13 (Palmé, 13:275).

71. *De motivo Incarnationis*, dub. 1, §3, no. 15 (Palmé, 13:276).

72. *De motivo Incarnationis*, dub. 1, §3, no. 15 (Palmé, 13:276–77). The core of their refutation of the counterargument follows that of Vásquez, *In III Thomae*, q. 1, a. 3, disp. 10, chap. 4, nos. 42–43 (Sanchez Crespo, 1:135–36).

true if the object truly possesses no heat whatsoever. If the object lacks the sun's heat but does have the heat of fire in it, it is false to say that it has "no heat," even though it does lack a certain mode of heat. Similarly, no one would say that the king is not coming into the city simply because he is coming on horseback and not in a chariot. The final counterexample the Salmanticenses offer is the one they consider the most damning. If the denial of one mode of occurrence suffices for absolute negation, then one could truly say "Christ will not come at the end of the world," since he will not come in passible flesh. In fact, one could even say truly that "Christ has not come" because he did not come in impassible flesh. Returning to the scriptural example, the Salmanticenses explain that "I am not going up" (Jn 7:8) has to be taken as the Lord's response to the disciples' request for him to go up publicly, to show his works to the crowds (Jn 7:3–4). In other words, taken in context, "I am not going up" is not an absolute negation at all.

Finally, the Salmanticenses argue against the applicability of the distinction between the incarnation's substance and its modality.[73] Granted that we can speculatively consider the incarnation without considering passibility or impassibility, God can only practically decree the incarnation in some determinate mode. Just because the incarnation *per se* is logically prior to its modality does not mean that two decrees are needed. If it did, there would have to be a new decree for every additional circumstance. There would be a decree for Christ's coming, another for his passibility, another for the redemptive value of his suffering, and so forth for every concrete aspect of the incarnation that does not follow of necessity from the previous decrees.[74]

In any case, it is incompatible with God's nature to will in a vague or confused way and then to will in a particular way. The Salmanticenses' own two-*signa* approach, they say, is more respectful of the

---

73. *De motivo Incarnationis*, dub. 1, §3, no. 16 (Palmé, 13:277).
74. *De motivo Incarnationis*, dub. 1, §3, no. 17 (Palmé, 13:279).

divine simplicity and the scope of God's most perfect providence.[75] In the first *signum in quo*, God knew all possible combinations of things, and in the second he actualized those he wished. In this way, the free exercise of the divine will extended effectively to all particulars from the beginning.

Replies to Suárez

Next, the Salmanticenses turn to Suárez. As Pfisterer has pointed out, the Salmanticenses' arguments against Suárez in this section draw on Gonet.[76] The Salmanticenses begin by summarizing Suárez's argument that God first willed the incarnation in the best way and then, foreseeing sin through middle knowledge, decreed it fully for redemption, which he then foresaw would be the best way.[77]

The first counterargument the Salmanticenses give is simply pointing out that what Suárez says, effectively, is that God's only actual decree of the incarnation has been redemptive.[78] This suffices to deny that Christ would have come by virtue of the present decree regardless of sin. If the present decree is efficacious in bringing about the redemptive incarnation, why posit an additional decree prior to it? And, if God's will for the incarnation independently of sin is not an efficacious decree but only a kind of velleity, then Christ would *not* actually come by virtue of it.[79]

Further, they attack Suárez's assertion that God initially willed the incarnation "in the best way." How does Suárez know this?[80] Even if it were the case, is it true that the redemptive incarnation really has occurred in the best possible way? After all, God could have

---

75. *De motivo Incarnationis*, dub. 1, §3, no. 16 (Palmé, 13:277).
76. Pfisterer, "El motivo de la Encarnación según los Salmanticenses," 226n18. This is evident by comparing Gonet, *Clypeus theologiae Thomisticae* III, tract. 1, disp. 5, §3, nos. 23–29 (Vivès, 5:477–78), with the Salmanticenses, *De motivo Incarnationis*, dub. 1, §4, nos. 23–24 (Palmé, 13:284–86).
77. *De motivo Incarnationis*, dub. 1, §4, no. 19 (Palmé, 13:280–81).
78. *De motivo Incarnationis*, dub. 1, §4, no. 20 (Palmé, 13:281).
79. *De motivo Incarnationis*, dub. 1, §4, no. 20 (Palmé, 13:281–82).
80. *De motivo Incarnationis*, dub. 1, §4, no. 20 (Palmé, 13:282).

willed for Christ to have more habitual grace, since habitual grace can be increased without limit. Or God could have redeemed all of humanity as he redeemed Mary through the grace of her Immaculate Conception. Both would be better than what God has actually done in Christ.

In any case, what Suárez says about God's middle knowledge of Adam's sin is "altogether false."[81] It simply cannot be the case that in the identical scenario in which Adam fell, God could also have foreseen that he would not fall. No matter how the difference between merely sufficient and actually efficacious grace is explained, there must be *some difference* between the situation of Adam wherein he fell and the situation wherein he would not have fallen. But if this means (whether we accept middle knowledge or not) that God decided to permit Adam to be in a situation where he would fall and so decreed the incarnation in response to this, then once again there seems to be no point in positing another decree for the incarnation except the present decree connected with redemption.

So far, the Salmanticenses have pointed out problems arising from within Suárez's position itself. They also reiterate all their arguments against the Scotists since, they say, Suárez is just as guilty of presuming about God's free choices instead of grounding his position in Scripture and the Fathers.[82] Because the Fathers' express and universal denials that Christ would have come absent sin should be taken at face value, it would be amazing to think that Suárez has a deeper insight into God than they do.[83] As for the defense that Scripture does not deny that Christ would have come absent sin, the Salmanticenses repeat that in a matter of such importance to faith, lack of affirmation is equivalent to express negation. Similarly, the

---

81. "Falsum omnino." *De motivo Incarnationis*, dub. 1, §4, no. 20 (Palmé, 13:282).

82. "Iste, et illi procedunt divinando liberam Dei voluntatem absque Luce, et duce Scripturae, et SS. Patrum." *De motivo Incarnationis*, dub. 1, §4, no. 21 (Palmé, 13:282).

83. "Et mirum est quod Suarius plura in Deo introspexerit, magisque ipsum comprehenderit, quam sacri Doctores, ut plus quam illi affirmet, et contrariam ipsis decernat sententiam." *De motivo Incarnationis*, dub. 1, §4, no. 22 (Palmé, 13:283).

Bible does not say that there are *not* more than three divine persons, but it is hardly an open question.

We saw in the previous chapter that Suárez tries to account for the silence of Scripture and the Fathers about a motive unconnected with redemption by showing that the more principal motive of an act may remain unstated while a secondary motive is affirmed. He uses the example of Samuel's going to Bethlehem both to anoint David and to offer sacrifice, where Samuel mentions only the sacrifice.[84] The Salmanticenses respond that although Samuel himself left the principal motive of his trip unstated when explaining his departure to Saul, *Scripture* presents anointing David as the principal motive.[85] Samuel misdirects Saul, but the Bible does not misdirect its reader. Thus there is no parallel with the incarnation. If the same principle did apply to what Scripture says about the incarnation, as Suárez holds, then he would be affirming that the Bible reveals only a secondary motive (redemption) and conceals the primary motive from us.[86] How, then, would we ever know that there is a hidden motive, and what reason would lead the Bible to obfuscate the incarnation's primary motive in the first place?

The consideration of multiple motives for the same act then leads the Salmanticenses to attack the Suaresian theory that the incarnation (or any act) could even have two total and adequate motives.[87] Suárez introduced this theory to assert that God willed the incarnation totally for its own intrinsic excellence and then, taking sin into account, also totally for redemption.[88] This, say the Salmanticenses, is simply impossible. Instead, there are four ways an agent can act for two ends. First, the ends are both partial and together make up a total end. Second, one end is total and the other adds a

---

84. Suárez, *In III Thomae*, q. 1, a. 4, disp. 5, sect. 4, no. 23 (Vivès, 17:247).

85. *De motivo Incarnationis*, dub. 1, §4, no. 22 (Palmé, 13:283–84).

86. Indeed, this is what Suárez himself admits, his explanation being that the Bible focuses on redemption because that is what human beings are more obviously in need of. *In III Thomae*, q. 1, a. 4, disp. 5, sect. 4, no. 9 (Vivès, 17:242).

87. *De motivo Incarnationis*, dub. 1, §4, no. 23 (Palmé, 13:284–85).

88. Suárez, *In III Thomae*, q. 1, a. 4, disp. 5, sect. 4, no. 7 (Vivès, 17:241).

new fittingness. Third, one total end is subordinated to another total end. Fourth, the agent changes his mind, ceasing to act for one total end and beginning to act for the other. Here the Salmanticenses follow Vásquez: if one of the motives completely accounts for the whole act, then another (nonsubordinated) end can add an additional fittingness but cannot also thereby be said to account by itself completely for the whole act.[89] Taking up Suárez's example, they reply that someone going to Rome on business and subsequently realizing his friend is there cannot truly say, "I came to Rome for your sake," but he can say, "Because I was coming to Rome, I wanted to speak with you."[90]

The Salmanticenses essentially follow Vásquez's critique of Suárez on two total ends. They also follow Vásquez in understanding a total end in a way different from that of Suárez.[91] For Suárez, a total and adequate end means one that would be sufficient by itself to elicit the act. For Vásquez and the Salmanticenses, a total and adequate end is one that is both sufficient and necessary to elicit the act. It is no wonder, then, that Vásquez and the Salmanticenses think two total and adequate but nonsubordinated ends are impossible. Suppose that there are two ends, each of which is sufficient and necessary, and that neither is subordinated to the other. This being the case, if one of the ends were taken away, the agent would both act (since the remaining end is sufficient) and not act (since the absent end is necessary).[92] Therefore it is impossible to have two sufficent and necessary ends without subordinating one to the other.

As with Vásquez, the Salmanticenses are stricter than Suárez in holding to the numeric identity of the agent's act. If a new motive is added, then either the agent's act will change or else it will not

---

89. *De motivo Incarnationis*, dub. 1, §4, no. 24 (Palmé, 13:285–86). Cf. Vásquez, *In III Thomae*, q. 1, a. 3, disp. 10, chap. 8, no. 81 (Sanchez Crespo, 1:143).

90. *De motivo Incarnationis*, dub. 1, §4, no. 22 (Palmé, 13:283).

91. Cf. Vásquez, *In III Thomae*, q. 1, a. 3, disp. 10, chap. 8, no. 80 (Sanchez Crespo, 1:143).

92. *De motivo Incarnationis*, dub. 1, §5, no. 23 (Palmé, 13:284).

change. If it does change, then either the new motive only alters the existing act accidentally (e.g., by motivating the agent to act faster or with greater attention) or else the new motive changes the existing act substantially. If the agent's act is only altered accidentally, then the new motive is not really a total motive since it does not give rise to the whole act. Or if the new motive changes the agent's act substantially, then the agent is no longer engaged in the original act but has, in fact, begun to pursue a new, numerically distinct act. In this case, the original motive and the new motive are both partial and inadequate motives that together constitute a total and adequate motive distinct from the original. Alternatively, if the addition of a new motive does *not* change the agent's act, then the new motive is no motive at all, since it makes no difference whatsoever to the agent's acting.[93]

In other words, what matters is not just the material action the agent is undertaking (e.g., going to Rome) but the fact of that action's being undertaken precisely so as to satisfy a certain desire.[94] A man traveling to Rome on business may learn on the way that his friend happens to be there. In fact, he may wish to see his friend so strongly that he would have made a trip even if he had not already been going to Rome for business. This man continues in the same material act of traveling to Rome—he does not return home and start his journey over. But if the traveler arrives in Rome and is prevented from seeing his friend, the trip will no longer have fully satisfied his desires. Once the new motive of visiting his friend is added, the business aspect of the trip *no longer* remains a total and adequate motive, since it no longer suffices to satisfy the desire of the agent in acting. Thus, unless one motive is subordinated to or included under another, a single act numerically requires a single total and adequate motive.

---

93. Salmanticenses, *Cursus theologicus*, tract. 8, disp. 4, dub. 1, §2, no. 4 (Palmé, 5:130–31).

94. Salmanticenses, *Cursus theologicus*, tract. 8, disp. 4, dub. 1, §2, no. 4 (Palmé, 5:130–31).

A total motive in Suárez's sense is one that *would* motivate the whole act by itself, but the Salmanticenses understand a total motive to be one that *does* motivate the whole act. Suárez is quite right that someone could go to Rome wholly for business and could also go to Rome wholly to see a friend, but he is wrong to conclude from this that the same person can actually act totally for both of these as distinct motives at the same time.

As stated above, the difference in positions can be summarized by saying that Suárez holds a total motive to be one sufficient to motivate the act, whereas the Salmanticenses hold a total motive to be sufficient and necessary. In effect, Suárez's sufficiency must *become* necessity when actually chosen by an agent. Once an agent decides to act out of a certain motive, then unless that motive is just accidental (and thus not total), it becomes necessary if the agent's desire is to be satisfied.

Finally, Suárez's examples (like the man going to Rome) always involve someone's deciding on a course of action for one reason and then later discovering a new reason for the same action. But even if we allowed for the sake of argument that human beings could discover a new total motive and begin to carry out the self-same act also for that motive, the imperfection implied in this is altogether unfitting to God.[95] If God was able to comprehend all possible total motives for the incarnation at once (in the first *signum in quo*, as the Salmanticenses explain it), then there is no reason to suppose that he acted for one motive and then subsequently for another. But if this is the case, then redemption was always a total motive of the incarnation from the beginning. Thus, according to the Salmanticenses, Suárez's theory ends up being far less intelligible than Scotus's.[96]

---

95. *De motivo Incarnationis*, dub. 1, §5, no. 24 (Palmé, 13:285–86).
96. "Plane difficilior longe est Suarii opinio, quam sententia Scoti." *De motivo Incarnationis*, dub. 1, §4, no. 24 (Palmé, 13:285).

Other Thomistic Approaches

The Salmanticenses set the stage for explaining and defending their own theory in greater detail by looking at other Thomistic approaches. First of all, they feel the need to explain why they disagree with important Thomists who deny any sense in which Christ was willed and intended prior to the permission of sin.[97] By affirming that Christ is the first willed and intended by God, are the Salmanticenses actually forced into the Scotistic opinion? After all, if Christ is really the first willed and intended by God, then his futurity logically precedes that of sin.[98] But then Christ's being intended would be independent of sin, and so he would have come absent sin.[99]

The Salmanticenses hold the opinion of the Thomists who deny Christ's being prior to sin in any sense as "very probable" both in its argumentation and in the authorities on which it relies.[100] Two elements of this stricter position are especially praiseworthy. First, this position directly opposes Scotus. Second, it takes the scriptural and patristic authorities seriously. Nevertheless, the Salmanticenses are not satisfied by this opinion, since they also find the authorities in favor of Christ's primacy convincing.

It is precisely their commitment to revelation as the ground for theological assertions about God's free acts that thrusts the Salmanticenses into this dilemma, for there are weighty authorities both for the thesis that Christ would not have come absent sin and for the thesis that he is the first willed and intended by God. Presuming that

---

97. The Salmanticenses cite Cajetan; Francisco de Araújo, OP (1580–1664); Diego Álvarez, OP (ca. 1550–1635); Pedro Cornejo de Pedrosa, O. Carm. (1566–1618); John of St. Thomas; Vásquez; and Giuseppe Ragusa, SJ (d. 1624), as examples.

98. In discussions of God's providential planning, as in the present disputation, the *futuritio* of a thing is its going-to-be-ness or "futurity." The word has no temporal meaning in this context. Instead, the point is simply that a thing having futurity has the property that it will at some point actually exist. In this way, the thing is "future" in comparison with pure possibles, which are in the divine mind alone "before" God's free decree of what is actually going to exist.

99. *De motivo Incarnationis*, dub. 1, §5, no. 25 (Palmé, 13:286–87).

100. "Valde probabilis." *De motivo Incarnationis*, dub. 1, §5, no. 26 (Palmé, 13:287).

the authorities are compatible at their deepest level, the solution is to find a higher synthesis.[101]

The Salmanticenses note that they are not the only Thomists seeking to hold that Christ is the first willed and intended by God with a dependence on sin.[102] Juan Vicente de Astorga, OP (1544–95), for example, proposes that God willed the natural, gratuitous, and hypostatic orders from the first but that the hypostatic union was not yet willed in a determinate way. For him, only after foreseeing sin does God specify the person of the Word, the individual human nature, and the incarnation's passible mode.[103]

The Salmanticenses reject this approach for several reasons.[104] First, it has no basis in Scripture. Second, the distinction between the concrete incarnation and the abstract idea of an incarnation is mental, not real, and so affords no basis for an order of priority and posteriority. Third, as a result Vicente multiplies *signa rationis* needlessly, which awkwardly construes God as willing in an indeterminate and vague manner and then subsequently willing in a determinate and concrete manner.

Alternatively, Alfonso de Mendoza, OESA (d. 1591), and Pedro de Lorca, O. Cist. (1561–1612), hold that God first willed Christ *per se* but chose to bind Christ as the end to the permission of sin as the necessary means.[105] Similarly, they say, someone can resolve to

---

101. *De motivo Incarnationis*, dub. 1, §5, no. 26 (Palmé, 13:288). I noted above that the *finis cuius gratia*, being that on whose account other things are chosen, can be called the end *simpliciter*, even though it is not the total end by itself.

102. The Salmanticenses list Capréolus; Bartolomé de Medina, OP (1528–80); Pedro de Cabrera, OESH (d. 1616); Juan Vicente de Astorga, OP (1544–95); Giovanni Paolo Nazario, OP (ca. 1556–1645); Gregorio Cippullo, OP (d. 1646); Godoy; Philippe de la Trinité, OCD (1603–71); Juan Prudencio, O. de M. (1610–57); Antonio de la Parra y Arteaga, CRM (fl. 1668); Gonet; and Lawrence of St. Therese, OCD (d. 1670). Salmanticenses, *De motivo Incarnationis*, dub. 1, §5, no. 26 (Palmé, 13:288).

103. See, e.g., Juan Vicente, *Relectio de habituali Christi salvatoris nostril sanctificante gratia*, q. 6 (Rome: Ex typographia Pauli Diani, 1591), 683–84.

104. *De motivo Incarnationis*, dub. 1, §5, no. 27 (Palmé, 13:289).

105. See Alfonso de Mendoza, *Fratris Alphonsi Mendozae, ex Ordine eremitarum D. Augustini, in florentissima Salmanticensium academia, sacrae theologiae magistri et vesperarii professoris, quaestiones quodlibeticae et relectio de Christi regno ac dominio*, q. 1, no. 5

make a journey but then freely bind this intention to a determinate means, such as a horse, in such a way that, lacking a horse, he would not make the journey.

The Salmanticenses argue against this approach because it posits in God a kind of potential and confused intention for Christ.[106] God's will, they insist, extends to all the determinate means from the first. It makes no sense for God to will an end precisely as an end apart from the means. After all, the end God wills is not an end from his own perspective but in relation to the means that God orders to it. God's willing an end just is his establishing the order between certain means and a certain end.[107]

Alternatively, if God first willed Christ and *then* willed the need for redemption to be the means for Christ, as Mendoza and Lorca would have it, the Salmanticenses pose this dilemma: would Christ have come by virtue of that first willing or not?[108] If they say yes, then they are asserting that Christ would have come absent sin, which is to abandon the Thomistic position. If they say no, then either God's initial willing was not really an effective intention or else God changed his mind.

The Salmanticenses' View

Leaving aside these approaches, the Salmanticenses turn to the core of their own position.[109] As I have already noted, their argument relies on the distinction of species of causality in combination with precisely two *signa in quo*. Thus, God's first intention includes Christ together with the permission of sin and the redemption of humanity through Christ. In this way, Christ has priority as *finis*

(Salamanca: Excudebat Petrus Lassus, sumptibus Francisci Martini, 1596), 13–14; and Pedro de Lorca, *Commentariorum, ac disputationum in tertiam partem D. Thomae, tomus primus, continens priorum viginti sex quaestionum expositionem*, q. 1, a. 3, disp. 10, memb. 2, nos. 34–35 (Alcalá de Henares: Apud viduam Andrea Sanchez de Ezpeleta, 1616), 76–77.

106. *De motivo Incarnationis*, dub. 1, §5, no. 28 (Palmé, 13:290).
107. *De motivo Incarnationis* (Palmé, 13:263). Cf. *ST* I, q. 19, a. 5 (Leonine, 4:239–40).
108. *De motivo Incarnationis*, dub. 1, §5, no. 28 (Palmé, 13:290).
109. *De motivo Incarnationis*, dub. 1, §5, nos. 29–31 (Palmé, 13:291–94).

cuius gratia, redeemed humanity has priority as *finis cui*, and permitted sin has priority as the matter addressed (*materia circa quam*).

"Priority" here means priority from a certain causal perspective among the objects themselves, not a succession of divine acts. Thus, nothing prevents God from knowing this whole complex reality as possible in the first *signum in quo* and then willing it in the second *signum in quo*. And the priority based on the distinct kinds of causality found among the objects willed is the basis for saying that God wills one or the other of them before the others in terms of that cause. For example, in material causality, God wills matter prior to form, and in formal causality, he wills form prior to matter. Further, there is no difficulty in one object's being willed only in conjunction with other objects while being prior to them. Priority does not necessarily mean independence. For instance, the end is willed with a dependence on the means, and the composite substance is willed prior to its accidents but cannot exist without them.[110]

In this way, the Salmanticenses harmonize the authorities affirming Christ's primacy in God's intention and those asserting that Christ would not have come apart from sin. Taking a similar example, they note that God willed to bestow glory on the elect precisely as a crown for merits. Thus, he established a link between glory and merits such that glory was willed first as final cause and does not depend on merits in this kind of causality. At the same time, God also willed glory to depend on merits in terms of moral efficient causality, so that without merits there would not be glory.[111]

In fact, say the Salmanticenses, Aquinas himself expresses the relation between Christ as *finis cuius gratia* and redeemed humanity as *finis cui* when he says:

God loves Christ not only more than the whole human race but even more than the whole universe of creatures, i.e., in that he willed him a greater good, since he "bestowed on him the name which is above every name": his being true God. Nor has his excellence been diminished by the

---

110. *De motivo Incarnationis*, dub. 1, §5, no. 30 (Palmé, 13:292).
111. *De motivo Incarnationis*, dub. 1, §5, no. 30 (Palmé, 13:292).

fact that God gave him over to death for the salvation of the human race, for in fact he thereby became a glorious conqueror.[112]

In this way, Christ enjoys the greatest share in goodness but is also meant for the salvation of the human race. These two facts, as Aquinas articulates them here, are uncontroversial.

However, the Salmanticenses see in them the ground for classifying Christ as *finis cuius gratia* and humanity as *finis cui*. Are the Salmanticenses, then, guilty of an unwarranted leap, especially in regard to *finis cuius gratia*? After all, they seem to be arguing that because the God-man is the greatest good, he is *finis cuius gratia*, which would be concluding to priority in intention from priority in dignity.[113] This is Scotus's *ordinate volens* principle applied in a way that is vulnerable to the criticisms of both Thomists like Cajetan and Scotists like Rada.[114]

However, there are two crucial differences between how Scotus applies *ordinate volens* and how the Salmanticenses do. First, the Salmanticenses do not argue *a priori* from the *ordinate volens* principle. Instead, they argue from authority for Christ as *finis cuius gratia* and then use the *ordinate volens* principle to elucidate why or how this is so. At most, they use the *ordinate volens* principle as an argument of fittingness, but they do not view it as conclusive by itself.[115] Second,

---

112. "Deus Christum diligit, non solum plus quam totum humanum genus, sed etiam magis quam totam universitatem creaturarum: quia scilicet ei maius bonum voluit, quia *dedit ei nomen, quod est super omne nomen*, ut verus Deus esset. Nec eius excellentiae deperiit ex hoc quod Deus dedit eum in mortem pro salute humani generis: quinimo ex hoc factus est victor gloriosus." ST I, q. 20, a. 4, ad 1 (Leonine, 4:256). The Salmanticenses quote this passage in *De motivo Incarnationis*, dub. 1, §5, no. 30 (Palmé, 13:292–93).

113. "Quod enim Christus Redemptor fuerit primum volitum, et intentum a Deo per modum *finis cujus gratia* ... constat ex dictis ... , id praesertim exigente excellentissima ipsius dignitate." *De motivo Incarnationis*, dub. 1, §5, no. 30 (Palmé, 13:292).

114. In particular, we may recall Cajetan's point that just because something is more willable does not mean it is more willed.

115. The Salmanticenses are quite sensitive to the problem with reasoning from fittingness to fact in God's free choices. E.g., they even remark: "Sicut se communicare hypostatice [*sic*] posset esse Deo conveniens attenta natura boni inclinantis ad sui communicationem: ita se non communicare hypostatice posset esse Deo conveniens in ordine ad alios fines altissimos, et nobis occultos, quos ipsius sapientia posset excogitare." *De motivo Incarnationis*, dub. 2, §2, no. 50 (Palmé, 13:314).

the Salmanticenses affirm again and again that Christ is first specifically from the perspective of *finis cuius gratia* but not from other perspectives. Each cause has priority in its own order, and a complete account requires consideration of all those perspectives taken together.

In effect, whereas Scotus conceptualizes God's "decision-making process" in a strictly linear fashion, the Salmanticenses envision it in a three-dimensional fashion. The object of God's will is a complex reality that can be examined from various angles, so that a certain facet is first from one perspective while a different facet is first from another. God wills this whole object all at once with all of its interrelated components. The Salmanticenses suspect that their account may even include what Cajetan really meant by his three-order distinction. In particular, they postulate that his three-order distinction (wherein God wills nature, then grace, then the hypostatic union) is correct from the perspective of material cause and the order of execution.[116]

Next, the Salmanticenses explain that just as God's willing glory does not presuppose his foreseeing merits, neither does his willing to redeem the human race presuppose an antecedent permission of sin and foreseeing of sin.

For such an intention of raising up [from] human misery, it was not necessary to presuppose that misery was foreseen and going to be by virtue of another antecedent decree. Rather, it was enough that on the part of the object willed it would entail the permission of sin and its remedy. For misery preceded Christ predestined in a given genus by the very fact that out of divine mercy he would be its remedy.[117]

---

116. "In quo sensu admittimus sententiam Cajetani ..., et forte ipse aliud non voluit, quam constituere praedictum ordinem, non absolute, sed in genere causae materialis, et attenta praedictorum objectorum executione." *De motivo Incarnationis*, dub. 1, §5, no. 31 (Palmé, 13:293).

117. "Ad hujusmodi intentionem sublevandi miseriam humanam opus non fuit praesupponere miseriam praevisam, et futuram ex vi alterius decreti antecedentis: sed satis fuit, quod ex parte objecti voliti inferret permissionem peccati, et remedium illius: nam eo ipso miseria praecessit in aliquo genere Christum praedestinatum, ut ex divina misericordia esset remedium illius." *De motivo Incarnationis*, dub. 1, §5, no. 31 (Palmé, 13:293).

This point is crucial. According to the Salmanticenses, in the order of intention, God did *not* first permit sin, then foresee sin, and then will Christ as redeemer. After all, if this were the case, then Christ would not be the first willed and intended by God as *finis cuius gratia*.[118] Instead, they say, God first intended Christ the redeemer. But this intention of its very nature logically entails the permission of sin, which will, in turn, entail the actual commission of sin due to human frailty. In this way, Christ is the *finis cuius gratia* even of the permission of sin, since his being intended as redeemer is what gives rise to the permission of sin in the first place. This is enough to make it true that from the perspective of material cause, God's permitting and foreseeing humanity's fall *do* precede the predestination of Christ the redeemer.[119]

The Salmanticenses explain that "predestination" in the most formal sense (*sensu formalissimo*) is "a practical act of the intellect directing and entailing the execution of the preintended good."[120]

---

118. It would also require multiple divine decrees and thus further *signa in quo*, since God would have to permit sin, then foresee actual sin, and then decree Christ as redeemer. In other words, in such a view, God could not logically will Christ as redeemer until he had already seen that humanity would sin, which would, in turn, require God's permission of sin in the first place.

119. In other words, although there are multiple causal perspectives, the perspective of *finis cuius gratia* is the most important and gives rise to the others. So if God first wills Christ the redeemer as *finis cuius gratia*, this entails the permission of sin. This also makes it true that from the perspective of material cause, the permission of sin precedes the predestination of Christ the redeemer. But the point is that the order of material cause itself here *derives* ultimately from the order of *finis cuius gratia*. The permission of sin only precedes Christ's predestination materially (as the *materia circa quam*) *because* from the more fundamental order of *finis cuius gratia*, God first willed and intended Christ the redeemer.

120. "Actus practicus intellectus dirigens, ac inferens executionem boni praeintenti." *De motivo Incarnationis*, dub. 1, §5, no. 31 (Palmé, 13:294). The background to their explanation is the technical delineation of stages in the process of willing. They enumerate: *iudicium, simplex volitio* (*benevolentia*), *simplex complacentia, dilectio, imperfecta fruitio, iudicium* concerning the attainability of the end through certain means, and *intentio*. These comprise the first order of intention. Next are: *consilium, consensus, iudicium* in the strict sense, and *electio*. These constitute the order to the means as related to the intention. Finally there are: *imperium, usus passivus* (the carrying-out of the means), *consecutio et possessio finis*, and *fruitio perfecta*. These latter acts belong to the order of execution. See

The Salamanca Theory

This directive act presupposes intention and election, which properly pertain to the order of intention. In other words, "predestination" is used "most properly for the act of command directing the use or execution. In this way it signifies the dispatching to the aforementioned end and supposes both the end and the means as foreseen and going to be, with at least the inchoate, though infallible, fact that they will exist."[121]

This is how the Salmanticenses account for Aquinas's statement that predestination presupposes knowledge of future things.[122] God's carrying out the election of Christ (to natural divine filiation) presupposes his knowing that there will be sin. This is because God's initial intention for Christ is precisely as redeemer. In this way, God does not foreknow sin and then intend Christ. Instead, by intending Christ as redeemer, he foreknows that there will be sin. The initial intention does not presuppose foreknowledge of the fact of sin, but carrying out the intention (predestination *sensu formalissimo*) does.

Replies to Objections

The Salmanticenses next address five objections to their theory. The first objection is that redeemed humanity seems rather to be the *finis cuius gratia*, since the word "for" (*propter*), as in the Creed's "for us men and for our salvation," usually refers to the *finis cuius gratia*.[123] Similarly, a sick person takes bitter medicine "for his health" (*propter salutem*), where health is clearly the *finis cuius gratia*. Along the same lines, Christ himself receives more glory and exaltation

---

Salmanticenses, *Cursus theologicus*, tract. 12, *De virtutibus, Arbor praedicimentalis*, §1, no. 6 (Palmé, 6:418). The point here is that "predestination" in the most proper sense does not mean the intention for Christ but the *imperium* that follows through with the plan to carry out that intention.

121. "[Praedestinatio sumitur] ... propriissime pro actu imperii dirigentis usum, sive executionem: quo pacto significat transmissionem in praedictum finem, supponitque tam finem, quam media praevisa, et futura saltem futuritione inchoata, sed infallibili." *De motivo Incarnationis*, dub. 1, §5, no. 31 (Palmé, 13:294). They allow, of course, that we commonly use "predestination" in a less proper sense for the choice or election itself.

122. *ST* III, q. 1, a. 3, ad 4 (Leonine, 11:14).

123. *De motivo Incarnationis*, dub. 1, §6, no. 32 (Palmé, 13:294).

than anyone else from the incarnation, and so he, not redeemed humanity, seems to be the *finis cui*.

The Salmanticenses respond by clarifying that "for" (*propter*) does often indicate the *finis cuius gratia*, but not always. The particular context controls the interpretation, though as a general rule what is more perfect will be the *finis cuius gratia*. Thus, Christ's coming "for us men and for our salvation" means the *finis cui*, not the *finis cuius gratia*. In support of this they cite Aquinas, who says that the one to whom the benefit comes can be said to be the one for whom the action is done, as when we say that the king is "for" (*propter*) the peasant or the heavenly bodies are for lower bodies.[124] Finally, there is no difficulty in saying that Christ as man also falls under the *finis cui* of the incarnation, seeing as he receives utmost glory from his work of redemption, even as the king also benefits from well-being and peace among the peasants.

The second objection is that if the incarnation were prior to the permission of sin in final causality *simpliciter*, then why should it have a necessary connection with the permission of sin?[125] Willing one object can only *require* willing another object if the objects have a mutual connection such as end-means or effect-cause. But if Christ is prior *simpliciter* as final cause with respect to the permission of sin, there seems to be no reason why the permission of sin should be required, and this would amount to the Scotistic opinion.

Here, the Salmanticenses acknowledge an apparent difficulty with two aspects of their view. They say both that God decrees Christ along with everything else all at once and also that everything else is for Christ as *finis cuius gratia*. The objector could then rightly observe that, for the Salmanticenses, God decrees Christ together with, for instance, a given housefly, and the same objector could equally observe that in their view God even orders the fly to Christ

---

124. *De motivo Incarnationis*, dub. 1, §6, no. 32 (Palmé, 13:295), citing Aquinas, *Super II Sent.*, d. 15, q. 1, a. 1, ad 6 (Mandonnet, 2:369–70); and *ST* II-II, q. 39, a. 2, ad 2 (Leonine, 8:309).

125. *De motivo Incarnationis*, dub. 1, §6, no. 33 (Palmé, 13:295–96).

as *finis cuius gratia*. Does this mean, then, that the Salmanticenses are forced to say that Christ would not have come absent the fly? If not, how is the permission of sin any different?

The Salmanticenses, of course, deny that Christ's coming depends on the fly.[126] They explain that the fly was made for Christ and sin was permitted for Christ, but not in the same way. The difference is that God did not will a relation of dependence between Christ and a given housefly, whereas he did will a relation of dependence between Christ and the permission of sin. This dependence does not arise from the very nature of the objects willed (as would be the case, for example, between an end and its necessary means) but instead comes about only because God wills it.[127] Similarly, glory does not of its nature depend on merits, but God has willed to bestow glory precisely as a crown for merits. This establishes a connection of dependence between glory and merits. This is also the case for Christ and the permission of sin, "since [God's] first intention of Christ regarded him as Redeemer, in passible flesh, and with all the circumstances that he had in execution."[128] Again, the Salmanticenses' two-*signa* approach is controlling for them: when God wills Christ, as when he wills anything at all, he already knows all the possible circumstances

---

126. *De motivo Incarnationis*, dub. 1, §6, no. 33 (Palmé, 13:296). Their argumentation here follows the observations of Cajetan, *Commentary on* Summa theologiae III, q. 1, a. 3 (Leonine, 11:16.10); and Vásquez, *In III Thomae*, q. 1, a. 3, disp. 11, chap. 2, no. 19 (Sanchez Crespo, 1:157). The problem is that if the Salmanticenses are correct that each and every thing willed by God is referred to Christ as to the *finis cuius gratia*, then this means that each individual entity that will ever exist bears a reference to Christ in God's decree. The problem arises for the Salmanticenses in a special way because of their two-*signa* theory. For them, God chooses the entire complex order of history all at once, meaning that if a single entity were different, then it would be a different order of history and thus a different initial choice (in some way) on God's part. Does the fact that God only ever chose Christ together with each individual entity that will ever exist create a relation of dependence between Christ and that entity? In other words, if God only ever chose Christ in the order of history that also contains a fly, does this mean that he would not have chosen Christ without the fly?

127. *De motivo Incarnationis*, dub. 1, §6, no. 33 (Palmé, 13:296).

128. "Cum prima intentio Christi illum respexerit ut Redemptorem, in carne passibili, et cum omnibus circumstantiis quas in executione habuit." *De motivo Incarnationis*, dub. 1, §6, no. 33 (Palmé, 13:296).

and interdependencies. And so, if God knows that it is possible for Christ's coming to be essentially a response to sin, he can equally will the incarnation as a response to sin from the first.

The third objection is that if the permission of sin is an *effect*[129] of Christ's predestination in terms of final causality, then the decree of Christ's predestination seems to be complete prior to the permission and foreknowledge of sin.[130] After all, a cause is complete in itself prior to its effect. But if the decree of Christ's predestination is complete prior to the permission of sin, then we again are left with the Scotistic opinion.

The Salmanticenses answer that because the decree of Christ's predestination regarded him precisely *as redeemer*, it includes a reference to the permission of sin and cannot be totally complete apart from this.[131] Christ is the *finis cuius gratia*, but the *finis cui* of redeemed humanity and the permission of sin with its reparation come together with the *finis cuius gratia* to form a single total end.

Similarly, when we analyze God's causality with respect to a material substance, the matter is prior to the form in the order of material cause. This does not mean, however, that God's causality extends to the matter in a *complete* way apart from the form.[132] After all, it is the substantial composite that is the adequate object of God's causality—even God cannot make prime matter exist on its own, since this is a contradiction in terms.[133] But if prime matter cannot actually exist on its own, this is precisely because matter is relative to form and the notion of matter is relative to the notion of form.[134] Thus, even if

---

129. We must not confuse "effect" from the perspective of final cause with the more common notion of "effect" from the perspective of efficient cause. The effect of the final cause is that which is chosen because of the final cause. In this way, the agent's intending the *finis cuius gratia* is what gives rise to his intending other things, which then count as the *finis cuius gratia*'s effects. For example, the physician intends medicine for the sake of health, so from the perspective of final cause, medicine is an effect of health.

130. *De motivo Incarnationis*, dub. 1, §6, no. 34 (Palmé, 13:296).

131. *De motivo Incarnationis*, dub. 1, §6, no. 34 (Palmé, 13:296–97).

132. *De motivo Incarnationis*, dub. 1, §6, no. 34 (Palmé, 13:297).

133. Cf. *ST* I, q. 66, a. 1 (Leonine, 5:154–55).

134. In particular, matter and form are related as potency and act, meaning that the notion of matter and the notion of form are also related as the notion of potency

matter is prior to form in the order of material cause, it always bears a reference to form.

Or to take another example, the intention of giving the saints glory in heaven as a *reward* is not complete without reference to merits. Thus, even though in the order of intention glory is prior to foreseen merits, it cannot be conceived of in isolation from merits. When God intends the crown of glory, in fact, what he is intending is that merits will precede glory in a different causal order (moral efficient cause). To put it generally, for two objects of intention A and B, A can be prior to B while also including a reference to B. Further, A's reference to B entails that from a different causal perspective B will be prior to A.

As applied to Christ's predestination, however, the Salmanticenses clarify even further: from the perspective of final cause, some effects of predestination are mere effects, whereas others are effects that also belong to the *finis cui*. The decree of predestination may be conceived of as complete apart from reference to the former, but not apart from the latter.[135] For example, looking at the predestination of Christ himself, Christ's natural filiation from God is the *finis cuius gratia* with respect to his humanity (Christ as subsisting in this humanity), but this does not mean that the decree of Christ's predestination can be considered as complete independently of his humanity, which is the *finis cui* of his predestination. Likewise, in the order of *finis cuius gratia*, redeemed humanity is an effect of the incarnation (i.e., it is chosen for the sake of the incarnation), but redeemed humanity is simultaneously the *finis cui* of the incarnation, part of the overall total end of the decree. Thus, the decree of the incarnation cannot be complete without reference to human redemption. Christ

---

is related to the notion of act. Just as it makes no sense to have a notion of potency that is complete without reference to the notion of act, so also it makes no sense to have a notion of matter that is complete without reference to the notion of form. Thus, besides the fact that it is impossible to *imagine* prime matter, it is also impossible to *conceptualize* prime matter except by relating it to form, e.g., as that which serves as the substrate for substantial change or that which can receive any material form.

135. *De motivo Incarnationis*, dub. 1, §6, no. 34 (Palmé, 13:297).

the redeemer is the *finis cuius gratia*, but there can be no redeemer without someone redeemed.

The fourth objection is that original justice was not an effect of Christ's predestination, but if it was produced for the sake of Christ and thus with a dependence on him as final cause, it would have to be.[136] To this, the Salmanticenses respond that the grace of original justice was indeed produced for Christ as final cause, but whether Christ *merited* the grace of original justice is a distinct question. They put off this inquiry to a subsequent disputation.[137] However, the Salmanticenses note that this objection comes up in a different form in the present disputation, where they offer a fuller response.

The fifth objection is that original sin cannot have been an effect of Christ's predestination.[138] But if original sin is not an effect of Christ's predestination, then it can only arise from a separate and prior providence of God. This is because we assign priority and posteriority within a given kind of causality based on causal relationships of that same kind. In other words, the only way for Christ to be prior to original sin as its final cause is for original sin to be an effect of Christ's predestination from the viewpoint of final causality.

The Salmanticenses reply that sin in itself, including its malice, is not an effect of Christ's predestination.[139] The *permission* of sin, however, is. And due to the frailty of human nature, the permission of sin infallibly entails the commission of sin. At the same time, they insist that Christ did not come for the sake of sin but to remedy it. Nor did God will sin for the sake of Christ but instead willed and directed the permission of sin to this end. They further add that this present difficulty comes up in the case of *anyone's* predestination, since

---

136. *De motivo Incarnationis*, dub. 1, §6, no. 35 (Palmé, 13:297–98).

137. They refer to Salmanticenses, *Cursus theologicus*, tract. 21, disp. 7, *De causa meritoria Incarnationis sive unionis hypostaticae*, dub. 4 (Palmé, 13:661–700). But see also Salmanticenses, *Cursus theologicus*, tract. 21, disp. 16, *De gratia Christi capitali*, dub. 4 (Palmé, 14:593–614).

138. *De motivo Incarnationis*, dub. 1, §6, no. 36 (Palmé, 13:298).

139. *De motivo Incarnationis*, dub. 1, §6, no. 36 (Palmé, 13:298).

in the case of any sin committed by one of the elect, God permits it and orders it somehow to the person's ultimate beatitude.

But, the objector insists, if God permitted sin in order to heal mankind through Christ, would he not be cruel, like a physician permitting a patient to fall ill just to have a chance to cure him?[140] Further, if God willed Christ for the remediation of sin, how do the Salmanticenses escape the charge that God must have willed sin itself, since one who wills the end wills the means?

To these further difficulties, the Salmanticenses reply that God would be cruel to allow the infection of sin *only* as an occasion to cure humanity. In point of fact, however, in Christ God has given much more than a bare remedy.[141] He has not just restored humanity to its former state but has elevated it far beyond this through the hypostatic union. Similarly, a physician who permitted an illness in order to ultimately bring the patient to *greater* health and to manifest the power of the medicine would not be cruel. To give an example that the Salmanticenses themselves do not use, we might compare God's permission of sin in the incarnation to allowing a child to catch certain illnesses so as to build up a greater adult immunity. While allowing a child to fall ill for no reason is cruel, doing so for the reason just mentioned is beneficent.

As for the charge that God must have willed sin, the Salmanticenses repeat that God willed to *permit* sin (which then entails sin due to human weakness) but that he did not will sin itself.[142] In any case, we should not lose sight of the fact that *any* account of the rationale for the incarnation suffers the same difficulty. Everyone must concede that God has, in fact, permitted evil and that the incarnation has responded to it. The problem of God's permitting evil in conjunction with the incarnation cannot, therefore, be lodged as

---

140. *De motivo Incarnationis*, dub. 1, §6, no. 38 (Palmé, 13:298). Cf. Suárez, *In III Thomae*, q. 1, a. 4, disp. 5, sect. 3, no. 9 (Vivès, 17:236–37); and Vásquez, *In III Thomae*, q. 1, a. 3, disp. 11, chap. 4, nos. 41–43 (Sanchez Crespo, 1:162).

141. *De motivo Incarnationis*, dub. 1, §6, no. 37 (Palmé, 13:298–99).

142. *De motivo Incarnationis*, dub. 1, §6, no. 37 (Palmé, 13:299).

an objection against the Salmanticenses in particular. In fact, only a theory such as theirs makes sense of *why* God allowed evil in the first place, since they explain that the permission of sin is directed to Christ the redeemer.

The Scotistic View and Salamanca Replies

The Salmanticenses next present the opinion that Christ would have assumed flesh by virtue of the present decree even absent sin. They offer five arguments for it, responding to each in turn. The first argument they relate for this opinion is from three authorities: first, Augustine, where he says that matrimony would have existed absent sin, adding that matrimony signifies the union of Christ and the Church; second, Bernard, who says that the devil knew of the incarnation prior to the fall; and third, Aquinas, who holds that Adam himself knew of the incarnation prior to the fall.[143] These arguments are some of the earliest in favor of the Scotistic opinion. We encountered them in Robert Grosseteste and Alexander of Hales.[144]

In response, the Salmanticenses note first of all that Augustine holds to their own position in many passages.[145] His words about matrimony can easily mean simply that matrimony would have existed absent sin and that it would be the kind of thing that could signify the union of Christ and the Church (potentially). However, even if it signified the actual union of Christ and the Church, then *ipso facto* it would signify the union of Christ the redeemer, who suffered, died, and rose, with the Church redeemed by him. Thus, also, the Fathers commonly hold that the formation of Eve from the side of Adam prefigures the formation of the Church from the pierced

---

143. *De motivo Incarnationis*, dub. 1, §7, no. 38 (Palmé, 13:300). See Augustine, *De nuptiis et concupiscentia* I, chap. 21 (CSEL 42:236); Bernard of Clairvaux, Sermon 1 on Advent, nos. 2–4 (Leclercq and Rochais, 4:162–64); and Aquinas, *ST* II-II, q. 2, a. 7 (Leonine, 8:34).

144. See Alexander of Hales, *Summa fratris* III, pars 1, inquisitio unica *De Verbo incarnato*, tract. 1, q. 2, tit. 2, co. (Quaracchi, 4:42); and Grosseteste, *De cessatione legalium* III.1.20–21 (Auctores Britannici, 7:127–28).

145. *De motivo Incarnationis*, dub. 1, §7, no. 39 (Palmé, 13:300–1).

side of Christ. There is no reason why matrimony prior to sin could not signify a future reality that was to come about because of sin. Similar replies can be made to the devil's knowledge of the incarnation prior to sin (if what the devil knows can even be taken as a good argument) and to Adam's. As Aquinas observes, "Not everyone who knows the effect knows the cause."[146]

The second argument for the opinion that Christ would have come absent sin is an argument drawn from the words of St. Cyril of Alexandria (ca. 376–444).

If [God] produced him from nothing, as the heretics say, to provide for us and other creatures through the Son of God, then he will be made for us, not us for him. And thus we will be more prominent than he in creation, while he will be the instrument to create other creatures. Why, then, does he not thank us, who is for us? ... If the Son was made for us, not us for the Son, we will be much more prominent than the Son, which is most absurd.... Add that, impelled by necessity, since otherwise he could not create us, he produced the Son, whom, according to them, he would not have produced if he had not willed to create us. For this reason, with us having been created, the Son seems needless, since once creatures are produced the Father has no need of him.[147]

---

146. "Non enim quicumque cognoscit effectum, cognoscit et causam." *ST* III, q. 1, a. 3, ad 5 (Leonine, 11:14). See *De motivo Incarnationis*, dub. 1, §7, no. 38 (Palmé, 13:301–2).

147. "Si ut nos, caeterasque creaturas per filium Dei procuret; ipsum, ut haeretici dicunt, a nihilo produxit; erit ipse propter nos factus, non nos propter illum: et ita nos praestantiores ipso erimus creatura, ipse vero instrumentum ad creandas caeteras creaturas. Cur ergo gratias nobis non aget, qui propter nos est? ... Si propter nos factus est filius, et non propter filium nos; erimus nos filio multo praestantiores, quod absurdissimum est.... Adde, quod necessitate impulsus, quoniam aliter nos creare non posset, filium produxit, quem secundum ipsos non produxisset, nisi creare nos voluisset. Quare nobis creatis supervacaneus videtur filius, cum ipso pater, creaturis productis non indigeat." *De motivo Incarnationis*, dub. 1, §7, no. 38 (Palmé, 13:302). The Latin translation of Cyril of Alexandria's *Thesaurus* V, chap. 3, that the Salmanticenses quote here is that found in *Divi Cyrilli patriarchae Alexandrini [...] opus insigne, quod Thesaurus inscribitur*, trans. Georgius Trapezontius (Basel: Apud Andream Cratandrum, 1524), 252. The content of the Latin varies slightly from Migne's Greek text (PG 75:257–59). The version given by the Salmanticenses more strongly echoes Athanasius, *Oratio II contra Arianos*, no. 30 (Savvidis, 1.1.2: 206–7). Cyril's argument here is put forward for the Scotistic position by Juan de Rada in *Controversiae theologicae* III, contr. 5, a. 3, obs. 4 (Ioannes Crithius, 3:159). Cyril is a patron of the Carmelites, which may be a factor in the Salmanticenses' selection of this argument for the Scotistic position as one deserving a special reply.

Cyril's argumentation here is a *reductio ad absurdum* against Arianism: if the Son is for other creatures, then other creatures are more important than he is, and so he should be grateful to other creatures, and he even seems unnecessary once his purpose has been served. The Salmanticenses borrow this quotation because the objector can similarly argue against the God-man's existence being essentially for human redemption.

The Salmanticenses respond that if the argument proves anything, it proves too much.[148] Cyril's argument is directed against heretics saying that the Son of God is a creature. If this argument is applied to the true incarnation, then its unfitting conclusions could be leveled against *all* theologians, since *de facto* Christ did come in passible flesh for human redemption. In other words, if the same argument does not force one to say that Christ as he has actually come is an occasioned good and is superfluous once redemption has been accomplished, then it does not force this conclusion even if Christ has only come on the condition of sin. Christ *has come* as redeemer. The fact that God has decreed this proves it is not unfitting and can, therefore, be used as a theological premise. In any case, the Salmanticenses do hold that Christ enjoys pride of place as *finis cuius gratia* of all the divine works, and he is hardly less perfect for having come precisely as redeemer.[149]

The third argument for the incarnation absent sin is that *de facto* Christ has come into the world for many other reasons besides redemption: for example, to testify to the truth (Jn 18:37), to be the exemplar for humanity (Jn 13:15; Ti 2:11–12), and to exalt human nature (1 Cor 2:7).[150] The Salmanticenses reply, citing Aquinas, that all these other benefits are connected with redemption.[151] The scriptural and patristic authorities, they say, always speak of redemption as

---

148. "Respondetur hoc argumentum excessive probare, si quid probat." *De motivo Incarnationis*, dub. 1, §7, no. 40 (Palmé, 13:302).

149. *De motivo Incarnationis*, dub. 1, §7, no. 40 (Palmé, 13:303).

150. *De motivo Incarnationis*, dub. 1, §7, no. 41 (Palmé, 13:303).

151. *De motivo Incarnationis*, dub. 1, §7, no. 41 (Palmé, 13:303), quoting *ST* III, q. 1, a. 3, ad 1 (Leonine, 11:14).

The Salamanca Theory

the principal motive, relating other aspects of the incarnation to this motive.[152] Even the passages the argument cites refer, in their larger context, to Christ's redemptive passion.

The fourth argument is that if God had intended Christ principally as redeemer, then for the same reason he would reprobate the damned because of their foreseen demerits, a position the Salmanticenses reject. This follows because Christ's predestination is the cause and exemplar of the predestination of the elect. His predestination is, therefore, prior to the predestination of the elect and thus also prior to the reprobation of others. Therefore, whatever comes before Christ's predestination comes before reprobation. So if sin comes before Christ's predestination, then it also comes before reprobation. But this is against the authority of St. Paul, when he writes: "They were not yet born and had done nothing either good or bad ... not because of works but because of his call.... As it is written, 'Jacob I loved, but Esau I hated'" (Rom 9:11, 13).[153]

The argument can be strengthened by applying it to the angels: Christ's predestination is the exemplar cause of the angels' predestination, inasmuch as his natural divine filiation is the exemplar of any adoptive divine filiation (human or angelic). But if Christ's predestination includes an essential dependence on Adam's sin, then we would also have to say that the angels would not have been predestined if Adam had not sinned, which is absurd.[154]

In response, the Salmanticenses note that "reprobation" (like

---

152. *De motivo Incarnationis*, dub. 1, §7, no. 41 (Palmé, 13:304).
153. *De motivo Incarnationis*, dub. 1, §8, no. 42 (Palmé, 13:304). The Salmanticenses note in passing that Bartolomé de Medina struggles especially hard with this argument. In fact, Medina goes through five possible replies to it, complaining that none of them is truly sufficient, and ends up explaining that when we say Christ's predestination presupposes foreknowledge of sin we mean not sin already committed but future sin. Thus, God predestined Christ because he saw that Adam was going to fall, not that he had fallen, like a physician who prepares medicine in advance. Reprobation, however, is not for future sins but only for sins already committed. See Bartolomé de Medina, *Expositio in tertiam D. Thomae partem*, q. 1, a. 3, in *Expostitio in tertiam D. Thomae partem usque ad quaestionem sexagesimam complectens tertium librum Sententiarum* (Salamanca: Typis haeredum Mathiae Gastii, 1580), 80–81.
154. *De motivo Incarnationis*, dub. 1, §8, no. 42 (Palmé, 13:304–5).

"predestination") in the most proper sense means the command that effectively implements the divine plan.[155] In this sense, there is no difficulty in reprobation's presupposing demerits. If, on the other hand, "reprobation" is taken in the sense of nonelection (i.e., a lack of effective choice in the order of intention), then another distinction is needed: as a punishment, reprobation presupposes demerit, but as the mere withholding of an undue benefit, it does not.

We must be careful, the Salmanticenses note, not to cross from one kind of causality into another. Sin is prior to Christ's being predestined as the matter to be destroyed (*per modum materiae destruendae*), but not from the perspective of final cause. Christ is the final cause *cuius gratia* of both the predestination and reprobation of human beings. In other words, Christ is the reason why God chooses some and omits choosing others.[156] Thus, from the perspective of final causality *cuius gratia*, Christ remains prior, and election and nonelection follow him. Nonelection from this causal perspective is *not* because of foreseen sins, just as election is not because of foreseen merits. Rather, it is the other way around: the nonelection of a person logically entails his demerit, just as the election of a person logically entails his merit.

As for the angels' predestination, the Salmanticenses concede an indirect dependence on Adam's sin by virtue of the present decree.[157] The angels were created and predestined for Christ's glory as *finis cuius gratia* by virtue of the present decree, whereby Christ also would not have come if Adam had not sinned. The Salmanticenses acknowledge the argument's logic and thus embrace the conclusion that in this sense the angels' predestination did depend on Adam's sin.[158] This does not mean, however, that God willed the angels' pre-

---

155. *De motivo Incarnationis*, dub. 1, §8, no. 42 (Palmé, 13:305).
156. "Deus namque elegit aliquos, et exclusit aliquos a regno ob majorem Christi gloriam." *De motivo Incarnationis*, dub. 1, §8, no. 42 (Palmé, 13:305).
157. *De motivo Incarnationis*, dub. 1, §8, no. 42 (Palmé, 13:305–6).
158. "In quo sensu evincitur probatione inducta, ut eam nescimus negare, nec in ea videamus aliquod inconveniens." *De motivo Incarnationis*, dub. 1, §8, no. 42 (Palmé, 13:305).

destination *because of* Adam's sin directly. Instead, God willed it for Christ, and he willed Christ for the remediation of Adam's sin. Further, we should not forget the qualifier "by virtue of the present decree." If Adam had not been going to sin, God may well have had some other decree of the angels' predestination, but it would not be the present one.

The fifth argument for Christ's coming independently of sin is that Christ's predestination seems to have effects that could not have depended on Adam's sin.[159] After all, Adam himself was created in original justice. If he had not sinned, he would have remained in original justice. Thus, original justice did not depend on his future sin. Further, original justice must be an effect of Adam's predestination, since if he had remained in it, he would have merited eternal life. But Christ's predestination is the cause and exemplar of Adam's. Therefore, Christ's predestination could not have depended on Adam's sin, since it has effects that did not depend on Adam's sin (original justice, Adam's own predestination).

The Salmanticenses reply first of all by reminding us that Christ "did not merit through what he was able to have or in accord with a state that he was able to have. Rather, he merited really in that state and through those things that he *de facto* did have. And it would be altogether absurd to imagine something else."[160] In other words, we may well say that Adam's merits depended on Christ's merits, but all of Christ's merits have *de facto* been in passible flesh and with an order to human redemption. It is not a question of comparing the state of original justice to a nonexistent and impossible version of the incarnation but of comparing it to the *actual* incarnation that has occurred.

This means that the stated argument can be turned back against the Scotistic opinion: if the argument is correct that original jus-

---

159. *De motivo Incarnationis*, dub. 1, §8, no. 43 (Palmé, 13:306).
160. "Non enim meruit per ea, quae potuit habere, nec secundum statum, quem potuit habere: sed meruit re ipsa in illo statu, et per illa quae habuit de facto. Et absurdum omnino esset aliud imaginari." *De motivo Incarnationis*, dub. 1, §8, no. 43 (Palmé, 13:306).

tice must have depended on Christ and his merits, then *ipso facto* it proves that even if Adam had not sinned, Christ would have come in passible flesh. Therefore, it is better to say that the state of original justice is *not* an effect of Christ's merits but instead falls under another providence.[161] For this reason, too, any merits that Adam had in the state of original justice would not revive, since they were not founded on Christ.[162]

However, even granting for the sake of argument that original justice was an effect of Christ's predestination and that Adam's merits therein were founded on Christ's merits, the Salmanticenses offer another response.[163] Even in this case, they say, their two-*signa* doctrine accounts for everything, since God could confer grace on Adam, allow its loss, and decree its restoration all for the sake of Christ. This would mean that the state of original justice would have had an indirect dependence on original sin, inasmuch as God would have bestowed it with a view to the future redeemer.

Is this just an arbitrary assumption, or do the Salmanticenses have some basis for affirming it?[164] Further, how can the grace of original justice, which had the real possibility of continuing, have been bestowed with a dependence on its future loss? And how can original justice be considered redemptive? To these questions, the Salmanticenses reply that if it is logically possible to affirm that Christ merited original justice, then our default presumption should

---

161. As I noted above, the Salmanticenses address this question elsewhere. An important distinction that they make in that discussion is between the *person* of Adam and his *state*. Adam, as a given person, was predestined to salvation only through Christ, but this does not mean that every state of Adam's is an effect of Christ's merits. Instead, we can say that the whole providence governing Adam included the permission of sin, whereby he fell from the state of original justice, and his subsequent healing through the future Christ. In this way, Adam's predestination is an effect of Christ's predestination, but the state of original justice need not be, since it is precisely the state whose continuance would have precluded Christ's coming. See Salmanticenses, *Cursus theologicus*, tract. 21, disp. 7, dub. 4 (Palmé, 13:661–700); and tract. 21, disp. 16, dub. 4 (Palmé, 14:593–614).

162. *De motivo Incarnationis*, dub. 1, §8, no. 43 (Palmé, 13:307).

163. *De motivo Incarnationis*, dub. 1, §8, no. 44 (Palmé, 13:307–8).

164. "Nec refert, si opponas *primo* haec voluntarie dici." *De motivo Incarnationis*, dub. 1, §8, no. 45 (Palmé, 13:308).

be that he did, since this would redound to Christ's glory.¹⁶⁵ This would not mean that original justice carried the seed of its own destruction within it but that God both bestowed original justice and permitted its loss with a view to Christ the redeemer. In this view, it is not that Christ suffered and died so that Adam would have original justice but instead that, in his suffering and dying, Christ merited original justice. As in the case of Mary's Immaculate Conception, original justice can be an effect of Christ's redemptive merits without actually entailing the forgiveness of a committed sin.

This rebuttal to the fifth argument for Christ's coming independently of sin concludes the Salmanticenses' treatment of the major doubt in their disputation *De motivo Incarnationis*. They combine what I have called the two keys to their position (distinct species of final cause and precisely two *signa in quo*) to argue that Christ is the first willed and intended by God while his coming was also only on the condition of sin. In their disputation, they develop and respond to various arguments in the Thomistic, Scotistic, and Suaresian veins. Having examined their argumentation on the first doubt in some detail, I will now give a brief outline of the remaining three doubts in the disputation *De motivo Incarnationis*.

THE OTHER THREE DOUBTS

The second doubt of the disputation *De motivo Incarnationis* serves as a follow-up to the first and most important doubt. While the first doubt asks whether, by virtue of the present decree, Christ would come if Adam had not sinned, the second doubt asks "whether, if Adam had not sinned, Christ would come by virtue of another decree that God would have."¹⁶⁶ As I explained in the previous chapter, this is a common approach among later Scholastics. The first question, though hypothetical in form, looks at the present order of his-

---

165. *De motivo Incarnationis*, dub. 1, §8, no. 45 (Palmé, 13:309).
166. "An si Adamus non peccasset, veniret Christus ex vi alterius decreti, quod Deus haberet?" *De motivo Incarnationis*, dub. 2 (Palmé, 13:309).

tory and identifies whether sin has been the *sine qua non* condition for the incarnation in this order of history. In contrast, the second question is hypothetical in the purest sense, asking directly whether God would have founded another order of history that would have included the incarnation had Adam not been going to sin.

Given that the Salmanticenses have argued that sin has indeed been the *sine qua non* condition for the incarnation in the present providential order, one might expect them to echo this conclusion in this second doubt, but that would belie a failure to grasp the real heart of their approach. It is in this second doubt that they show themselves to be full-fledged and methodical Thomists: "The difficulty is reduced to the Incarnation absolutely. Nor should we make our decision only by focusing on the object's possibility or only from the elements of appropriateness we imagine. Rather, [we should decide] through reasonable foundations that positively determine our understanding at least with probability to one side. For knowledge that does not reach at least this point hardly pertains to theology and should be spurned by a theologian."[167] In other words, theology is a rational inquiry into the mysteries of faith, not conclusions based on preconceived notions of how God would freely act. The theologian investigates mysteries by the lights of reason and faith; he does not engage in aprioristic divination.

Thus, the Salmanticenses immediately continue with St. Thomas's principle: what depends on God's free will alone becomes known to us through being revealed.[168] This leads them to three conclusions as to what theology can say about the content of other divine decrees if Adam had not sinned. First, theology cannot determinately affirm that God would decree Christ's coming by anoth-

---

167. "Unde difficultas reducitur ad Incarnationem absolute. Nec decidi debet attenta sola objecti possibilitate, nec ex solis congruentiis imaginatis; sed per rationabilia fundamenta, quae positive determinent intellectum saltem probabiliter ad unam partem. Notitia enim, quae ad id saltem pertingit, minime pertinet ad Theologiam, et debet a Theologo sperni." *De motivo Incarnationis*, dub. 2 (Palmé, 13:309–10).

168. *De motivo Incarnationis*, dub. 2, §1, no. 46 (Palmé, 13:310).

er decree.[169] Second, theology cannot determinately deny that God would decree Christ's coming by another decree.[170] Third, the matter is therefore uncertain and cannot be settled by theologians.[171]

In the preceding doubt, the Salmanticenses presented evidence from Scripture and the Fathers to the effect that God willed Christ only in connection with sin. But there is simply no evidence as to whether God would have willed Christ for some other reason in some totally nonexistent order of history. They even observe: "Just as communicating himself hypostatically could be fitting to God, focusing on the nature of the good inclining to its communication, so also not communicating himself hypostatically could be fitting to God in an order to other ends, most lofty and hidden to us, such as he could think up in his wisdom."[172] One could not ask for a more rigorous application of the Thomistic principle that God's free acts are only made known through revelation. The coming of Christ as savior may be the greatest good we can dream up, but we need the humility to leave open the possibility that God can envision and choose goods beyond creaturely imagination.

The third and fourth doubts of the disputation *De motivo Incarnationis* ask whether Christ would have come, by virtue of the present decree, if there had been original sin but no actual sins (the third doubt),[173] or if there had been actual sins but not original sin (the fourth doubt).[174] Following Aquinas, the Salmanticenses hold that Christ came for the remediation of all human sins, but "more principally" for original sin.[175] It is not just the aggregate of individual

---

169. *De motivo Incarnationis*, dub. 2, §1, nos. 46–47 (Palmé, 13:310–11).
170. *De motivo Incarnationis*, dub. 2, §1, no. 48 (Palmé, 13:311–12).
171. *De motivo Incarnationis*, dub. 2, §1, no. 49 (Palmé, 13:312–13).
172. "Sicut se communicare hypostatice [*sic*] posset esse Deo conveniens attenta natura boni inclinantis ad sui communicationem: ita se non communicare hypostatice posset esse Deo conveniens in ordine ad alios fines altissimos, et nobis occultos, quos ipsius sapientia posset excogitare." *De motivo Incarnationis*, dub. 2, §2, no. 50 (Palmé, 13:314).
173. *De motivo Incarnationis*, dub. 3 (Palmé, 13:315–27).
174. *De motivo Incarnationis*, dub. 4 (Palmé, 13:328–32).
175. *ST* III, q. 1, a. 4 (Leonine, 11:17).

sinners that Christ came to save but the fallen human race as such. Thus, he came more principally to remedy the infection of the nature than to remedy the sins committed by individuals alone. Thus, the Salmanticenses prefer to say that, by virtue of the present decree, Christ would have come for original sin absent actual sins but that he would not have come for actual sins absent original sin.

In this latter case, absent original sin, would God then provide some *other* remedy for those individuals who would fall into actual sins while the rest of the human race remained in original justice? The Salmanticenses repeat that the matter is uncertain to us, seeing as God has revealed nothing along these lines. They add: "Even so, we should presume of the divine piety that it would not leave men fallen in actual sins bereft of every remedy, even lacking original sin. But as to what sort of remedy this would be, since there can be many, this is hidden to us in such a way that we cannot determine a certain one."[176] With these words, they conclude the final doubt of the disputation *De motivo Incarnationis*.

CONCLUSION

In this chapter, I have identified two key principles underlying the Salmanticenses' theory: the distinction between *finis cuius gratia* and *finis cui* and the identification of exactly two conceptual stages (*signa in quo*) in the divine "decision-making process." The Salmanticenses combine these principles in order to articulate how Christ has a true primacy in God's intention as the end of all God's other works and, simultaneously, how God willed Christ himself precisely as a response to human sin.

Their reason for trying to hold both of these assertions together is above all the testimony of Scripture and the Fathers. They believe

---

176. "Praesumendum tamen est de divina pietate, quod homines lapsos in peccatis actualibus, licet originale deficeret, non relinqueret destitutos omni remedio: sed quale foret, cum plurima esse possint, sic latet nos, ut non valeamus unum aliquod determinare." *De motivo Incarnationis*, dub. 4, §1, no. 71 (Palmé, 13:332).

that Scripture is consistent and intelligible when it presents Christ as primary in God's plan and when it says that his coming is essentially redemptive. The Salmanticenses develop and apply their key principles in an effort to articulate how this can be the case. They build on Cajetan's distinction of causal perspectives and take up the Scotistic *ordinate volens* principle. They avoid the polarization of extremists, like Juan de Rada and Gabriel Vásquez, as well as Suárez's tangled attempt to harmonize the Scotistic and Thomistic views. In short, for the Salmanticenses, mercy through Christ the redeemer is the foundation and defining feature of the present economy.

Overall, the Salmanticenses' approach is elegant and respectful of God's divine simplicity and immutability. Their decisive methodological principle is that knowledge of God's free acts is founded on revelation. This comes across with particular force in the second doubt of the disputation, where they profess the inability of theology to decide whether God would have decreed the incarnation by virtue of some other decree if Adam had not sinned. This shows their commitment to being rooted in the mysteries of faith as God has revealed them. They employ logical subtleties and arguments from fittingness, but precisely as an act of *fides quaerens intellectum*, not *a priori* demonstrations. Despite the rigor and thoroughness of their argumentation, there are still criticisms of their position. I will address these in the next chapter.

4

A Defense of Salamanca

In the previous chapter, I outlined how the Salmanticenses hold together that Christ is the first willed and intended by God and that he would not have come absent sin. Their theory relies on the combination of the distinction between *finis cuius gratia* and *finis cui* with their two-*signa* approach to divine providence. In the course of summarizing their argument, I related their own responses to objections.

In the present chapter, I will deal with further objections against the Salmanticenses in particular or against essential elements of their approach in general. First, I will address the legitimacy of *signa rationis*. Second, I will respond to the charge that the Salmanticenses' two-*signa* approach is sophistical. Third, I will reply to the objection that the Salmanticenses abuse the distinction between *finis cuius gratia* and *finis cui*. Fourth, I will examine whether they betray the Thomistic view of the divine economy, especially vis-à-vis original justice. Fifth, I will argue that the Salmanticenses' theory does not entail that God wills sin. Sixth, and finally, I will respond to four further criticisms from Francesco Maria Risi, OH (1834–1907).

SIGNA RATIONIS ARE METHODOLOGICALLY INAPPROPRIATE

Some theologians take issue with *signa rationis* as a conceptual instrument. Hervaeus Natalis was an early objector, rejecting the application of *signa rationis* to the natural process of generation as well as to the divine act of creation.[1] Ockham criticizes Scotus's use of *signa originis* for the Trinitarian processions as "simply false or too abusive."[2] Even Molina—hardly a stranger to the multiplication of conceptual distinctions in God—complains about the Scotistic *signa*.[3] Nevertheless, as we have seen, theologians from all schools, from the thirteenth century onward, have used *signa rationis* to demarcate conceptual priority and posteriority in God's acts.

Should theologians really speak of the divine knowledge and will in terms of successive stages? Maurice de la Taille, SJ (1872–1933) argues that, while conceptual distinctions are needed, *signa rationis* go too far: "The use of a simple distinction of reason between divine attributes without formal succession, without placing one determining element over another determinable element, does not of-

---

1. Hervaeus Natalis, *Tractatus de formis*, pars 2, ad q. 10, ad supp. 1, no. 326 (Studia artistarum, 30:111–12); and *De esse et essentia*, pars 2, chap. 4, ad 3, no. 227 (Studia artistarum, 35:96).

2. "Modus loquendi est simpliciter falsus vel nimis abusivus." Ockham, *Ordinatio* I, d. 9, q. 3 (Opera theologica, 3:295). Walter Chatton (ca. 1290–1343) remarks that contemporary continental theologians similarly regarded Scotus's use of *signa* for the Trinitarian processions as silly: "Sed ista quaestio iam cassata est per multa argumenta: ponere scilicet in Deo quaecumque talia signa originis nisi tantum quod una persona est ab alia, et hoc esse ab hoc, et omnis alia imaginatio signorum frivola reputatur ultra mare et citra." Walter Chatton, *Reportatio super librum primum Sententiarum*, d. 4, q. 3, a. 1, no. 5, in *Reportatio super Sententias*, ed. Joseph C. Wey and Girard J. Etzkorn, Studies and Texts 141 (Toronto: Pontifical Institute of Mediaeval Studies, 2002), 1:356.

3. Molina, *In I Thomae*, q. 23, aa. 4–5, disp. 1, memb. 7 (Prost, 1:311). The censor of his work remarked that Molina himself did not seem able to avoid speaking of priority and posteriority in divine acts. See *Ludovici Molina liberi arbitrii cum gratiae donis, divina praescientia, providentia, praedestinatione et reprobatione concordia*, ed. Johann Rabeneck, Societatis Iesu selcti scriptores (Oña: Collegium maximum S. I., 1953), 47*. Molina later added an appendix, explaining that he would allow *signa rationis* as long as one *signum* really did not imply the other. *In I Thomae*, q. 23, aa. 4–5, disp. 1, memb. 8 (Prost, 1:314–15).

fend against the privileged position of the pure act, but this is not the case for the aforementioned *instantia rationis*."[4] The problem for de La Taille is not that human beings need conceptual distinctions when confronted with God's simplicity. He allows, for example, that we can distinguish conceptually between God's essence and his attributes.[5] De la Taille's objection to *signa rationis* centers on the notion of succession implying indeterminacy. Thus, de La Taille prefers to speak of an "operative knowledge" in God to avoid the impression that God knows his works first as possible before willing them as actual.[6]

In response, I concede, first of all, that *signa rationis* can certainly be abused. The Salmanticenses themselves complain of theologians who assign eight, ten, or even more *signa*.[7] Such approaches indeed foster an overly anthropomorphic and ultimately misleading view of the divine acts, as if God really does go through a discursive process. However, the question at hand is not whether *signa rationis* can be

---

4. "L'emploi d'une simple distinction de raison entre attributs divins sans succession formelle, sans superposition d'un élément déterminant à un élément déterminable, n'a rien d'offensant pour la prérogative de l'acte pur; au contraire, pour les instants de raison ci-dessus mentionnés." Maurice de la Taille, "Sur diverses classifications de la science divine," *Recherches de Science Religieuse* 13 (1923): 537–38. Elsewhere, he says: "Associer l'idée de Dieu et l'idée de potentialité est manifestement un abus; et c'est dans cet abus que tomberait celui qui prêterait à Dieu une science de l'idée simple, antérieure à la science du plan, et une science du plan antérieure à la science de l'existence." "Associating the idea of God with the idea of potentiality is manifestly an abuse, and this is the abuse one would fall into by attributing to God a knowledge of the simple idea prior to knowledge of the plan and knowledge of the plan prior to knowledge of its existence." De la Taille, "Sur diverses classifications de la science divine," 10.

5. De la Taille, "Sur diverses classifications de la science divine," 537.

6. "La science divine, pas plus qu'aucune autre science ouvrière, ne cause rien dans l'objet que ce qui s'y trouve de conforme aux idées mises en ouvre." De la Taille, "Sur diverses classifications de la science divine," 21. "Unlike other kinds of operative knowledge, divine knowledge does not cause anything in the object besides what conforms with the idea put into effect." And: "En Dieu, vue et science pratique ne font pas deux sciences échelonnées commedans l'ouvrier humain, mais bien une seule et même connaissance, réellement et logiquement indivisible." "In God, vision and practical knowledge do not form two knowledges separated out as in the human agent, but rather one and the same cognizance, really and logically indivisible." De la Taille, "Sur diverses classifications de la science divine," 17.

7. *De motivo Incarnationis*, dub. 1, §1, no. 5 (Palmé, 13:268).

misused but whether they are inappropriate *per se*, and particularly at interest is the Salmanticenses' own application.

De la Taille worries that *signa rationis* imply indeterminacy in God. But since *signa* are based on the *objects* of God's knowledge and will, they need not give the impression of indeterminacy in God. Instead, they indicate the composition of determinable and determining elements in the objects God knows and wills and, most basically, their contingent existence.[8] The objects that God is knowing and willing might not have been. God's knowledge and will are necessary, but this does not make their objects necessary.[9]

Therefore, if de La Taille is right about the danger in conceptually distinguishing between the situation *before* God decides and *after* he decides, there is also the danger in *not* so distinguishing. In particular, there is the false impression that God could not have acted otherwise than he does. God's knowledge and will can be compared with his essence, in which case his knowledge and will are really identical, simple, eternal, and immutable. But they can also be compared with their creaturely objects.[10] Considered as identical with the divine essence, God's knowledge and will are not characterized by succession, indeterminacy, or mutability, but God's knowledge and will can also be considered in their extension to objects *ad extra*, where there are succession, indeterminacy, and mutability.[11]

As for the fact that one *signum* is "prior" to another, this, too, reflects the structure of the objects known and willed by God. Aquinas writes: "As the Philosopher says in *Metaphysics* 5, we speak of 'prior'

8. Thomas Gornall, "A Note on Imagination and Thought about God," *The Heythrop Journal* 4, no. 2 (1963): 137. Cf. his introductory essay on God's knowledge in vol. 4 of *Summa theologiae: Latin Text and English Translation, Introductions, Notes, Appendices and Glossaries* (Cambridge: Cambridge University Press, 2006), xxv–xxvi.

9. *ST* I, q. 19, a. 8 (Leonine, 4:244).

10. The fact that God knows these objects in and through knowing himself does not preclude the comparison, since they remain objects really distinct from God.

11. Cf. Salmanticenses, *Cursus theologicus*, tract. 5, *De praedestinatione*, disp. 9, *De modo quo Deus elegit praedestinatos ad gloriam*, dub. 3, §6, no. 109 (Palmé, 2:453); and Michael J. Dodds, *The Unchanging God of Love: Thomas Aquinas and Contemporary Theology on Divine Immutability*, 2nd ed. (Washington, D.C.: The Catholic University of America Press, 2008), 177–80.

and 'posterior' with reference to their relation to a given principle. Now order includes within it a given manner of 'prior' and 'posterior.' Hence wherever there is a given principle, there must also be a certain order."[12] In other words, the intelligible constitution of creatures in relation to God as their principle serves as the basis for our conceptual ordering.

Further, it is not only various objects that are related to the same first principle but various *aspects* of objects. Thus, "we take note of the order of the divine will not with reference to the different things willed but with respect to one and the same thing willed on account of the differences found in it."[13] God, in fact, is the source of the order found within and among the objects he wills. "It is necessary for the pattern [*ratio*] for the order of things to the end to pre-exist in the divine mind."[14]

For example, in terms of final causality, God first wills the end and then wills the means, not because of indeterminacy in God but because he determines the relation between the end and the means, seeing as "he wills this to be on account of that, but it is not on account of this that he wills that."[15] The means are on account of the end, whereas the end is not on account of the means. Of this principle, François Daguet, OP, observes, "This kind of affirmation about the absence of causality in God and about the will of the order from a means to the end safeguards Saint Thomas from any charge of anthropomorphism and, at the same time, justifies the doctrine of *in-*

---

12. "Sicut Philosophus dicit, in V *Metaphys.*, prius et posterius dicitur secundum relationem ad aliquod principium. Ordo autem includit in se aliquem modum prioris et posterioris. Unde oportet quod ubicumque est aliquod principium, sit etiam aliquis ordo." *ST* II-II, q. 26, a. 1, co. (Leonine, 8:209).

13. "Ordo divinae voluntatis non attenditur secundum diversa volita, sed respectu ad unum et idem volitum propter diversa in eo reperta." Aquinas, *De veritate*, q. 23, a. 2, ad 2 (Leonine, 22:657). John of St. Thomas emphasizes this in *Cursus theologicus* III, q. 1, disp. 3, a. 1, nos. 3–4 (Vivès, 8:91).

14. "Necesse est quod ratio ordinis rerum in finem in mente divina praeexistat." *ST* I, q. 22, a. 1, co. (Leonine, 4:263).

15. "Vult ergo hoc esse propter hoc: sed non propter hoc vult hoc." *ST* I, q. 19, a. 5, co. (Leonine, 4:239).

stantia rationis, that of the order of effects or divine decrees."[16] In other words, the methodology of *signa rationis* does not offend against the divine simplicity or immutability, since it is only a conceptual distinction grounded in the relations existing among the objects of the divine will.[17]

Applying the maxim *causae ad invicem sunt causae (sed in diverso genere)*, it is possible to assign priority to each kind of cause within its own order. In this way, from the perspective of material cause, matter is prior to form, and so one can say that God wills matter "first" (at a prior conceptual moment) in the order of material cause. This means nothing other than the fact that God wills the priority matter enjoys from its own perspective. And from the perspective of formal cause, the converse is true. The complementarity of determinable and determining elements exists not in God but in the composite object. It is, however, a complementarity that God wills. As explained in the preceding chapter, the Salmanticenses call the priority of matter relative to form (from the perspective of material cause) "priority *a quo*" to indicate that it always implies the priority of form relative to matter from the opposite perspective. Priority and posteriority *a quo* ground corresponding *signa a quo*.

Applying this to the motive of the incarnation is what allows the Salmanticenses to say that God wills Christ "first" from the perspective of *finis cuius gratia* while also knowing sin "first" from the perspective of *materia circa quam*. "First" here denotes priority *a quo*, since we are analyzing distinct and complementary aspects of the single willed object.

At the most basic level, however, the fundamentally contingent existence of creatures is the basis for our saying that God knows

---

16. "Une telle affirmation sur l'absence de causalité en Dieu et sur la volonté de l'ordre d'un moyen à la fin met Saint Thomas à l'abri de tout reproche d'anthropomorphisme et, en même temps, justifie la doctrine des instants de raison, celle de l'ordre des effets ou des décrets divins." François Daguet, *Théologie du dessein divin chez Thomas d'Aquin: Finis omnium Ecclesia*, Bibliothèque thomiste 54 (Paris: Librairie philosophique J. Vrin, 2003), 222.

17. Daguet, *Théologie du dessein divin*, 222.

them first as possible and then wills and knows them as actual. This leads to the distinction between God's knowledge of simple intelligence and his knowledge of vision. It also grounds the Salmanticenses' two *signa in quo*, based on priority and posteriority *in quo*, which exclude mutual entailment.

This is how the Salmanticenses avoid undue anthropomorphism while still accounting for God's freedom and the resulting contingency in creatures. Alternatively, if we fail to distinguish pure possibles from what is actual, we either end up identifying nonbeing with being or else risk an error once made by Peter Abelard (1079–1142)—and repeated by Gottfried Leibniz (1646–1716). Abelard emphasized the real unity of the divine attributes (especially wisdom, benevolence, and power) to the point of concluding that God must will the best possible.[18] The way to avoid this dilemma is to recognize that the real distinction between pure possibles and what is actual can serve as a *fundamentum in re* for speaking about what God "could have done" in distinction from what he "has done."[19] This real *fundamentum* means that a distinction following on it (such as that between God's knowledge of simple intelligence and his knowledge of vision or that between the Salmanticenses' two *signa in quo*) is not *merely* conceptual, even though it does not reflect indeterminacy within God himself. In Scholastic terms, it is a *distinctio rationis ratiocinatae*, not a *distinctio rationis ratiocinantis*.[20]

The limitations of human thought and language force us to conceive of and speak of God's active potency as "before" his free exer-

---

18. Peter Abelard, *Theologia scholarium* III, nos. 27–64, in *Theologia 'scholarium,'* ed. E. Buytaert and C. Mews, Opera theologica 3, CCCM 13 (Turnhout: Brepols, 1987), 511–27. See also Marcia L. Colish, "Peter Lombard and Abelard: The *Opinio nominalium* and Divine Transcendence," in *Studies in Scholasticism* (Hampshire, UK: Ashgate, 2006), VI, 14–15.

19. J. M. Dalmau, *De Deo uno et trino* I, chap. 3, a. 2, thesis 12, no. 147, in *Sacrae theologiae summa*, 3rd ed., Biblioteca de autores Cristianos 90 (Madrid: Biblioteca de autores Cristianos, 1958), 2:118–19.

20. See Sven K. Knebel, "Aureol and the Ambiguities of the Distinction of Reason," in *Philosophical Debates at Paris in the Early Fourteenth Century*, ed. Stephen F. Brown, Thomas Dewender, and Theo Kobush (Leiden: Brill, 2009), 334.

cise of that potency. This is not a temporal priority, but it is a logical one. It is true that God has always been willing what he wills, but there seems to be no more straightforward way to affirm God's freedom than by saying that he "could have" willed otherwise.[21] As long as it is true to say with Aquinas that "God could have become incarnate even if sin did not exist,"[22] there are two conceptually distinct stages, or *signa rationis*.

THE TWO-*SIGNA* APPROACH IS SOPHISTICAL

Having defended the legitimacy of *signa rationis*, I will now consider the opposite criticism—that the Salmanticenses do not use enough of them. Francesco Maria Risi, for example, criticizes the Salmanticenses' two-*signa* approach as nothing but "sleight of hand."[23] He begins by observing that "only one *signum* is no *signum* at all" because the entire rationale for *signa* as a theological instrument is to articulate a conceptual order of prior and posterior in the single simple divine act.[24] He claims that the Salmanticenses' approach of assigning a single *signum* for the divine intellect (knowledge of simple intelligence) and another for the divine will (free will and, consequently, knowledge of vision) is merely a pretense.

In reality, he says, they multiply further *signa* without calling them such in violation of one of their own key principles.[25] As a supporting example, Risi quotes from the Salmanticenses: "In the order pertaining to execution, the production of men was willed *first, then* eleva-

---

21. Cf. Dodds, *Unchanging God of Love*, 178–80.
22. "Potuisset enim, etiam peccato non existente, Deus incarnari." *ST* III, q. 1, a. 3, co. (Leonine, 11:14).
23. "Il sistema dei Salmaticesi è un giuoco di prestigio." Francesco Maria Risi, *Sul motivo primario della incarnazione del Verbo, ossia, Gesù Cristo predestinato di primo intento per fini indipendenti dalla caduta dell'uman genere e dal decreto di redenzione* (Brescia: Tipografia Mucchetti & Riva, 1897), 1:313. Pancheri repeats his criticism in *Universal Primacy of Christ*, 59.
24. "Un solo segno è un segno nullo." Risi, *Motivo primario della incarnazione*, 1:315.
25. Risi, *Motivo primario della incarnazione*, 1:316.

tion to the state of grace, *further* the permission of sin, and *afterwards* the remedy through Christ the Redeemer and the efficacious election of the predestined and their glorification."[26] The result, Risi says, is that the Salmanticenses' system amounts to Molinism, since the first *signum* of all possible things does not correlate precisely to God's knowledge of simple intelligence but ends up functioning as middle knowledge, which the Salmanticenses purport to reject.[27]

In response, I first note that the context for the quotation Risi adduces is a comparison of causal perspectives. The Salmanticenses preface the above quotation as follows: "Granted that Christ was willed and foreseen prior to other things in the genus of final cause, ... in the genus of material cause and in the order pertaining to execution, the production of men was willed first."[28] In this passage, the Salmanticenses are not comparing the two *signa in quo* but are instead comparing final and material causal perspectives. *Within* each of these causal perspectives (here material cause), there are degrees of proximity to what is ultimate in that given perspective. These can indeed be compared in terms of prior and posterior and could, therefore, serve as the basis for *signa rationis* within that causal perspective, but we would not be talking about the two macro-level *signa in quo* that include all the causal perspectives taken together.

I have established that when comparing two causal perspectives (e.g., material and formal cause), each is prior in its own order *a quo*, since each implies the other. I have also established that pure possibles are prior *in quo* to actuals, since there is not mutual entailment. So the question arises: what sort of priority governs the *signa rationis* assigned *within* a given causal perspective? For example, in the quo-

---

26. "In ordine ad executionem *prius* fuit volita productio hominum, *deinde* elevatio ad statum gratiae, *ulterius* permissio peccati, *postea* remedium per Christum Redemptorem, et electio efficax praedestinatorum, et eorum glorificatio." Salmanticenses, *De motivo Incarnationis*, dub. 1, §5, no. 31 (Palmé, 13:293). Risi adds the emphasis in *Motivo primario della incarnazione*, 1:315.

27. Risi, *Motivo primario della incarnazione*, 1:316.

28. "Licet in genere causae finalis Christus fuerit prius volitus, et praevisus, quam alia ... nihilominus in genere causae materialis, et in ordine ad executionem prius fuit volita productio hominum." *De motivo Incarnationis*, dub. 1, §5, no. 31 (Palmé, 13:293).

tation above, the Salmanticenses have identified that from the perspective of material cause, the production of human beings is first, followed by their elevation to grace, then the permission of sin, then sin's remedy through Christ, and finally the predestination and glorification of the elect.

At first blush, it seems that this cannot be priority *a quo*. For example, there is nothing in the production of human beings that entails necessarily their elevation to grace: grace presupposes nature, but nature does not strictly entail grace.[29] Must they, then, be *signa in quo*? Here caution is needed. We can speak from within the perspective of material cause in two senses: in isolation or in the larger context. If we *only* traced the elements enumerated within the material causal perspective, we would indeed be left with *signa in quo* for the reason noted above: the elements do not mutually entail one another. However, if we look within the material causal perspective but keep in mind that this perspective has been willed by God *precisely as such*, then the situation changes.

In fact, this latter perspective is the one that should be used when discussing *signa rationis*, since this conceptual distinction arises not just from the objects themselves but from their being willed as such by God. Therefore, while the creation of human beings considered *per se* does not entail their elevation to grace, God's concrete act of creating human beings, taken in the whole providential context, may. God can choose to create human beings with a view to elevating them to grace, as he has actually done. The mere idea of creating human nature does not imply elevation to grace, but God's efficacious decree to create and elevate human nature does.[30]

---

29. Granted that this is a contentious subject in contemporary theology, the Salmanticenses, whose view is at issue, certainly do not think that the creation of human nature *per se* entails its elevation to grace. See their *Cursus theologicus*, tract. 14, *De gratia Dei*, disp. 1, chap. 2 (Palmé, 9:13–26).

30. This latter consideration is what leads to the objection about the fly mentioned in the last chapter, which boils down to a challenge that the Salmanticenses' theory relies *only* on the fact that all the objects God wills are included in the same decree to establish that there is a *sine qua non* connection among them.

The Salmanticenses insist time and again that God's effective choice extends not only to the proximate end of his works but also to all the means and circumstances connected with the end, whether this connection is necessary from the nature of the work or one freely imposed by God. Therefore, when looking at the production of human beings within God's efficacious decree, we cannot consider it as isolated from the elevation of human beings to grace. Or when looking at the permission of sin, we cannot consider this permission in isolation from Christ the redeemer. Thus, the priority and posteriority at work in such a consideration is not strictly *in quo*, since all the objects related as prior and posterior have been decreed precisely in conjunction with one another. Therefore, the Salmanticenses do not need to multiply their comprehensive *signa in quo* to account for the priority and posteriority of the objects of the divine will considered from within each causal perspective.

As an analogy, one might imagine an immense room filled with gemstones of different kinds, varying in color, size, and cut. Any of the gemstones can be picked up, rotated, and viewed from any angle. The farthest facet from one perspective becomes the nearest from another. The observer can peer through the stone, tracing a linear path from near to far. As the stone is rotated, the order of the stone's successive parts from the observer's vantage point changes.

Similarly, prior to the determination of the divine will, all possible configurations of created reality are available to God, and he can choose to actualize any of them or none of them.[31] The two com-

---

31. Paul Galtier objects to comparing the divine decree of the incarnation to a composite physical object (like a living body). It may well be the case, he says, that soul and body enjoy complementary priorities from formal and material perspectives, but this does not hold in the case of an "object" of God's intention. See Paul Galtier, *Les deux Adam* (Paris: Beauschesne et ses fils, 1947), 102n1. I reply that the concept of an object is applied analogously. In the case of a living body, there are really distinct formal and material principles and a single substance arising from them. In the case of the decree of the incarnation, there are really distinct elements (sin, Christ, redeemed humanity) and the simple act of the divine will that unifies them in a single plan. In the latter, the elements are not *of themselves* connected in the way that soul and body are by nature, but they are *de facto* connected by the divine intention itself.

prehensive *signa in quo* describe this. However, any given configuration can also be viewed from various perspectives, and the order of the configuration's parts can be described from that perspective. This is what the Salmanticenses are doing in the quotation above when they compare the logical sequence from the point of view of final cause with that of material cause. Any *signa* assigned within a given causal perspective, on the basis of the priority and posteriority found therein, are such precisely as part of the whole configuration and are, therefore, not strictly separable from one another.[32]

This is why further macro-level *signa in quo* are not needed. It is true, for example, that the permission of sin and the sending of Christ are not connected by necessity, but they are connected *within this particular configuration*. We do not need to add another *signum in quo* to express the non-necessity of the connection, since it is enough to say that God could have chosen a different overall configuration in the first place, just as the observer could choose a gemstone with different features instead of altering the one he is currently holding.

Next, as far as the charge of occult Molinism goes, while Molina and the Salmanticenses both aspire to eliminate needless *signa rationis* and, ultimately, embrace a single-decree theory, they achieve this differently.[33] Molina begins with God's knowledge of all possible future contingents.[34] For him, this means both God's knowledge of simple intelligence (which Molina prefers to call God's "necessary knowledge") and middle knowledge. Then, Molina says, God chooses whichever configuration of contingent realities he pleases. Through this, Molina intends to cut off a ground to Scotus's *ordinate volens* principle: because God envisions and wills the end and its determinate means simultaneously, there is no basis for a conceptual order of priority and posteriority that would divide the end and the

---

32. Cf. John of St. Thomas, *Cursus theologicus* III, q. 1, disp. 3, a. 1, nos. 13–14 (Vivès, 8:93–94).

33. Cf. Carol, *Why Jesus Christ?*, 488–89.

34. Molina, *In I Thomae*, q. 23, aa. 4–5, disp. 1, memb. 7 (Prost, 1:310–11).

means. Therefore, there is no conceptual moment when God wills the incarnation *prior* to willing it as redemptive.

The Salmanticenses differ from Molina by emphasizing the complementarity of causal perspectives within the single divine decree. This allows them to assign conceptual stages from each point of view (*signa a quo*), where Christ is the first willed and intended from the most significant perspective. Molina and the Salmanticenses both take a single-decree approach, and to this extent Molina is a real predecessor of the Salmanticenses. Nevertheless, while Molina distinguishes elements of final cause, stating that all other divine works are for Christ while at the same time Christ is for humanity in need of redemption, he does not use the language of *finis cuius gratia* and *finis cui* and, more drastically, does not identify conceptual stages for each causal perspective.[35] In other words, Molina does not have the benefit of the Salmanticenses' *signa a quo*. In fact, in an appendix that Molina added in response to his critics, he explains that he rejects conceptual stages when one presupposes or entails the other, although he otherwise allows them.[36] The lack of emphasis on causal perspective and concomitant analysis of priority and posteriority on the basis of it, using *signa a quo*, constitutes a major difference between Molina and the Salmanticenses.

Molina and the Salmanticenses also differ in how they conceive of the certitude of Adam's sinning by virtue of the present decree. Molina thinks that human free will is such that, with all other factors being equal, including God's grace, the will could really determine itself to either side.[37] Thus, in the circumstances in which he was created, including identical divine *concursus* and *auxilium*, Adam might

---

35. "Quare actu illo simul caetera omnia, quae ad naturam et gratiam spectant, ordinauit in Christum tanquam in finem: et incarnationem ipsam atque Christum, licet expetiuerit, vt ideo essent, quia in se ipsis sunt maius bonum quam caetera creata, vicissim tamen voluit, vt forent in reparationem generis humani, tanquam in partem finis integri, sine qua, iuxta verisimiliorem sententiam, non foret Christi incarnatio." Molina, *In I Thomae*, q. 23, aa. 4–5, disp. 1, memb. 7 (Prost, 1:313).

36. Molina, *In I Thomae*, q. 23, aa. 4–5, disp. 1, memb. 8 (Prost, 1:314).

37. Molina, *Concordia*, par. 4, q. 14, a. 13, disp. 47, no. 2 (Rabeneck, 293–94).

just as well have sinned or not sinned. For Molina, then, the will determines itself in a way that excludes being determined by anything else, even God.[38] However, God's middle knowledge penetrates the creaturely will entirely and thereby allows him to know what Adam would do in any circumstances. This gives God infallible certitude of Adam's choice without God's determining that choice *in actu secundo*. Instead, God gives Adam the capacity for free choice *in actu primo* and creates the world such that Adam will end up in the given circumstances. In other words, for Molina, the present decree—as far as the decision to create Adam in the circumstances in which he was really placed is concerned—could have remained exactly as it is and yet without Adam's sinning.

The Salmanticenses, in contrast, hold that God knows whether Adam would sin in any given circumstances precisely because God does move the will *in actu secundo*, determining it to determine itself.[39] In the case of Adam's sin, God knows that if he himself were not to provide the *auxilium* actually effective in producing Adam's resistance to temptation, then, because of human frailty, Adam would inevitably sin. In this way, God's knowledge of what he himself would do leads, by logical inference, to certitude about what Adam would do. This is entirely different from Molina's explanation.

Difficulties about the real sufficiency of inefficacious grace or about divine innocence do not, at this point, count against the Salmanticenses' view of the incarnation. These are indeed serious theological difficulties, ones that theologians can never exhaustively settle, but the Salmanticenses are not engaged in the controversy *de auxiliis* in the present disputation. Their theory about the motive of the incarnation does not rely on the theological resolution of that problem. In fact, they even allude to the fact that acceptance or rejection of Molinistic middle knowledge is immaterial to their argument

---

38. Molina, *Concordia*, par. 4, q. 14, a. 13, disp. 53, memb. 3, no. 10 (Rabeneck, 389–90).

39. The whole of the Salmanticenses' *Cursus theologicus*, tract. 14, disp. 7, *De gratia efficaci* (Palmé, 10:1–262), is essentially devoted to this point.

that the present decree includes sin as the *sine qua non* condition for the incarnation.[40] They themselves reject it, but one could accept it and still agree in substance with their doctrine on the incarnation. Their theory only requires acceptance that God can provide a help that is truly sufficient (however this sufficiency is accounted for) and at the same time know infallibly that the creature will not actually avoid sin. This much is clear from revelation, so that even if theology has not yet demonstrated or cannot demonstrate *how* it is true, it is no less certain *that* it is true.

Chrysostome Urrutibéhéty, OFM (1853–1935), also argues against the Salmanticenses' two-*signa* approach. His observations are particularly valuable because he is one of the few critics of the Salmanticenses to attend to the distinction between a *signum a quo* and a *signum in quo*.[41] Urrutibéhéty observes first that we cannot distinguish *signa in quo* in cases where the cause necessarily implies the effect. This is because priority *in quo* means one-way entailment, but when the cause necessarily gives rise to the effect, there is two-way entailment and thus priority *a quo*. Next, he recalls that in the present disputation we are dealing not with necessary causes but with free ones. We have God's freedom to account for, which the Salmanticenses do neatly with two *signa in quo*. However, Urrutibéhéty adds, we must also account for *human* freedom.

For example, Adam sinned not from his nature but from his free will. Adam's existence does not, therefore, logically and infallibly entail sin.[42] Similarly, redemption is a *free* gift, and Christ *freely* accepted the office of redeemer.[43] Human sin does not imply the redeemer in the way that the sun implies its illumination. In these examples,

---

40. "Requiritur auxilium efficax, quolibet modo explicetur." *De motivo Incarnationis*, dub. 1, §4, no. 20 (Palmé, 13:282). The point is that no matter how one explains the difference between Adam's sinning and not sinning, the situation in which he does not sin must be different from the situation that has actually obtained and, thus, does not fall under the same decree numerically as the present one.

41. Chrysostome Urrutibéhéty, *Le Motif de l'Incarnation et les principaux thomistes contemporains* (Tours: Librairie Alfred Cattier, 1921), 141–47.

42. Urrutibéhéty, *Le Motif de l'Incarnation*, 146.

43. Urrutibéhéty, *Le Motif de l'Incarnation*, 146.

the effect does not proceed inexorably from the cause, which means there is not two-way entailment. This means there is priority *in quo*, not *a quo*. Thus, further *signa in quo* are needed to account for these free decisions.

In reply, human acts can be viewed both in relation to their proximate source, which is the human being himself, and in relation to their ultimate source, which is the first cause. Looking within the human being considered in himself, there would have to be multiple *signa in quo* to account for the fact that the person's existence does not entail a given free act. However, looking at the same free act from the perspective of God's knowledge and will, there is no need for extra *signa in quo*. This is because in the first *signum in quo* in which God knows all possible things with all their possible combinations, he also knows which *concursus* and *auxilia* he could give. In other words, he knows simultaneously which creatures he could create and how he could move them in each and every act. From the perspective of the first cause, giving rise to the free creature and moving the free creature to act at distinct points in time occur within the same *signum in quo*.

The obvious objection to this is that it is deterministic and violates human free will. As before, this objection is really directed not against the Salmanticenses' theory about the incarnation's motive but against a Thomistic (Bañezian) account of God's transcendent causality. As long as it is true that God moves the created will to move itself and works intimately in all things, sustaining them and moving them in their proper operations,[44] then his knowledge of possible creatures includes his knowledge of what he himself can do in them. The Salmanticenses are decidedly not Molinists on this question, since they firmly believe that the first cause, even as it gives rise to secondary causes, also works within those causes, moving them according to their own proper modality, so that God can determine the free will to determine itself freely. And as far as sin goes,

---

44. *ST* I, q. 22, a. 4, co. (Leonine, 4:269); and q. 105, aa. 4–5 (Leonine, 5:474–76).

the Salmanticenses are clear that God does not move the creature to sin but simply refrains from efficaciously moving it to avoid sin, so that sin is logically entailed and thus infallibly foreseen but not caused by God as to its malice.[45]

The objector might further respond that, if this is the case, then the Salmanticenses' theory involves God's letting the human race fall into the ruin of sin *so as* to have occasion for the redemptive incarnation. As shown in the preceding chapter, the Salmanticenses accept precisely this view.[46] I will address whether it is unfitting below when considering whether the Salmanticenses' view entails that God intends sin.

THE SALMANTICENSES CONFUSE *FINIS CUIUS GRATIA* AND *FINIS CUI*

Francesco Saverio Pancheri, OFM Conv. (1920–86), writes that "in the position adopted by the *Salmanticenses*, the *finis cui* becomes the *motive* of Christ's existence and is thus automatically transformed into a *finis cuius gratia*."[47] It is irrelevant, he explains, that Christ's own intrinsic goodness surpasses that of all other divine works *ad extra*. For Pancheri, as long as God wills Christ as a means, as long as the human need of redemption is Christ's *raison d'être*, Christ cannot be the *finis cuius gratia*.[48]

In this criticism, Pancheri follows a thread common to Risi's critique of the Salmanticenses as well, one that reflects the heart of the strict Scotistic approach—namely, the application of the *ordinate volens* principle in a linear fashion without attention to the vari-

---

45. *De motivo Incarnationis*, dub. 1, §5, no. 31 (Palmé, 13:294).
46. *De motivo Incarnationis*, dub. 1, §6, no. 37 (Palmé, 13:298–99). In particular, God's primary intention of Christ the redeemer logically entails the permission of sin, which, in turn, logically entails humanity's actually sinning, due to the frailty of unaided human nature. *De motivo Incarnationis*, dub. 1, §5, no. 31 (Palmé, 13:293).
47. Pancheri, *Universal Primacy of Christ*, 60.
48. Pancheri, *Universal Primacy of Christ*, 60.

ous species of cause.[49] The criticism essentially arises because of the presumption that if Christ is first in God's intention in a true sense, then this precludes his being ordered to another object of the divine will in another sense. But Christ *is* the redeemer. He has come "to give his life as a ransom for many" (Mk 10:45). It is, thus, a theological starting point, a *datum* of revelation, that God has willed Christ *for* the good of humanity, constituting Christ as a "means" in some sense.

Indeed, Scripture is clear that Christ is for humanity and that humanity is for Christ. The mistake of theologians like Risi and Pancheri is to speak of God's intention as if it extends only to the individual objects of his will and not to the entire order among them all at once. By one single act of the will, God can will the complex interrelation of Christ for humanity and humanity for Christ, just as he can will matter for form and form for matter, as long as there are multiple senses of "for."

But this is nothing other than distinct kinds of finality, which the Salmanticenses take to be not multiple ends but multiple aspects of a single overall end. The fact that the *finis cuius gratia* is willed for its own sake does not preclude its being willed as a benefit to someone else at the same time. Similarly, loving God above all things for God's sake does not mean being indifferent to one's own beatitude, which arises from this love. To love God because he is the supreme good and simultaneously to love him because he is one's own happiness are two sides of the same coin. Neither is it incompatible for God to order all things to Christ because of the God-man's intrinsic excellence and at the same time to will Christ essentially for human redemption.

Pancheri allows for the application of the distinction between *finis cuius gratia* and *finis cui* provided that the *finis cui* "is wholly sub-

---

49. Thus, del Sagrado Corazón agrees that, in terms of the two-*signa* theory, "la explicación de los Salmanticenses representa, sin duda, un avance sobre la explicación escotista." Del Sagrado Corazón, "Juan Duns Escoto en la doctrina de los Salmanticenses," 508.

ordinated to" the *finis cuius gratia*.⁵⁰ He thinks that this is practically equivalent to the Scotistic solution because if the *finis cui* is wholly subordinated to the *finis cuius gratia*, then sin is no longer the *sine qua non* condition of the incarnation. However, Pancheri again fails to account for the fact that each kind of cause has priority in its own order. The *finis cui* is indeed subordinated to the *finis cuius gratia* viewed from the perspective of *finis cuius gratia*. But from the reverse perspective, the *finis cuius gratia* is subordinated to the *finis cui*. It is the false presumption that the *finis cuius gratia* is the complete end in itself that prevents seeing it as subordinate to another end in a different sense. However, since the *finis cuius gratia* and the *finis cui* come together to form a single complex end, there are complementary causal perspectives.

From the perspective of formal cause, the matter in a bodily substance is subordinated to its form, whereas the reverse is true from the perspective of material cause. There is no difficulty in this as long as one recognizes that both matter and form together constitute the single composite substance. Further, if we wish to identify one element as "for" the other *simpliciter*, then since form is more noble than matter, we will say that matter is for form *simpliciter* without thereby excluding the reverse perspective. Likewise, although God only ever willed Christ with reference to human redemption, Christ remains more noble than redeemed humanity and all other divine works. Hence we can say that all God's other works are for Christ *simpliciter*.⁵¹ In this way, God wills Christ *first* but not *unconditionally*.

Another objection of Urrutibéhéty's arises from two mistaken identifications. First, Urrutibéhéty equates *finis cuius gratia* and *finis qui*.⁵² Second, he takes the Salmanticenses to equate an action's *finis cui* with its effect because they say "as for the *finis cui*, or the effect."⁵³ These identifications lead Urrutibéhéty to object, "But if the

50. Pancheri, *Universal Primacy of Christ*, 59–60.
51. Salmanticenses, *De motivo Incarnationis*, dub. 1, §5, no. 30 (Palmé, 13:292).
52. Urrutibéhéty, *Le Motif de l'Incarnation*, 130–33. In fairness, they are closely related and sometimes refer to the same object materially, as I noted in the preceding chapter.
53. Urrutibéhéty, *Le Motif de l'Incarnation*, 131. I noted in the preceding chapter that

A Defense of Salamanca 137

finis cui is the effect, what difference is there between the *finis qui* and the *finis cui*?"[54] In other words, if the *finis cui* is what results from the action and the agent knows it will result from the action (as God always does), how can it be anything other than what the agent is trying to bring about when freely choosing the action?

To address Urrutibéhéty's objection, it is necessary to clarify that the Salmanticenses do not strictly identify *finis cuius gratia* and *finis qui*. Rather, they expressly state:

> We admit that Christ was the principal end *cuius gratia*, not only of this mystery but also of all the divine works, in accord with the infinite dignity of the God-man.... At the same time, it is quite coherent with this that God also first willed him to be the Redeemer of men and willed that he would assume flesh for our remedy and would regard us as the *finis cui* of his coming. Supposing this, there is a mutual dependence between the aforementioned ends, which are truly parts of one adequate and total *finis qui*, such that neither has existed or would have existed independently of the other in the different genera of cause.[55]

This is possible because some effects of the *finis cuius gratia* are not mere effects but are also parts of the end.[56] For example, when God wills glory (*finis cuius gratia*), he wills it for a member of the elect

---

the Salmanticenses often treat *finis cui* and *finis effectus* as functionally equivalent. See, e.g., *De motivo Incarnationis*, dub. 1, §1, no. 5 (Palmé, 13:268); dub. 1, §1 no. 7 (Palmé, 13:269); dub. 1, §6, no. 34 (Palmé, 13:296); dub. 1, §6, no. 36, (Palmé, 13:298); and dub. 1, §8, no. 42 (Palmé, 13:305).

54. "Mais si le *finis cui* est l'effet, quelle différence entre le *finis qui* et le *finis cui*?" Urrutibéhéty, *Le Motif de l'Incarnation*, 131.

55. "Cum fateamur Christum fuisse finem principalem *cujus gratia*, non solum hujus mysterii, sed etiam omnium operum divinorum, juxta infinitam dignitatem Dei hominis.... Cum quo simul cohaeret optime, quod primo etiam voluerit ipsum esse redemptorem hominum, et quod assumeret carnem ad nostrum remedium, nosque respiceret ut finem *cui* sui adventus. Quo supposito adest mutua dependentia inter praedictos fines, qui vere sunt partes unius finis adaequati, et totalis *qui*, ita quod neuter fuerit, aut futurus esset independenter ab alio in diverso genere causae." *De motivo Incarnationis*, dub. 1, §7, no. 40 (Palmé, 13:303). Cf. the Complutenses, *Artium cursus, Liber II Physicorum*, disp. 14, q. 1, §1, no. 1 (Chevalier, 2:231–32); and the Salmanticenses, *Cursus theologicus*, tract. 8, q. 1, no. 4 (Palmé, 5:3).

56. *De motivo Incarnationis*, dub. 1, §6, no. 34 (Palmé, 13:297). As explained in the preceding chapter, an "effect" of the *finis cuius gratia* in this sense is something willed on its account (e.g., the means to achieve it). See table 3–1 on p. 70.

(*finis cui*). Therefore, the person exists for the sake of being glorified and so is an effect of glory in the order of *finis cuius gratia*. But the person is not a *mere* effect, since he is also the *finis cui* and thus part of the total, adequate end willed by God. What God, in fact, wills objectively (*finis qui*) is "this glorified person." The *finis cui* (the person) enters into the *finis qui* (the glorified person), which is an aspect of the *finis cuius gratia* (glory). Nevertheless, the considerations are distinct, and so the terms are not equated.

Further, the *finis effectus*, considered in the strictest sense, is on the part of the *finis operis*—that is, it is what results from the agent's acting in a certain way. Considered in this way, it is not a cause. It is a cause, however, under the aspect of being intended by the agent, since from this perspective it gives rise to the agent's action. This may be why Urrutibéhéty thinks that the *finis effectus* (redemption) must really be a *finis cuius gratia*.

Indeed, this *can* be the case, but it *need not* be the case. For example, the action of painting tends to produce an image—say, a portrait. This makes the portrait the *finis effectus* of painting. However, when an artist chooses to paint so as to produce a portrait, the portrait is also the *finis cuius gratia* of the artist's act of painting. But what if the artist paints a portrait in order to give it to his friend? In this case, the friend is the *finis cui*, the one to whom the artist directs the portrait as a benefit. The artist is still free to paint the portrait precisely because of its own value and yet also *only* on the condition that he can give it to his friend. This does not necessarily transform the friend's reception of the portrait into the *finis cuius gratia*, especially if the portrait is exceedingly noble and worthy in itself.[57] So, too, God can will the surpassing good of the God-man and yet will him only on the condition of giving him over to and for the human race.

---

57. In technical terms, the portrait is the *finis cuius gratia*, the friend is the *finis cui*, the portrait as a gift is the *finis qui*, and the friend's reception of it is the *finis quo*. All together they form the total, adequate end intended by the agent. Similarly, a playwright may choose to devote himself to writing a play only if it will be performed for an audience, or a composer may produce a symphony only if it will be heard.

Although there are reasonable presumptions based on the dignity of the objects willed, *finis cuius gratia* and *finis cui* must be assigned as the agent wills them. For example, an artist could also paint a portrait purely to make a profit, in which case the profit is the *finis cuius gratia* and the portrait only a means to it. In the present discussion, then, what is really at stake is God's freedom. Is God free to will the incarnation with a *sine qua non* condition? If he is not, then he *must* will it absolutely or not will it at all. Since God is free not to will the incarnation, he is also free to will it conditionally. But if he can will it conditionally, he can will it on the condition of sin.

Now if God is free to will the incarnation on the condition of sin, are there grounds for saying that the added condition *must* unseat the God-man from his primacy as *finis cuius gratia*? In other words, does the conditional character of Christ's coming necessarily mean that God has not willed Christ (and everything else) for Christ's own sake? I argue that it does not. As Aquinas observes:

God loves Christ not only more than the whole human race but even more than the whole universe of creatures, that is, because he willed him a greater good, since he "bestowed on him the name which is above every name": his being true God. Nor has his excellence been diminished by the fact that God gave him over to death for the salvation of the human race, for in fact he thereby became a glorious conqueror.[58]

Therefore, given that the God-man himself surpasses the work of redemption and all the other divine works in dignity and given the testimony of Scripture along these lines, we ought to presume that the God-man remains the *finis cuius gratia*. Similarly, we would be unwarranted in saying out of hand that the artist who paints a portrait only on the condition that he can give it to his friend intends the portrait less principally than the artist who paints the portrait

58. "Deus Christum diligit, non solum plus quam totum humanum genus, sed etiam magis quam totam universitatem creaturarum: quia scilicet ei maius bonum voluit, quia dedit ei nomen, quod est super omne nomen, ut verus Deus esset. Nec eius excellentiae deperiit ex hoc quod Deus dedit eum in mortem pro salute humani generis: quinimo ex hoc factus est victor gloriosus." *ST* I, q. 20, a. 4, ad 1 (Leonine, 4:256). The Salmanticenses quote this passage in *De motivo Incarnationis*, dub. 1, §5, no. 30 (Palmé, 13:292–93).

unconditionally. The portrait may well remain the principal good motivating the act of painting, despite the additional condition of the friend's receiving it. Seeing as God, unlike the artist in our example, is not motivated by the acquisition of external goods, *a fortiori* do we have no basis for claiming that the addition of a *sine qua non* condition to his willing the incarnation makes the God-man less than *finis cuius gratia*.

Urrutibéhéty objects that in the Salmanticenses' scheme, salvation is really the *finis cuius gratia* and humanity is the *finis cui*, while Christ is only the means to securing salvation. The Salmanticenses themselves, he notes, call human redemption the "motive" (*motivum*) and the "reason" (*ratio*) why God decreed the incarnation.[59]

The key to overturning this objection is to bear in mind that the *finis cuius gratia* and the *finis cui* are not two ends: they are aspects of a single, overall end. The Salmanticenses do say that if Adam had not sinned, the motive or reason why God has actually decreed the incarnation would be lacking, but this does not mean that redeemed humanity is the entire end or *finis cuius gratia*. Rather, it means that God willed the *finis cuius gratia* (Christ) only in conjunction with a particular *finis cui* (humanity needing redemption). In this way, if Adam had not sinned, the incarnation's motive would be lacking, not because redemption is the total, adequate motive but because redemption is an *essential part* of it, even if not the most important part.

The fact that God wills Christ for human redemption does not make redemption into the *finis cuius gratia*. Both Christ and human redemption are components of a single end, but Christ is the greater good. He is the *finis cuius gratia*, since what has a greater share in goodness is characterized more by finality and *finis cuius gratia* is more radical than *finis cui*.[60] The *finis cui* is not just a happenstance

---

59. Urrutibéhéty, *Le Motif de l'Incarnation*, 140. See Salmanticenses, *De motivo Incarnationis*, dub. 1, §2, no. 8 (Palmé, 13:270).

60. The Salmanticenses do not establish that Christ is the *finis cuius gratia* only because he is the greater good. This would be the error that Cajetan notes—equating what is more willable with what is actually more willed. Instead, they think that Christ's status as *finis cuius gratia* is evident from Scripture and the Fathers.

beneficiary, not just the subject who *de facto* receives some good from the *finis cuius gratia* in the order of execution. Instead the *finis cui* enters into the agent's intention but without becoming the primary factor in that intention. In this way, the *finis cui* is really characterized by finality, since consideration of it, too, moves the agent to act. However, it is not as radically characterized by finality as the *finis cuius gratia*, which thus remains the most essential part of the overall motive and can be designated as the end *simpliciter*.

If we insist rigidly that the *finis cuius gratia* can only be willed unconditionally, for its own sake and not for anything else in another sense, then we are left with an absurdity. In the case of the incarnation, we would have to say that God's willing Christ as *finis cuius gratia* entails God's sending Christ independently of concern for other divine works *ad extra*, in the order of nature and in the order of grace. God would will Christ for his own sake so exclusively that any benefits accruing to anyone else would only be *per accidens*, seeing as God would send Christ without regard for those benefits.[61] If, on the other hand, we admit that God wills Christ to be the head of all his works and also wills the benefits Christ brings to those works, even as a good king benefits his kingdom, then we must say that God can will Christ as *finis cuius gratia* together with a *finis cui* other than Christ. But if God can will the incarnation in this way, he can also will it *only* in this way, since he is free to decree the incarnation or not decree it as he sees fit. This means that God can will Christ for his own sake (*finis cuius gratia*) and also for human redemption (*finis cui*) without the *finis cui* becoming a *finis cuius gratia*.

Urrutibéhéty goes through the examples that the Salmanticenses borrow from Aquinas in support of their application of the distinction between *finis cuius gratia* and *finis cui*: the heavenly bodies are for lower creatures; a king is for peasants; and angels are for human be-

---

61. As, for example, when Scotus claims that at an early conceptual moment God willed Christ even if nothing else would be created. Scotus, *Reportatio Parisiensis* III-A, d. 7, q. 4, no. 4 (Vivès, 23:303). Cf. Rada, *Controversiae theologicae III*, contr. 5, a. 3, obs. 3 (Ioannes Crithius, 3:157).

ings.⁶² The first example, he says, just means that the heavenly bodies are useful for lower creatures, while the second means that royal dignity is for the subjects, not that this man, the king, exists only because a peasant exists.⁶³ In fact, explains Urrutibéhéty, the Salmanticenses should have looked more carefully at what Aquinas says about the relationship between the angels and humanity.⁶⁴ The angels benefit humanity and are "for" human beings in this sense, but they would have existed apart from their ministry to human beings. Similarly, Urrutibéhéty argues, Christ benefits humanity, but this does not mean that his existence depends on his redemptive work for humanity.

What the Salmanticenses are really doing, according to Urrutibéhéty, is gaming their analysis of the preposition "for" to support a preconceived theory. They take "for" as an indication of *finis cuius gratia* ("Everything was created for the glory of Christ") or as an indication of *finis cui* ("Christ was willed for the salvation of human beings") as it suits them.⁶⁵ The reason, of course, is that, convinced by Scotus's *ordinate volens* principle and yet unwilling to sacrifice the Thomistic doctrine, the Salmanticenses have to make the complementary final causes work in order to allow sin and human redemption each to have priority from some perspective.⁶⁶ Thus, they have no choice but to parse otherwise formally identical propositions in distinct ways.⁶⁷

Actually, the Salmanticenses have already addressed these latter objections of Urrutibéhéty. It is not only the form of certain dogmatic propositions that matters but the entire weight of Scripture and

---

62. Urrutibéhéty, *Le Motif de l'Incarnation*, 134–35.
63. Urrutibéhéty does not say so, but in this argument, he is essentially following Licheto, who argues that a king would not reasonably confer a great honor on a high-ranking official if and only if the official's servant received a lesser honor or, *a fortiori*, if and only if there were such a servant. See Licheto's *Commentary on Scotus's* Quaestiones in tertium librum Sententiarum, d. 7, q. 3, no. 11 (Vivès, 14:357).
64. Urrutibéhéty, *Le Motif de l'Incarnation*, 136.
65. Urrutibéhéty, *Le Motif de l'Incarnation*, 131.
66. "Je vois bien la raison qui fait désirer cette diversité d'étiquette, sous laquelle se cache un même produit; c'est qu'il s'agit de faire dépendre les deux priorités de deux espèces de causes." Urrutibéhéty, *Le Motif de l'Incarnation*, 131–32.
67. Urrutibéhéty, *Le Motif de l'Incarnation*, 137.

Tradition, which contextualize them.[68] For example, Urrutibéhéty is right that the angels' ministry to human beings is not a *sine qua non* condition of their existence. But we can say this precisely because the Bible characterizes the angels as primarily pursuing ends independent of human beings—such as glorifying God (Ps 148:2; Dn 3:58; Is 6:3; Rv 4:8) and enjoying the beatific vision (Mt 18:10)—and secondarily ministering to human beings. Further, the existence of the angels is a good proportionate to the natural perfection of the universe. In contrast, the God-man is a strictly supernatural good—infinite in dignity and *supra omnem naturae exigentiam*—and the Bible always portrays his coming as directed to human salvation.

Therefore, far from twisting senses of "for" to fit a preconceived application of the distinction between *finis cuius gratia* and *finis cui*, the Salmanticenses actually start with the data they have gleaned from Scripture and the Fathers. From these sources, they are convinced both that the God-man is the first willed and intended by God, the proximate end of all other divine works, and also that God willed him essentially for human redemption. They apply the distinction between *finis cuius gratia* and *finis cui* to show the coherence of what has been revealed.

Finally, I would add that although the king's existence does not depend on the existence of his subjects, his existence *as king* does. So, too, if God wills Christ precisely *as redeemer*, then his coming depends on the existence of those who need redemption. In this way, the redeemed are for Christ, and Christ is for the redeemed.

IS THE SALMANTICENSES' VIEW OF THE DIVINE ECONOMY UN-THOMISTIC?

François Daguet raises the question of whether the Salmanticenses' theory cuts against Aquinas's view of original justice.[69] In particular, Daguet is concerned not to conflate the pre- and post-lapsarian

---

68. Cf. *De motivo Incarnationis*, dub. 1, §5, no. 31 (Palmé, 13:293).
69. Daguet, *Théologie du dessein divin*, 216.

states while, at the same time, acknowledging a continuity between them.[70] His own approach rightly emphasizes that from the beginning God ordered humanity to return to the Father through the missions of the Son and Holy Spirit. In the state of original justice, this *reditus* would have been accomplished by the invisible missions alone. After the fall, which mired humanity in sensible things, the return to the Father comes through the visible missions of the Son and the Holy Spirit, which, in fact, are ordered to the invisible missions. Thus, Daguet writes:

> The finality of the Word's visible governance is nothing other than that of his invisible governance prior to sin: God's purpose is unchanged. The visible missions of the divine persons have no other end than the invisible missions, but are instead subordinated to them.... The visible missions of the Word and of the Spirit, and in the first place the incarnation, do not have their proper term in themselves, but rather are ordered to the invisible missions as their end.[71]

In this way, there is a true succession of states but also a continuity, inasmuch as the end of humanity remains the same but the mode in which it is attained changes. And continuity is particularly found in the fact that the self-same Son and Spirit are sent and personally given both invisibly and visibly.

The difficulty is that the Salmanticenses' doctrine entails that the state of original justice is essentially dependent on the Word incarnate. This, in turn, would seem to reduce the pre- and post-lapsarian states into one in which the visible missions are anticipated as necessary from the beginning.

Daguet is right that, for Aquinas, the visible economy, with rites

---

70. Daguet, *Théologie du dessein divin*, 235–37.

71. "La finalité du gouvernement visible du Verbe n'est pas autre que celle de son gouvernement invisible avant le péché: le dessein de Dieu est inchangé. Les missions visibles des personnes divines n'ont pas une autre fin que les missions invisibles, mais elles leur sont subordonnées.... Les missions visibles du Verbe et de l'Esprit, et au premier chef l'incarnation, ne possèdent pas en elles-mêmes leur propre term, mais sont ordonnées aux missions invisibles comme à leur fin." Daguet, *Théologie du dessein divin*, 274.

of sacrifice from the time of Cain and Abel prefiguring Christ's paschal mystery and the sacraments of the Church flowing from it and applying it, is needed because humanity's fall entails a disordered turn to the sensible.[72] Thus, after the fall, the invisible missions are only restored through the visible missions. This occurs in two ways, as Aquinas explains:

> Christ as man is said to justify in two ways. In one way [he justifies] in accord with an action of his, inasmuch as he has merited for us and satisfied for us. And in this regard he could not have been called the head of the Church before the incarnation. In the other way [he justifies] through an operation of ours directed to him, insofar as we are said to be justified through faith in him. And in this way even before the incarnation he was able to be the head of the Church in his humanity.[73]

I have already noted that Aquinas also holds that Adam, in the state of original justice, had faith in Christ's incarnation.[74] On the other hand, Aquinas says in the same article of the *De veritate*: "Supposing the opinion that Christ would not have been incarnate if man had not sinned, before sin Christ would have been the head of the Church in his divine nature alone, but after sin he must be the head

---

72. See especially Aquinas, *Super epistolam ad Hebraeos lectura*, chap. 11, l. 2, nos. 561–79 (Cai, 2:460–63); *De veritate*, q. 29, a. 4, ad 3 (Leonine, 22:860); *ST* II-II, q. 2, a. 7 (Leonine, 8:33–35); and *ST* III, q. 61, a. 2 (Leonine, 12:15–16). In fact, Aquinas thinks that Adam, too, offered sacrifice to God, though this is not recorded in Scripture. *ST* II-II, q. 85, a. 1, ad 2 (Leonine, 9:215–16).

73. "Christus, secundum quod homo, dupliciter nos iustificare dicitur: uno modo secundum suam actionem, in quantum nobis meruit et pro nobis satisfecit, et quantum ad hoc non poterat dici caput Ecclesiae ante incarnationem; alio modo per operationem nostram in ipsum secundum quod dicimur per fidem eius iustificari, et per hunc modum etiam poterat esse caput Ecclesiae ante incarnationem secundum humanitatem." Aquinas, *De veritate*, q. 29, a. 4, ad 9 (Leonine, 22:860–61). William D. Lynn notes that Aquinas never seems to address explicitly whether or how Christ merited for the just who lived prior to the incarnation. Instead, Aquinas focuses on their faith in Christ's future coming. Lynn goes on to argue, however, that Aquinas's framework is open to seeing the graces received by the just prior to the incarnation through their faith in Christ's future coming as deriving from Christ's merits. William D. Lynn, *Christ's Redemptive Merit: The Nature of Its Causality According to St. Thomas*, Analecta Gregoriana cura Pontificiae universitatis Gregorianae edita 115 (Rome: Gregorian University Press, 1962), 162–65.

74. *ST* II-II, q. 2, a. 7, co. (Leonine, 8:34); and *ST* III, q. 1, a. 3, ad 5 (Leonine, 11:14).

of the Church also in his human nature."[75] This leads to the difficulty: can the Salmanticenses really say that the state of original justice was ordered to Christ incarnate as *finis cuius gratia*? After all, this makes original justice dependent on Christ, makes the invisible missions depend on the visible missions from the beginning, and seems to make Christ the head of Adam in original justice, thus collapsing the pre- and post-lapsarian states. Would this not require the abandonment of Aquinas's view and the embrace of pure Scotism?

The first thing to observe when addressing this difficulty is that our fundamental concern should not be to harmonize with Aquinas but to tell the truth about God. Only if Aquinas is right should we fear contradicting him. So I will note briefly some of the reasons for affirming a real distinction of pre- and post-lapsarian states. First, it would be contrary to Scripture to affirm that humanity's fall is anything other than a real loss, an offensive rejection of a gift from God that of itself was meant to continue. Second, God did not positively will sin. Third, in reality all of Christ's merits and the whole paschal mystery are redemptive in mode and connected with his passion and death. No matter what Christ *would have* merited if he had come as impassible, he actually came and merited in the wayfaring state, one marked by passibility and directed to his "hour." But the state of original justice cannot be an effect of Christ's passion, since *ex hypothesi* the continuation of original justice would have precluded the passion. Aquinas himself observes:

Since the work of the incarnation is principally ordered to the restoration of human nature through taking away sin, it is manifest that it was not fitting for God to have been incarnate from the beginning of the human race, before sin. For medicine is only given to those who are already sick. Hence the Lord himself says, "Those who are well have no need of a phy-

---

75. "Supposita illa opinione, quod Christus non fuisset incarnatus, si homo non peccasset, Christus ante peccatum fuisset caput Ecclesiae secundum divinam naturam solum, sed post peccatum oportet quod sit Ecclesiae caput etiam secundum humanam." Aquinas, *De veritate*, q. 29, a. 4, ad 3 (Leonine, 22:860).

sician, but those who are sick.... For I came not to call the righteous, but sinners." (Mt 9:12–13).[76]

Christ died to redeem Adam, not to give him original justice.

Having outlined these reasons why we should take seriously the distinction of the pre- and post-lapsarian states, I will explain why the Salmanticenses' theory does not violate this distinction. First, recall that the Salmanticenses raised this objection in their own treatment, where they remarked that the relation of Christ as head to Adam in the state of original justice would be treated outside their disputation *De motivo Incarnationis*. Nevertheless, they also indicated in this disputation how they would address this difficulty—that is, by distinguishing between Christ's final causality and his meritorious or physical efficient causality.[77] The fact that Christ is the *finis cuius gratia* of original justice and, indeed, of the very permission of sin does not mean that God bestowed original justice through Christ's merits or through his humanity as instrumental cause. Nor does Adam's faith in the future Christ contradict this, since even if Adam had faith *in* Christ prior to the fall, this does not mean that he had the virtue of faith *through* Christ.[78] The incarnation as the revealed object known by the theological virtue is one thing, and the incarnation as the cause of the infusion of that theological virtue is another.

Second, in the place where the Salmanticenses directly ask whether Christ was the head of Adam in the state of original justice,

76. "Cum opus incarnationis principaliter ordinetur ad reparationem naturae humanae per peccati abolitionem, manifestum est quod non fuit conveniens a principio humani generis, ante peccatum, Deum incarnatum fuisse: non enim datur medicina nisi iam infirmis. Unde ipse Dominus dicit, Matth. ix: *Non est opus valentibus medicus, sed male habentibus: non enim veni vocare iustos, sed peccatores.*" *ST* III, q. 1, a. 5, co. (Leonine, 11:19).

77. *De motivo Incarnationis*, dub. 1, §6, no. 35 (Palmé, 13:297–98). In this, the Salmanticenses differ from Godoy, who argues that Christ merited our very existence by his passion and death. Godoy, *Disputationes theologicae in tertiam partem*, tract. 14, disp. 57, §4, no. 51 (Hertz, 3:392).

78. As John of St. Thomas notes. *Cursus theologicus* III, q. 8, disp. 10, a. 2, no. 34 (Vivès, 8:269).

they answer in the negative.[79] At a minimum, this means that they do not view their own theory on the motive of the incarnation as running counter to two distinct states before and after the fall.

The essential distinction is between the *person* of Adam and his *state*.[80] From the first, Adam was predestined to salvation only ever through Christ, but this does not require that every *state* of his be an effect of Christ, or indeed of Adam's own predestination. Similarly, God can permit a member of the elect to fall into sin and can order that fall to the person's greater sanctity in the future, but this does not mean that the state of sin itself is, strictly, an effect of the person's predestination. It is the *ordering* of the state to future glory that falls under predestination. And so, in the case of Adam, God did not bestow original justice as an effect of Adam's predestination, which depended on Christ and thus indirectly on Adam's fall. But in terms of final causality, it is still true that God bestowed original justice and permitted its loss with a view toward Adam's ultimate salvation through Christ the redeemer.[81]

By analogy, the present state of health is not an effect of the future illness or of the medicine that will be given for it, but, by a single decision, God can grant the present health *and* permit the illness with a view toward the better state that will result from the medicine. In this way, the present health is not an effect (as to efficient cause) of the medicine, even though it is ordered (as to final cause) to the future health that will result from the medicine and even its own loss. This is how the Salmanticenses maintain the integrity of humanity's original providential state. Adam, not the God-man, was truly the head of the human race in original justice. Christ is not the "first Adam" but the "last" (1 Cor 15:45–48). There is, thus, a real succession of pre- and post-lapsarian states, which are part of a larg-

---

79. Salmanticenses, *Cursus theologicus*, tract. 21, disp. 16, *De gratia Christi capitali*, dub. 4, §1, nos. 48–51 (Palmé, 14:593–96).
80. Salmanticenses, *Cursus theologicus*, tract. 21, disp. 16, dub. 4 (Palmé, 14:593).
81. Salmanticenses, *De motivo Incarnationis*, dub. 1, §8, no. 43 (Palmé, 13:307); and *Cursus theologicus*, tract. 21, disp. 16, dub. 4, §1, no. 50 (Palmé, 14:595).

er, single providential plan but which are not, for this reason, to be identified.

This explanation emphasizes that the fall was a real loss. For the fact that the state of original justice did not come through Christ (as to efficient or meritorious cause) means precisely that it cannot revive after the fall. In contrast, if a Christian sins mortally, his merits can revive when he is restored to grace, since the principal root of those merits, namely Christ, remains. But this was not the case for Adam in original justice, and so when he fell from grace, his merits were irrevocably lost.[82]

This explanation also upholds the nonredemptive character of original justice. All the graces received through Christ, the Salmanticenses say, are redemptive. We cannot separate out some of Christ's merits or the graces given through him as redemptive and others as nonredemptive. In the concrete order of history, the Lord has come as redeemer, and theology knows nothing of graces that he would have merited or bestowed but only those he has merited and bestowed.[83]

Yet at the same time, the Salmanticenses are not at all forced to minimize the significance of Christ for all human beings, including Adam, since they still maintain that no one has ever been saved apart from Christ or his merits.[84] They can hold quite well to the *felix culpa*: the fall was ruin, but something greater has come out of it. In fact, because the Salmanticenses assign Christ the redeemer as the *finis cuius gratia* of this permission, they hold that God permitted sin precisely for the greater good of the redeemer. Thus, in their theory, there is an answer to the question of why God allowed sin and yet

---

82. Salmanticenses, *Cursus theologicus*, tract. 21, disp. 16, dub. 4, §4, no. 64 (Palmé, 14:609).

83. "Non enim meruit per ea, quae potuit habere, nec secundum statum, quem potuit habere: sed meruit re ipsa in illo statu, et per illa quae habuit de facto. Et absurdum omnino esset aliud imaginari." *De motivo Incarnationis*, dub. 1, §8, no. 43 (Palmé, 13:306).

84. Salmanticenses, *Cursus theologicus*, tract. 21, disp. 16, dub. 4, §3, no. 59 (Palmé, 14:604–5).

the mystery of evil is not explained away. In the only divine plan we know, Christ the redeemer makes the permission of sin intelligible, but we can still wonder about God's free choice of this plan when he could have planned not to permit sin or not to send Christ in response to it. This, in turn, leads us to the next objection.

DOES THE SALAMANCA THEORY IMPLY THAT GOD WILLS SIN?

Charles-René Billuart, OP (1685–1757), observes, "We have it from Scripture that the incarnation is for sin, but nowhere that sin is for the incarnation."[85] Perhaps the greatest difficulty with the position of Thomists—such as Godoy and the Salmanticenses—who hold that God intended Christ precisely *as redeemer* from the first is that this seems to make sin a necessary means to this end. Since, then, one who wills the end wills the means, God would have to will sin. This is the very difficulty that kept Suárez from embracing such a solution.[86]

Here one must not forget that in the present order of history, God *has* permitted sin and *has* sent Christ to redeem humanity from it. Therefore, if God cannot will sin, which is opposed to him, then the distinction between God's positive will and his permissive will is valid. Because this distinction is valid, it can be applied to the present matter. This means that God *permits* sin for the sake of Christ the redeemer without *willing* sin.[87]

As Garrigou-Lagrange points out, we must distinguish *sin as*

---

85. "Cum habeamus ex. S. Scriptura Incarnationem esse propter peccatum, neutiquam autem peccatum propter Incarnationem." Charles-René Billuart, *Summa accommodata*, tract. *De Incarnatione*, diss. 3, a. 3, resp. to obj. 6, in *F. C.-R. Billuart Summa sancti Thomae hodiernis academiarum moribus accommodata*, new ed. (Paris: Apud Victorem Palmé, 1872), 5:403.

86. Suárez, *In III Thomae*, q. 1, a. 4, disp. 5, sect. 3, no. 4 (Vivès, 17:234).

87. On the fact that God's antecedent permission of sin is not a cause of sin, see Taylor Patrick O'Neill, *Grace, Predestination, and the Permission of Sin: A Thomistic Analysis* (Washington, D.C.: The Catholic University of America Press, 2019), 83–87, 120–29, 286–90.

sin (peccatum ut peccatum) from *sin considered in light of redemption (peccatum ut redimendum)*.⁸⁸ Sin as sin may be the occasion for the incarnation, but it is not the cause or motive. In other words, sin has precedence as the matter addressed by Christ's coming (*materia circa quam*), but when we consider the incarnation's final cause, we cannot think of sin merely as an evil but instead must connect it with the good to which God orders it.⁸⁹ Thus it is not, strictly speaking, *fallen* humanity that is the *finis cui* of the incarnation but humanity *to be redeemed*.⁹⁰

But is not sin still related to redemption (and thus to Christ the redeemer) as the means to an end? Again, this argument cuts both ways. Christ has come as redeemer, and glory has redounded to him from his redemptive work, as all theologians admit. If, then, God intends the glory that Christ actually does enjoy as redeemer, must God have positively willed the sin that led to it? Clearly not. In fact, there are many other cases where we recognize that God intends a good occasioned by evil without thereby willing the evil precisely as evil. For example, "There will be more joy in heaven over one sinner who repents than over ninety-nine righteous persons who need no repentance" (Lk 15:7). God intends the sinner's repentance and the greater joy resulting from it, but the sin remains only permitted and foreseen—not intended. Similarly, God intends fraternal correction and the glory of the martyrs without thereby intending the sins that serve as the *sine qua non* conditions for these. Finally, God wills the existence, grace, and glory of children conceived through fornication or adultery without thereby willing fornication or adultery. In these and many other cases, it is clear that God brings good from evil, willing only the good and permitting evil for the good's sake.

Although he rejects the Salmanticenses' theory, Jean-François Bonnefoy, OFM (1887–1958), says of the view that God permitted

---

88. Garrigou-Lagrange, "De motivo Incarnationis," 34.
89. As Bonaventure essentially argues when addressing the question of how evil can be the *sine qua non* condition for the incarnation's great good. *In III Sent.*, d. 1, a. 2, q. 2, ad 6 (Quaracchi, 3:27).
90. Garrigou-Lagrange, "De motivo Incarnationis," 35.

sin for the sake of Christ the redeemer: "The importance of this thesis is beyond question; it eliminates from the Thomistic system a succession of divine plans, and from the Scotistic, the amendments to a single divine plan. It enables us to safeguard without restriction or attenuation Christ's universal finality and, therefore, his absolute primacy."[91] Bonnefoy's point is essentially that unless the permission of sin has some intended orientation to Christ, we must introduce either a succession of divine plans or modifications of the same plan (which arguably amount to the same thing, given that such modifications would have to be substantial). The resulting division within the divine plan would appear to safeguard God's innocence by emphasizing human sin as the ruining of a state of innocence that God intended to continue. Such, indeed, is what "strict" Thomists like Vásquez say, and such is the reason they enumerate multiple *signa rationis* and multiple decrees.

The problem is that such a schema cannot account for why God *permitted* sin in the first place. Precisely because the ruin of sin ruptures the divine plan so thoroughly, there is no way to link the permission of sin with the present decree. In such a view, Christ's coming can only be conceived of as a new and secondary plan of God introduced to make up for what was lost. But such a "backup plan" has no explanatory value as to why God would allow the disruption of the original plan in the first place.

If, on the other hand, the Salmanticenses are correct that God permitted sin with a view to Christ the redeemer, then there is no rupture in the divine plan (from the perspective of *finis cuius gratia*). God created, elevated to grace, and permitted sin all for Christ the redeemer. This does not mean that God wanted the malice of sin

---

91. Jean-François Bonnefoy, *Christ and the Cosmos*, ed. and trans. Michael D. Meilach, 1st American ed. (Paterson, N.J.: St. Anthony Guild Press, 1965), 347. Bonnefoy himself argues a developed version of the Scotistic thesis. Thus, Bonnefoy's final inference needs clarification. As far as the Salmanticenses are concerned, Bonnefoy is correct if "absolute primacy" means a primacy in the order of *finis cuius gratia* with respect to all other divine works without exception, but he is incorrect if "absolute primacy" means a primacy that is unconditional.

but only that he ordered sin to an infinitely greater good and that he planned to do this from the beginning.

Here, the explanation for the permission of sin is drawn not from *a priori* arguments but from reflection on the present decree: we know why God permitted evil because we know Christ.[92] As the *Catechism of the Catholic Church* observes: "If God the Father almighty, the Creator of the ordered and good world, cares for all his creatures, why does evil exist? To this question, as pressing as it is unavoidable and as painful as it is mysterious, no quick answer will suffice. Only Christian faith as a whole constitutes the answer to this question."[93] For Christian faith to answer the question, as the *Catechism* says, there must be a link—in God's intention—between the permission of sin and the coming of Christ. In other words, the permission of sin is ordered to Christ as its final cause. No calamity or crime is permitted the human race save for the sake of Jesus, whose cross lends suffering all its intelligibility and power. Apart from him, evil has no meaning.

FINAL OBJECTIONS FROM RISI

In addition to the objections I have already considered, Francesco Maria Risi alleges that the following four irrational conclusions follow from the Salmanticenses' doctrine:

a) All the good willed by God in his direct intention depends in such a system on an occasioned good, one *accidentally* related to the intention of God creating a complete world as he envisions it (Jesus Christ willed on the occasion of fault is directly intended by God the *redeemer* but is *outside the direct intention of God the creator*). b) A being willed *exclusively for a particular end* becomes *a universal end, actually, in name only*, while it *would have no reason to exist* among the beings whose end it is. c) The decree of the objective end is *posterior* to the decree of everything ordered

---

92. See Garrigou-Lagrange, "De motivo Incarnationis," 14.
93. *Catechism of the Catholic Church*, 2nd ed. (Washington, D.C.: United States Catholic Conference, 1997), no. 309.

to the end. d) Everything existing in the divine decree is directed to a *possibility* as an end.[94]

I will address each in turn.

To Risi's objection (a), I respond that the unfittingness of this conclusion does not follow from the Salmanticenses' doctrine. They hold that from the perspective of final cause *cuius gratia*, all other divine works are ordered to Christ, whether of the natural or supernatural order.[95] It is true that from the perspective of material cause, creation, elevation, the permission of sin, and Adam's sin precede Christ as the *sine qua non* conditions of his coming. In a sense, this does give all the goods intended by God an indirect dependence on Adam's sin, as the Salmanticenses themselves admit, using the example of the angels' predestination.[96] However, such an indirect dependence is not unfitting in the way Risi purports precisely because this discussion is only over *the present decree*.

We must not confuse the order of material cause and the order of final cause *cuius gratia*. From the perspective of final cause *cuius gratia*, which is the most important perspective, Christ is the first willed and intended by God. But this is *Christ as he has actually come*, not just the idea of hypostatic union. If we admit that Christ the redeemer is the end of all the divine works *cuius gratia*, as the Salmanticenses do, then we must also admit an indirect dependence of all the divine works on Adam's sin. If, on the other hand, we hold that all the divine works depend on Christ but *not as redeemer* (so as to avoid

---

94. "a) Tutto il bene voluto da Dio d'intenzione diretta, in tal sistema dipende da un bene occasionato, e *per accidens* rapporto all'intenzione di Dio creante a suo genio un mondo perfetto. (Gesù Cristo voluto all'occasione della colpa è d'intenzione diretta di Dio *Redentore* ma è fuori *dell'intenzione diretta di Dio Creatore*. b) Un essere voluto esclusivamente *per un fine particolare*, diviene *per solo titolo di fatto fine universale*, mentre *non avrebbe ragione di esistere* tra gli esseri di cui è fine. c) Il decreto del fine obbjettivo è *posteriore* al decreto di tutti gli ordinati al fine. d) Tutti gli esistenti nel decreto divino sono diretti come a fine *ad un possibile*." Risi, *Motivo primario della incarnazione*, 1:317. For objection A, see also Carol, *Why Jesus Christ?*, 247.

95. *De motivo Incarnationis*, dub. 1, §1, no. 4 (Palmé, 13:266); and dub. 1, §5, no. 29 (Palmé, 13:291).

96. *De motivo Incarnationis*, dub. 1, §8, no. 42 (Palmé, 13:305–6).

the indirect dependence on Adam's sin), we would actually have to hold that they do not depend on *Christ* at all but only on the idea of a hypostatic union. Either the natural order, the angels, the state of innocence, and all the rest depend on Christ the redeemer, or they do not depend on Christ at all. If they do not depend on Christ at all, then the Scotistic system that Risi defends cannot stand. If, however, they depend on Christ the redeemer, then they depend indirectly on Adam's sin, as the Salmanticenses hold, and, therefore, this is not unfitting.

The Salmanticenses would have it that creation and the permission of sin, then, are wrapped up in a single decree with Christ the redeemer. They do not, as Risi does in the objection, presume that multiple divine decrees are required. Thus, Risi's objection would have force, perhaps, against a strictly Cajetanian approach, in which distinct ontological orders (creation and elevation or redemption) are mapped onto distinct divine decrees, but this is not what the Salmanticenses hold. Instead they are clear that God made the natural and the supernatural by a single decree and that he made the former out of love for the latter, not in the sense that the supernatural is proportionate to the natural or necessarily connected with it but as an end surpassing proportion to the natural in nobility.[97]

In Risi's objection (b), the difficulty seems to be this: if God intends Christ only for a particular purpose, such as human redemption, then Christ is *not* the reason why God has willed everything else and is not, therefore, the universal end.[98] In Risi's view, being willed only for a particular purpose *ipso facto* precludes being the universal end. If the universal end is willed only for a particular purpose, then we have the following dilemma: either everything else is also willed for that particular purpose,[99] or everything else is willed

---

97. Salmanticenses, *Cursus theologicus*, tract. 5, *De praedestinatione et reprobatione*, disp. 5, dub. 1, §3, no. 23 (Palmé, 2:352).

98. This objection is very close to the objection I considered above that if God wills Christ for human redemption, redemption must be the *finis cuius gratia* of the incarnation.

99. For example, if God created the world for the sake of Christ as its end and yet

independently of the universal end. Both possibilities are absurd. Therefore, the universal end cannot be willed only for a particular purpose.

Risi's fundamental error is taking a strictly linear approach. This leads to equating being willed *first* with being willed *unconditionally*, since the intended end is the reason why everything else is willed. This means that, for Risi, if God wills Christ as the end, he must will Christ prior to all other considerations and independently of them. It is no wonder, then, that he thinks Christ cannot be willed only for some other purpose, since from a strictly linear point of view, this would place that purpose prior to Christ in the causal chain.

The Salmanticenses' approach, in contrast, embraces complementary causal perspectives: God wills Christ as the *finis cuius gratia* and, simultaneously, wills that in the order of material cause, sin will precede Christ as the matter addressed by his coming. In this way, for the Salmanticenses, God wills Christ *first* from the most important causal perspective (*finis cuius gratia*), but he never wills Christ unconditionally or independently. As I noted above, the Salmanticenses' approach is not strictly linear but is three-dimensional, admitting of examination from various, mutually complementary perspectives.

To will Christ primarily is not necessarily to will him independently. Actually, to will the incarnation with radical independence would not be to will Jesus of Nazareth but would be to will only an abstract idea. What God wants most of all in the world he has made is Christ—not just the idea of the God-man but *Christ* as he has come, the redeemer and first-born of all the elect, whom God chose in him before the world's founding (Eph 1:4).

Finally, I will consider Risi's objections (c) and (d) together. In both, the unfitting conclusion arises only by overlooking the complementarity of the causal perspectives within the single complex object of the divine will. The Salmanticenses insist time and again

---

Christ came because of human sin, then God created the world only because he knew humanity would sin.

that from the perspective of *finis cuius gratia*, which is the radical element of the overall motive, God willed all other divine works for the sake of Christ. Thus, from this perspective, Christ precedes all other divine works and is the reason for their being willed or permitted. This makes him the first willed and intended by God—even *simpliciter*—as they state.

As for the charge that the divine works are directed to a mere possibility, it is true that human sin (a free act) is the *sine qua non* condition or occasion for Christ's coming. But this does not render Christ's coming a mere possibility. Instead, God's intention to send Christ is the reason why he permits sin in the first place, and, with sin having been permitted, the actual commission of sin follows with certainty, since absent an efficacious *auxilium*, wayfarers cannot avoid sin. In this way, although Christ's coming is *conditional*, it is not *uncertain*. God's intention to send Christ the redeemer guarantees that the condition will be met, which is to say that the redeemer's priority as *finis cuius gratia* entails the permission of the sin that will become the incarnation's *materia circa quam*.

Again, when the Salmanticenses speak of Christ as the end of all the divine works, they do not have in mind the possibility or the abstract idea of Christ. They have in mind *Jesus of Nazareth with all the concrete circumstances of his actual coming*. It is he who is the first willed and intended by God. Theology has no knowledge of what God would have chosen by virtue of another decree. In the only world we know—the world of the present decree—there is no Christ but the redeemer.

CONCLUSION

As seen in the previous chapter, the Salmanticenses are thorough in addressing objections to their theory. In this chapter, I have considered further objections and concerns. I have argued that the Salmanticenses' doctrine, based on the distinction between *finis cuius gratia* and *finis cui* and on the two-*signa* approach, is logically coherent as applied, does not promote an un-Thomistic view of original justice, does not entail that God intends sin, and does not imply the unfitting conclusions alleged by Risi.

Having defended the Salamanca theory, I will now show how it can aid contemporary Christocentric aspirations. Over the next two chapters, I will present the Christocentric theologies of Karl Rahner and Hans Urs von Balthasar and explain how the Salmanticenses can preserve key insights of theirs while avoiding certain pitfalls.

5

Christ the Apex
Karl Rahner and the Salmanticenses

Karl Rahner's Christocentrism is especially focused on Jesus Christ as the apex of God's self-communication to the world. For him, the Son's incarnation is the pinnacle of a universal process without an essential reference to sin. In this chapter, I will show how a recovery of the Salmanticenses can preserve this emphasis while correcting certain problems with Rahner's theology, particularly methodological overreach and ontological confusion that do not adequately respect the distinction between God and the world. I will also consider a way in which Rahner's ascending Christology can harmonize with and illuminate the Salmanticenses.

THE SHAPE OF RAHNER'S CHRISTOCENTRISM

There are two main periods in Karl Rahner's approach to Christology.[1] In his early work, prior to the mid-1950s, Rahner's approach was essentially "from above," concerned with Christ as God's word to humanity. Around this time, scriptural exegesis separated from dog-

---

1. For this summary, I draw especially on John M. McDermott, "The Christologies of Karl Rahner," *Gregorianum* 67, no. 1 (1986): 87–123; and "The Christologies of Karl Rahner – II," *Gregorianum* 67, no. 2 (1986): 297–327.

matic theology, and Catholics embraced the historical-critical method, which at that time largely denied the historicity of John's Gospel. In this milieu, Rahner began to approach Christology "from below," emphasizing Christ as the peak of human openness to God. Finally, in his 1976 work *Grundkurs des Glaubens* (*Foundations of Christian Faith*),[2] Rahner synthesized these two approaches.

This synthesis is possible because the framework allowing for both Rahner's descending and ascending approaches was already laid in his 1939 and 1941 works *Geist in Welt* (*Spirit in the World*) and *Hörer des Wortes* (*Hearer of the Word*).[3] This consists especially in his transcendental approach, which characterizes the human person as spirit and matter, open to the infinite while simultaneously bound by time and space. The result is that humanity can recognize the existence of an infinite, free God and respond in faith if God should choose to reveal his mysteries in a concrete, historical way.

This revelation actually does occur in Jesus, in whom is realized not only God's speech to the world but the Son's personal presence (cf. Heb 1:1) and the epitome of human receptivity to God. In other words, Rahner's commitment to the Chalcedonean formula, applied in terms of his transcendental method, is what synthesizes his earlier and later views. Christ himself is divine and human, from above and from below (Jn 3:13; 1 Cor 15:45–47). Therefore, descending and ascending Christologies converge. I will discuss Rahner's Christocentrism from the perspective of this synthesis, touching on other aspects of his approach to nature and grace or Christology only as needed.

In *Hearer of the Word*, Rahner is concerned with the human capacity to receive divine revelation, prescinding from the question of grace as such.[4] In later works when he turns not just to God's

---

2. Karl Rahner, *Foundations of Christian Faith: An Introduction to the Idea of Christianity*, trans. William V. Dych (New York: The Crossroad Publishing Company, 1987).

3. English translations are Karl Rahner, *Spirit in the World*, trans. William V. Dych (New York: Herder, 1968); and *Hearer of the Word: Laying the Foundation for a Philosophy of Religion*, trans. Joseph Donceel (New York: Continuum, 1994).

4. As Rahner observes, e.g., in *Hearer of the Word*, 16.

speech about himself but to God's *gift* of himself, it is clear that God's self-communication to the world attains its apex in Christ, the God-man.[5] It is on the basis of divine gift and human receptivity that Rahner highlights the continuity of the natural, gratuitous, and hypostatic orders: "If a man receives this human essence from God in such absolute purity and integrity and so actualises this relationship with God that he becomes God's self-expression and his once-for-all pledge of himself to the world he calls into existence, we have what we call 'Incarnation' in a dogmatically orthodox sense."[6]

God's communication to the man Christ and Christ's acceptance of this communication are, then, two sides of the same coin: "This Saviour, who represents the climax of [God's] self-communication, must therefore be at the same time God's absolute pledge by self-communication to the spiritual creature as a whole *and* the acceptance of this self-communication by this Saviour; only then is there an utterly irrevocable self-communication on both sides, and only thus is it present in the world in a historically communicative manner."[7] This means, in turn, that faith in Christ is possible for other human beings because of Christ's own human acceptance of God's self-communication.

In other words, Jesus is the exemplar of human transcendence, openness to God, properly and supremely exercised. Jesus' full humanity entails his full divinity: "The Incarnation of God is the unique and *highest* instance of the actualization of the essence of human reality, which consists in this: that man is insofar as he aban-

---

5. See especially Karl Rahner, "Christology within an Evolutionary View of the World," trans. Karl-H. Kruger, in *Theological Investigations* (London: Darton, Longman, and Todd, 1966), 5:185–87.; *Mary, Mother of the Lord*, trans. W. J. O'Hara, paperback ed. (Wheathampstead, Hertfordshire: Anthony Clarke Books, 1974), 10–12; *Foundations of Christian Faith*, 192–98; and *The Trinity*, trans. Joseph Donceel, Milestones in Catholic Theology (New York: The Crossroad Publishing Company, 2004), 28–30. This chapter frequently cites *Theological Investigations* [henceforth *TI*], various trans., 23 vols. (London: Darton, Longman, and Todd, 1961–92).

6. Karl Rahner, "'I believe in Jesus Christ': Interpreting an Article of Faith," trans. Graham Harrison, in *TI* (1972), 9:167. See also Rahner, *Foundations of Christian Faith*, 218.

7. Rahner, "Christology within an Evolutionary View of the World," in *TI*, 5:176.

dons himself to the absolute mystery whom we call God."[8] Human nature's transcendence is its defining quality. Therefore, the fuller the openness, the fuller the humanity. This means that the universal human struggle toward openness to God points to the perfection of that openness that is found *de facto* in Jesus. This continuity between grace in general and the grace of union in particular constitutes Jesus as humanity's awaited savior. The result is that the proclamation of Christ must be relevant to all human beings as such. In fact, because human beings are a union of spirit and matter ("spirit in the world"), the relevance of Jesus to humanity entails his relevance to all of creation, including the material world and the angels. More precisely, the apex reached in the hypostatic union is the goal of the whole spirit-matter cosmos.[9]

As for the continuity between nature and grace, while Rahner agrees with thinkers such as Joseph Maréchal, SJ (1878–1944), and Henri de Lubac, SJ (1896–1991), that grace is not merely layered on top of nature, he holds, contrary to them, that the orientation of human beings to the beatific vision (God as he is in himself) is already a gratuitous work.[10] If God were not to elevate human nature, mankind would still have a true, finite end, which would amount to contemplation of God through the mirror of his creation as the mysterious, free, and unknown Being.[11] In this case, "we would reach the peak of our spiritual and religious existence by listening to the silence of God."[12]

To state the matter differently, the orientation to God in himself is not an element of human nature as such. Instead, it requires an antecedent, gratuitous decision on God's part to communicate him-

---

8. Rahner, *Foundations of Christian Faith*, 218.

9. Rahner, "Christology within an Evolutionary View of the World," in *TI*, 5:176–84. See also Rahner, "The Unity of Spirit and Matter in the Christian Understanding of Faith," trans. Karl-H. Kruger and Boniface Kruger, in *TI* (1969), 6:177.

10. Karl Rahner, "Concerning the Relationship between Nature and Grace," trans. Cornelius Ernst, in *TI* (1961), 1:297–317.

11. Rahner, "Concerning the Relationship between Nature and Grace," in *TI*, 1:315.

12. Rahner, *Hearer of the Word*, 9.

self to the rational creature. For de Lubac and others of the *nouvelle théologie*, this decision partly constitutes the rational creature *per se*, so that if God had not decided to communicate himself, the rational creatures he might make would be specifically different from those he has actually made. For Rahner, in contrast, God's free offer of himself (whether accepted or rejected) modifies the human essence in its concrete existence. Borrowing a Heideggerian term, Rahner calls this modification, which is not yet grace but is gratuitously produced, the "supernatural existential" (*übernatürliches Existential*).[13]

One of Rahner's main concerns in positing the supernatural existential is to uphold the gratuity of God's self-communication in accord with the teaching of Pius XII's *Humani generis*.[14] Leaving aside any evaluation of the supernatural existential, it is clear that Rahner holds that God is free to produce rational creatures—endowed with the same natures they would otherwise have—without the offer of his self-communication.[15] Therefore, for Rahner, the creation of rational beings does not necessitate grace.

Neither, then, does creation necessitate the incarnation. "There could of course be men, if the Logos had not become man. The lesser can exist without the greater, though the lesser is always founded on the possibility of the greater and not vice versa."[16] But this state-

---

13. Presented in Rahner's response to Émile Delaye's 1950 article, "Ein Weg zur Bestimmung des Verhältnisses von Natur und Gnade": Rahner, "Eine Antwort," *Orientierung* 14, no. 12/13 (1950): 141–45. The article cited above, "Concerning the Relationship between Nature and Grace," in *TI*, 1:297–317, is a developed version of this. As David Coffey shows, Rahner refined his understanding of the supernatural existential over the course of his career but without contradicting his earlier thought. David Coffey, "The Whole Rahner on the Supernatural Existential," *Theological Studies* 65 (2004): 95–111. See also Anton Losinger, *The Anthropological Turn: The Human Orientation of the Theology of Karl Rahner*, trans. Daniel O. Dahlstrom (New York: Fordham University Press, 2000), 35–38.

14. See, e.g., Rahner, "Concerning the Relationship between Nature and Grace," in *TI*, 1:300–5, 312–13.

15. Although Rahner does not devote much attention to human nature in a "pure" state, he does acknowledge it as something real, even if—being a "remainder concept" (*Restbegriff*)—we only have access to it by abstracting out the modifications resulting from the *de facto* divine self-communication.

16. Karl Rahner, "On the Theology of the Incarnation," trans. Kevin Smyth, in *TI* (1966), 4:115–16.

ment is revealing: it is not because God can create that he can become incarnate, but because he can become incarnate that he can create. In particular, it is the Father's ability to express himself in his Word (immanently and economically) that grounds creation. "Man is possible because the exteriorization of the Logos is possible."[17] From the other side, if human nature is viewed primarily in terms of its transcendence, then *ipso facto* the power of God to assume human nature is logically prior to his power to create it, since the hypostatic union is nothing other than the highest fulfillment of human transcendence. This is to say that assumability features in the very definition of human nature: the Word's ability to be uttered economically and the aptitude of human nature to express the Word are correlative.

Even so, no one could prove the possibility of the incarnation just by reflecting on human nature, since the characteristic openness of that nature is mysterious.[18] Transcendence would not be transcendental but only categorical if its horizons could be charted out in advance. This is why the ascending approach is a "searching Christology."[19] It begins with humanity's openness to God and the corresponding duty to seek out whether and where God fills up that openness in history.

Once we encounter the fact of the incarnation, we come to understand the real depth of human transcendence. Man is the creature capable of being assumed into personal union with the Word. Or to put it differently, human nature is what God would make if he wanted to become something other than divine. "If God wills to become

---

17. Rahner, *The Trinity*, 33.

18. Rahner, "On the Theology of the Incarnation," in *TI*, 4:110. Rahner's general cautions about God's freedom to reveal or not reveal himself apply as well. In other words, the human person is by nature open to the reception of a divine revelation and, therefore, obliged to respond to one if God should reveal himself, but this does not necessitate that God must reveal himself or that the contents of revelation could be deduced from a study of human nature. On this point, see the entirety of Rahner's *Hearer of the Word*.

19. Karl Rahner, "Jesus Christ and Christology," in *A New Christology*, by Karl Rahner and Wilhelm Thüsing, trans. David Smith and Verdant Green (New York: The Seabury Press, 1980), 5.

non-God, man comes to be."[20] Again, because of God's universal saving will, human beings are concretely destined for divinization. Therefore, it is not so easy to parcel out what belongs to the pure nature of the human being and what is an effect of God's gratuitous decision to communicate himself.[21]

In this way, Rahner views the gratuitous and hypostatic orders as even more closely linked than the gratuitous and natural orders: if it is hard to believe that God would make spiritual creatures without communicating himself to them in grace and glory, it is much more incredible that he would communicate himself to them in grace and glory without communicating himself hypostatically. The possibility of the incarnation, not glory or created grace, is what grounds the possibility of human nature, as stated above. Therefore, it is supremely fitting that God would freely choose to communicate himself in this highest way. For Rahner this means that the incarnation cannot be primarily meant to address something gone wrong in creation. Instead, God "establishes this world to begin with as the materiality which is to become his own."[22] The result is that creation and the incarnation can be described as "two moments and two phases of the *one* process of God's self-giving and self-expression."[23]

This being the case, Rahner highlights a further continuity between the gratuitous and hypostatic orders—namely, his claim that all grace is Christic. After all, if God has created the world to allow for the incarnation (the apex of his self-communication), then it makes sense that the grace given to rational creatures (the lesser degree of his self-communication) bears an essential reference to the incarnation. Here it is worth quoting an important passage from Rahner at length.

---

20. Rahner, "On the Theology of the Incarnation," in *TI*, 4:116. Cf. Rahner, *The Trinity*, 32–33, 88–90; and *Foundations of Christian Faith*, 224–27.
21. Rahner, "Concerning the Relationship between Nature and Grace," in *TI*, 1:301–2.
22. Rahner, *Foundations of Christian Faith*, 197.
23. Rahner, *Foundations of Christian Faith*, 197.

Is there anything in Catholic principles to prevent us taking the Scotist point of view and considering the primal act of God, in which everything else is in fact given, as the self-exteriorization of God who is the love which gives itself in the incarnation? And then the order of grace would already be instituted, which would (probably) be unthinkable without such a decree of God with regard to his personal communication. Are there any valid arguments against the position which holds that the *possibility* of creation rests on that of the Incarnation, even though the fact of creation (as nature) does not necessarily imply the actual realization of the self-exteriorization of God in the Incarnation? Let us assume this position, which is recommended by its lofty simplicity, not to mention its more positive support in the Logos-theology of pre-Nicene and pre-Augustinian theology. Then grace has a much more radically Christological character. The Logos who has become part of the world is not merely the *de facto* mediator of grace by his merit—which only became necessary because Adam had cast this grace away—he is also the person who by his free Incarnation creates the order of grace and nature as his own presupposition (nature) and his milieu (the grace of the other spiritual creatures). This would enable us, as we have already said, to reach a deeper understanding of the immanent Trinity. The Logos would not be merely one of the divine persons who could become man if they wished: he would be the person in whom God communicates himself hypostatically to the world. The Incarnation would mirror the personal propriety of the second divine person, the Logos as such. The Trinity of the economy of redemption would enable us to have some insight into the immanent Trinity. This is not impossible, because the axiom that the efficient causality of God *ad extra* is common to the one God without distinction of persons cannot be applied to this quasi-formal causality.[24]

In this quotation, Rahner states his preference for the Scotistic view precisely because it does not divorce God's actual offer of grace from the Son's incarnation.

Further, Rahner adds to the Scotistic view his characteristic emphasis on the convertibility of the economic and immanent Trinity, as expressed in his *Grundaxiom*: "The 'economic' Trinity is the 'immanent' Trinity and the 'immanent' Trinity is the 'economic' Trinity."[25] Rahner's concern is especially that God's self-communication

24. Rahner, "Nature and Grace," trans. Kevin Smyth, in *TI* (1966), 4:176–77.
25. Rahner, *The Trinity*, 22.

be truly a *self*-communication. In other words, "God for us" is also "God in himself."[26] God does not keep his true self behind the scenes. "The Trinity is a mystery of *salvation*, otherwise it would never have been revealed."[27]

This implies that the Son's incarnate life must reveal him precisely as the Son in relation to the Father and the Holy Spirit. For this reason, Rahner holds that only the Son could become incarnate.[28] If *any* of the divine persons could become incarnate, then the incarnation would reveal the Trinity only extrinsically or "verbally."[29] For the incarnation to reveal the Son *per se*, there must be something about the Son that makes the incarnation uniquely possible to him.

Rahner explains this by locating the hypostatic union within a broader ontological discussion of divine self-communication *ad extra*.[30] The lynchpin of this is Rahner's reversal of the typical Scholastic approach to created and uncreated grace. In the typical approach, God's self-gift results from a modification in the creature. Rahner's reversal puts uncreated grace first: it is because God gives himself that creaturely reality is changed. Thus, God's self-communication in the Son's incarnation results in Christ's humanity, and his self-communication in the grace of the Spirit results in created grace in the soul.[31]

This also means that God's self-gift should not, first of all, be described in terms of efficient causality. As efficient cause, God may produce something that represents him, but he does not give *him-*

---

26. Rahner, *The Trinity*, 44.
27. Rahner, *The Trinity*, 21.
28. Rahner, *The Trinity*, 28–30; "On the Theology of the Incarnation," in *TI*, 4:105–7; and *Foundations of Christian Faith*, 222–23.
29. Rahner, *The Trinity*, 39. See also especially Rahner, "The Theology of the Symbol," trans. Kevin Smyth, in *TI* (1966), 4:237–39.
30. See especially Rahner, "Some Implications of the Scholastic Concept of Uncreated Grace," trans. Cornelius Ernst, in *TI* (1961), 1:319–46; and *Foundations of Christian Faith*, 116–26. See also Guy Mansini, "Quasi-Formal Causality and 'Change in the Other': A Note on Karl Rahner's Christology," *The Thomist* 52, no. 2 (1988): 293–306; and Michael Purcell, "Quasi-Formal Causality, or the Other-in-Me: Rahner and Lévinas," *Gregorianum* 78, no. 1 (1997): 80–84.
31. Rahner, *The Trinity*, 99–101.

self.[32] No amount of finite, created effects can add up to God's personal presence. Instead, when God communicates himself in Christ, the Son is the "quasi-formal" cause of Christ's humanity, and when he communicates himself in grace, the Spirit is the quasi-formal cause of the justified soul. The "quasi" in "quasi-formal" is meant to safeguard divine transcendence and immutability against the impression that God actually combines with the creature in any way. Rahner admits, too, that "God's being a quasi-formal cause with regard to a creature can never be positively understood."[33] Still, Rahner only prepends "quasi" out of an abundance of caution. He takes the "quasi" in "quasi-formal" to be no more restrictive than the "quasi" that "must be prefixed to every application to God of a category in itself terrestrial."[34]

Rahner derives the category of quasi-formal cause in his discussion of divine self-communication from the notion of the beatific vision—the perfect flowering of grace—where God himself takes the place of the *species impressa* in the created intellect. When Rahner applies this to grace in general, he argues that uncreated grace precedes created grace (logically and by nature, though not chronologically) in the way that a formal cause precedes the final material disposition for that form.[35] In fact, Rahner holds that "supernatural reality and reality brought about by a divine self-communication of quasi-formal, not efficient type, are identical concepts."[36] Consequently, the incarnation and the indwelling of the Trinity both involve proper (non-appropriated) and distinct relations of the divine

32. Rahner, "Divine Trinity," in *Sacramentum mundi: An Encyclopedia of Theology*, ed. Karl Rahner et al. (New York: Herder, 1970), 6:298.

33. Rahner, "Divine Trinity," in *Sacramentum mundi*, 6:299.

34. Rahner, "Concept of Uncreated Grace," in *TI*, 1:330. For this reason, the "quasi" in "quasi-formal" could be dropped (as, e.g., we usually speak of God as the "efficient cause" and not the "quasi-efficient cause" of the world). Rahner does omit "quasi" in *Foundations of Christian Faith*, 120–22.

35. In this way, created grace remains a requirement for uncreated grace (as the material disposition is for the reception of the form) while being in a more fundamental sense its consequence.

36. Rahner, "The Concept of Mystery in Catholic Theology," trans. Kevin Smyth, in *TI* (1966), 4:67.

persons to the world.³⁷ This, in turn, is what truly constitutes the revelation of the Trinity: because God gives himself as he really is and because his economic self-communication is Trinitarian, God's immanent life is Trinitarian.³⁸

In terms of Christology, this also means that grace is not primarily a *thing* that Christ merits that God then applies to others (as efficient cause).³⁹ Instead, the one God shares himself as incarnate (the Son) and as divinizing from within (the Spirit) while simultaneously remaining the transcendent source of these self-communications (the Father).⁴⁰ The Father expresses himself in the incarnate Son and imparts acceptance of adoptive filiation in other human beings through the Holy Spirit, who is sent from the Father and the Son. All of this is possible in non-appropriated terms because of quasi-formal causality, which applies both to the Son's hypostatic union and to the grace of the Spirit in general.

In other words, Rahner's account assumes "the necessary unity of the divinization of the world and the Incarnation as two correlative factors of God's one free self-communication to the creature."⁴¹ Just as the immanent processions of the Son and Spirit necessarily imply each other, so also the Father can only communicate himself economically through their missions taken together.⁴² Again, "the dependence of the self-communication of God to the created spirit in glory with regard to the incarnation does not indicate a merely moral relationship, arising from the fact that the incarnate Logos

---

37. Rahner, "Concept of Uncreated Grace," in *TI*, 1:343–46; and "The Concept of Mystery in Catholic Theology," in *TI*, 4:65–67.

38. Rahner, *The Trinity*, 34–38; and *Foundations of Christian Faith*, 136–37.

39. Rahner, "Current Problems in Christology," trans. Cornelius Ernst, in *TI* (1961), 1:199–200; "Personal and Sacramental Piety," trans. Karl-H. Kruger, in *TI* (1963), 2:113–14, 119–22; "The Theology of the Symbol," in *TI*, 4:244; "Theological States of Man," in *Sacramentum mundi* (1970), 6:174; and *The Trinity*, 10–15.

40. Rahner, *The Trinity*, 32–33, 63–66.

41. Rahner, "Jesus Christ: IV. History of Dogma and Theology," in *Sacramentum mundi* (1970), 3:204. See also Rahner, "The Concept of Mystery in Catholic Theology," in *TI*, 4:67–68.

42. Rahner, *The Trinity*, 86–87, 98–99; and "Divine Trinity," in *Sacramentum mundi*, 6:298–300.

once 'merited' this glory for us in time. The relationship is a real and permanent ontological one."[43] In other words, the Father could not give himself to the world except through Christ, Christ could not come without giving the Spirit, the Spirit could not be given without Christ's coming, and humanity could not be glorified without Christ and the Spirit.

Because the incarnation and grace are connected not only *de facto* by divine decree but necessarily (on the supposition of God's free decision to communicate himself to the world), one can approach Christology from the perspective of theological anthropology, and vice versa. Rahner thinks the former approach, in fact, has important apologetic advantages. If theology can develop a "transcendental Christology"—that is, an approach to Christ that speaks to the openness to God and aspiration for him common to every human being—then the Gospel becomes universally intelligible and appealing.[44]

Hence Rahner argues that the modern world needs a transcendental Christology. "Without it the traditional christology would today be in the gravest danger of being regarded as a mythology which is no longer capable of being made real to the man of today."[45] A transcendental Christology would articulate in general terms "the 'idea' of a bringer of salvation in the absolute, a manifestation in history of the irreversibility and the victory of God's self-communication over the denial of the unbelief of the world."[46] At the same time, Rahner does not want to lose sight of the historical Jesus of Nazareth, in whom the idea has actually been realized. "A transcendental Christology only becomes historically possible and necessary when man encounters the factual Christ-event."[47]

---

43. Rahner, "The Theology of the Symbol," in *TI*, 4:244.
44. Rahner, "Jesus Christ: IV. History of Dogma and Theology," in *Sacramentum mundi*, 3:196–98.
45. Rahner, "Reflections on Methodology in Theology," trans. David Bourke, in *TI* (1974), 11:96.
46. Rahner, "Reflections on Methodology in Theology," in *TI*, 11:95–96.
47. Rahner, "Jesus Christ: IV. History of Dogma and Theology," in *Sacramentum mundi*, 3:197.

Rahner then goes on to describe transcendental Christology's essential features. To quote him at length:

> Taking as its starting-point the principle of God's will to save all men, in other words a self-communication on God's part which supports the whole of history and supplies it with its goal, and also taking as a starting-point the principle of a historical development in this transcendental self-communication of God to the world which is necessary of its very nature, such a christology in transcendental theology would have to develop the concept of an absolute mediator of salvation. In other words it would have to show that a historical development of the transcendental self-communication of God in this sense (provided that it does not lead to the absolute perdition of the world) must necessarily be developed to a point at which this self-utterance of God appears as addressed to the world irreversibly (as "effective" and not merely "sufficient" grace for the world in its power to lay hold of this grace in the dimension of history), and at which it is freely accepted as such. Further a christology of this kind in terms of transcendental theology would of course have to do something more than to enable men to understand that the event of God's self-communication as posited in history and as made irreversible on the one hand, and the definitive acceptance of this on humanity's part on the other, implicitly expresses in the unity of both these aspects precisely what the classic doctrine of the hypostatic union, on any right understanding of this, is intended to convey. Over and above this this transcendental christology would also have to enable men to understand how the endowment of the world as a whole with grace and the hypostatic union constitute the necessary unity of a mutually conditioning relationship, how, in other words a supralapsarian christology and a universal christocentricity are the necessary postulates for any christology to be credible today. Such a christology would also have to enable men to understand, likewise in terms of transcendental theology, why a hypostatic union exists only in a single instance, and how this fact does not mean that the universal God-manhood inherent in the spiritual creature as such is not in some sense degraded to a secondary category such that in and for itself it could conceivably be surpassed.[48]

In other words, transcendental Christology must begin with God's will to save. Rahner understands this as God's desire to give himself

---

48. Rahner, "Reflections on Methodology in Theology," in *TI*, 11:96–97.

to the world. God's self-gift and the human acceptance of this gift occur together concretely in the single person of the God-man. This means, in turn, that the God-man is the center of God's whole plan for the universe, especially humanity's elevation to grace. This elevation is nothing less than humanity's participation in the God-man's acceptance of God's self-gift. In this way, there is ontological continuity between the hypostatic union and the grace enjoyed by other human beings. On this last point, Rahner highlights the need to maintain the uniqueness of the hypostatic union without denigrating God's self-gift to other human beings.

It is important to note that in the preceding quotation, the notion of salvation does not *per se* entail sin. Instead, it means God's self-communication together with the proper human acceptance. The emphasis is entirely on God's offer of himself to humanity, which even partly constitutes what it concretely means to be human in the first place (via the supernatural existential), and humanity's free acceptance of this gift, an acceptance that the God-man makes *par excellence*. Whether or not humanity has refused the divine self-gift through sin prior to the God-man's definitive acceptance of the gift is accidental to Rahner's account.

Along these lines, of particular interest is Rahner's claim that "a supralapsarian christology and a universal christocentricity are the necessary postulates for any christology to be credible today." This is to say that Rahner finds the notion of Christ's having come only as a response to human sin untenable to the modern world. We can make sense of humanity's general openness to what is beyond (transcendence) and so, in these terms, make sense of the union of God (the absolute beyond) with human nature, but to see the realization of this union as essentially a corrective to human sin is dangerously mythological. Only if God intends the God-man prior to any other consideration (supralapsarianism) and only if the God-man thus stands as the apex of a divinization common to all human beings can Christology be credible to the modern world.

Rahner again supports the legitimacy of his opinion by comparing it to the Scotistic view:

> It should be stated, first of all, that there is quite a long established school of thought among Catholic theologians (usually called the "Scotist school") which has always stressed that the first and most basic motive for the Incarnation was not the blotting-out of sin but that the Incarnation was already the goal of the divine freedom even apart from any divine fore-knowledge of freely incurred guilt. This School holds therefore that—seen as the free climax of God's self-expression and self-effacement into the otherness of the creature—the Incarnation is the most original act of God anticipating the will to create and (presupposing sin) to redeem, by including them, as it were, as two of its moments. In the light of this conception—which has never been objected to by the Church's *magisterium*—it is therefore impossible to say that the view of the Incarnation proposed by us could arouse some real misgivings on the part of the *magisterium*.[49]

Naturally, Rahner maintains that the incarnation has actually been redemptive—that is, that it has overcome human sin—but he does not see the incarnation as essentially a response to sin. Instead, the overcoming of sin is simply included within the self-communication accomplished in the incarnation: "In a history which, through the free grace of God has its goal in an absolute and irrevocable self-communication of God to the spiritual creature—in a self-communication which is finally established through its goal and climax, i.e. through the Incarnation—the redeeming power which overcomes sin is necessarily found precisely in this climax of the Incarnation and in the realization of this divine-human reality."[50] In other words, God wills to give himself to humanity. This self-gift culminates in Christ, who also freely accepts the gift in its fullness. Whether sin is present or not is a secondary consideration. The fall does not determine God's decision to communicate himself. Rather, God's initial, free decision to communicate himself in Christ is virtu-

---

49. Rahner, "Christology within an Evolutionary View of the World," in *TI*, 5:184–85.
50. Rahner, "Christology within an Evolutionary View of the World," in *TI*, 5:186.

ally redemptive. It holds within itself the remission of any sins that might be there.

One of Rahner's concerns is that sin (a human act) not be taken as the determining factor in God's will to communicate himself *ad extra*. Sin does not force God to abandon or correct his original plan. If salvation is conceived of as a response to sin, we have not soteriology but only "hamartiology."[51] Accordingly, salvation must primarily consist in elevation to divinity. What Jesus *saves* creation from, then, is nonfulfillment of its capacity for the divine. The result is that salvation includes original justice and the grace of the angels, making both of these *gratia Christi*.[52] Given that the hypostatic and gratuitous orders belong to the same decision of God to communicate himself to the world, "the mysteries of soteriology can undoubtedly be reduced to the mystery of the Incarnation; ... the whole doctrine of the redemption follows from the mystery of the Incarnation."[53]

Just as God's salvific will is not prompted by the human act of sin, neither, in Rahner's view, does Christ's cross somehow persuade God to give grace to fallen humanity. In both cases, God's universal will to save precedes any other consideration. "It is not Christ's action which causes God's will to forgiveness, but vice versa."[54] But God's will to forgiveness must not be construed as essentially distinct from his will to communicate himself. There is a single process of divine self-communication that includes humanity's elevation to grace, the incarnation as its high point, and the remission of any sins that might be committed.

51. Rahner, "Salvation: IV. Theology: C. Soteriology," in *Sacramentum mundi* (1970), 5:435.
52. Rahner, "Theological States of Man," in *Sacramentum mundi*, 6:174; "Salvation: IV. Theology: C. Soteriology," in *Sacramentum mundi*, 5:435–36; *The Trinity*, 90; and Rahner and Herbert Vorgrimler, *Dictionary of Theology*, trans. Richard Strachan, David Smith, Robert Nowell, and Sarah O'Brien Twohig, 2nd ed. (New York: Crossroad, 1988), s.v. "Christocentrism."
53. Rahner, "The Concept of Mystery in Catholic Theology," in *TI*, 4:65.
54. Rahner, "Christology within an Evolutionary View of the World," in *TI*, 5:186. See also Rahner, "The One Christ and the Universality of Salvation," trans. David Morland, in *TI* (1979), 16:207–8; "The Christian Understanding of Redemption," trans. Hugh M. Riley, in *TI* (1988), 21:247–52; and *Foundations of Christian Faith*, 282–85.

In this self-communication and in its climax (i.e. in the Incarnation), the world becomes the history of God himself. And so if and in so far as it is found in the world, sin is from the outset embraced by the will to forgive and the offer of divine self-communication becomes necessary. For, since on account of Christ this offer is not conditioned by sin, it becomes necessarily an offer of forgiveness and of victory over guilt; indeed, sin is permitted merely because, being finite human guilt, God knew it to remain always, imprisoned within his absolute will regarding the world and his offer of himself.[55]

In this way, "on account of Christ," God's plan to communicate himself to humanity is "not conditioned by sin." The very fact that God's self-gift is *not* conditioned by sin means that it becomes an offer of forgiveness if sin happens to be present. Sin will be overcome precisely because it is not the decisive factor in how God relates to the world.

To put it differently, God's will to forgive is only an aspect of his ineluctable will to communicate himself to the world, which means, ultimately, to become human. Forgiveness is that self-communication insofar as it overcomes resistance on the part of the recipient. "We have always emphasized that this self-communication of God necessarily exists either in the mode of its acceptance, which is usually called justification, or in the mode of its rejection, which is called disbelief and sin."[56]

I have said that one of Rahner's concerns is the credibility of the Gospel and the plausibility of the individual's response of faith. Closely connected is his general soteriological concern. How can the message of Christ be truly a *saving* message capable of reception by all human beings? In this vein, Rahner writes:

We can and must see God's free will to salvation as the *a priori* cause (a cause conditioned by nothing outside God himself) of Christ's incarnation and cross as well; so that from this point of view, too, it is not easy to see how the cross of Christ could be the reason for God's saving will towards other people, if this saving divine will after all precedes the cross of

---

55. Rahner, "Christology within an Evolutionary View of the World," in *TI*, 5:186.
56. Rahner, *Foundations of Christian Faith*, 193.

Christ, as its cause and not as its effect, and must then be viewed as being related to all men.[57]

Jesus does not undergo the cross to change God's mind. This would be a mythological view, like something out of a fairy tale, and, therefore, unacceptable in today's world. Instead, it is God's saving will that causes Jesus to take up the cross.

In Rahnerian terms, then, the cross is a *Realsymbol*.[58] This is to say that it is the concrete, historical realization of God's self-communication to humanity.[59] If not for the cross, that self-communication would never have been brought to actual, definitive completion and would have remained only a rejected offer.[60] To be more precise, the salvation that is God's self-communication to the world occurs first of all in Christ himself through his supreme openness to receive this communication in its highest form (hypostatic union). But the death of a human individual is what brings his free actions within history to a close and thus renders them definitive.[61] Therefore, it is Christ's death unto Resurrection, his entrance into a definitive and "pancosmic" relation to historical reality, that is the actualization of God's saving will for the whole world.[62] The death of any human being is what completes his life, sealing his relationship to the world of time and space. In Christ's case, this means

---

57. Rahner, "Jesus Christ in the Non-Christian Religions," trans. Margaret Kohl, in *TI* (1981), 17:45. See also Rahner, "Christology within an Evolutionary View of the World," in *TI*, 5:186; and especially "The One Christ and the Universality of Salvation," in *TI*, 16:207–8.

58. On *Realsymbol*, see Rahner's essay "The Theology of the Symbol," in *TI*, 4:221–52.

59. See especially Rahner, "The Christian Understanding of Redemption," in *TI*, 21:247–52; and "The One Christ and the Universality of Salvation," in *TI*, 16:214–15. See also the discussion in Jerry T. Farmer, "Four Christological Themes of the Theology of Karl Rahner," in *The Myriad Christ: Plurality and the Quest for Unity in Contemporary Christology*, ed. T. Merrigan and J. Haers, Bibliotheca ephemeridum theologicarum Lovaniensium 152 (Leuven: University Press, 2000), 450–55.

60. Rahner, "The One Christ and the Universality of Salvation," in *TI*, 16:214.

61. Rahner, *On the Theology of Death*, trans. C. H. Henkey and W. J. O'Hara, 2nd English ed., Quaestiones disputatae (New York: Herder, 1965), 26–31.

62. Rahner, *On the Theology of Death*, 57–58, 63–67; and *Foundations of Christian Faith*, 279–80, 296–97.

that death finalizes his existence as the one who was fully human (fully open to God) to the point of being fully divine. This itself is the definitive concretization of salvation (God's gift of God's self) in relation to the world.[63]

This means that the cross does not merely make humanity aware of the gift it has already received but actually effects human salvation by a kind of sacramental causality. The cross is the "universal primary sacrament of the salvation of the whole world."[64] For Rahner, this means that God's saving will has chosen to make use of the cross and Resurrection as concrete instruments so that salvation can be realized historically. An ahistorical self-communication of God to humanity would, after all, be a contradiction in terms, since the human person is precisely a spirit *in the world*, capable of the infinite but bound by time and space.

Rahner also highlights the relation of the incarnation and cross to the Holy Spirit.

> We can only emerge from these difficulties (and others which we have not mentioned) if we see the incarnation and the cross as what scholastic terminology calls the "final cause" of God's universal self-communication to the world, given with God's saving will, which knows no reason outside itself and which we call the Holy Spirit; and if we view the incarnation and cross in this sense as the cause of the imparting of the Holy Spirit at all times and in all places in the world.... Jesus is the "cause" of the Spirit, even if the reverse relationship is equally true, as is the case in unity and difference, and the mutually conditioning relationship between efficacious and final causes. Since the efficacious cause of incarnation and cross (i.e., the Spirit) has its goal within itself, as inner entelechy, and fulfils its own being (as communicated to the world) only in the incarnation and cross, the Spirit is from the outset the Spirit of Jesus Christ.[65]

Joseph H. Wong has characterized Rahner's approach here as "pneuma-Christocentric."[66] The action of the Spirit, which Rahner char-

63. Rahner, "Jesus Christ and Christology," 32–41.
64. Rahner, "The One Christ and the Universality of Salvation," in *TI*, 16:215.
65. Rahner, "Jesus Christ in the Non-Christian Religions," in *TI*, 17:46.
66. Joseph H. Wong, "Anonymous Christians: Karl Rahner's Pneuma- Christocentrism and an East-West Dialogue," *Theological Studies* 55, no. 4 (December 1994): 619–30.

acterizes as an efficient cause, is complemented by the influence of Christ as final cause. What the Spirit seeks to do in the world has its goal in Christ—is done for the sake of Christ—while Christ himself is brought into the world by the Spirit.

Rahner's application of final causality is especially important because it allows him to articulate how God's supreme self-communication to humanity together with human acceptance of this self-communication can reach a pinnacle that is also normative for the whole process of self-communication.[67] In other words, graces given prior to Christ's coming are Christic because Christ is their goal. The God-man is not only the outcome or the happenstance apex of the universal process of spirit-matter development and divinization, he is also what gives rise to and governs that process as its final cause. Christ is, therefore, first in God's intention when acting *ad extra*. "The end is the absolute beginning."[68]

Given the synthesis of Rahner's descending and ascending approaches to Christology, achieved on the basis of his transcendental method, it is no surprise that he also professes a methodological Christocentrism. Rahner's method is anthropological, yes, but Christ is the supreme exemplar of humanity and the final cause of humanity's creation. Thus,

> Christology is the beginning and end of anthropology, and this anthropology in its most radical actualization is for all eternity theology. It is first of all the theology which God himself has spoken by uttering his Word as our flesh into the emptiness of what is not God and is even sinful, and, secondly, it is the theology which we ourselves do in faith when we do not think that we could find Christ by going around man, and hence find God by going around the human altogether.[69]

In Christ, our understanding of human nature is radically deepened. "The finite itself has received infinite depths."[70]

---

67. Rahner, *Foundations of Christian Faith*, 194–95.
68. Rahner, *Foundations of Christian Faith*, 191.
69. Rahner, *Foundations of Christian Faith*, 225–26. See also Rahner, "On the Theology of the Incarnation," in *TI*, 4:116.
70. Rahner, *Foundations of Christian Faith*, 226.

Therefore, Rahner's Christocentrism emphasizes Christ as the goal of the self-communication for which God made the world. To this extent, Rahner is a Scotist, since he holds that the incarnation is not essentially a response to sin. Rahner puts his own spin on the Scotistic view, however, by articulating it within his transcendental Christology and especially by positing the quasi-formal nature of the divine self-communication to the creature. Because human nature is essentially transcendent, full humanity and full divinity are correlative. Thus, for Rahner, hypostatic union is the apex of grace, meaning that Christ is continuous (although unique as exemplar and final cause) with other human beings in their openness to God and that all grace is Christic. Christ is simultaneously God's word to humanity and supreme human receptivity to that word. By this approach, Rahner hopes to explain how Christ is relevant to human beings *as such* on the basis of their experience of openness to the beyond and, thus, to overcome modern rejection of the Gospel as mythological.

THE SALMANTICENSES AND RAHNER

The Salmanticenses and Rahner agree that Christ is the apex of God's plan for history and, therefore, primary in God's intention. However, for Rahner the Son's incarnation is essentially bound up with the offer of grace, resulting in a *de iure* Christocentrism, whereas the Salmanticenses hold that Christ's primacy is a matter of God's *de facto* providential plan. Further, in their view, Christ's coming is directed to the cross essentially, not accidentally, which Rahner loses sight of.

Here, I will argue that there are three major areas where the Salmanticenses offer a corrective to Rahner. First, Rahner limits God's economic freedom. Second, Rahner deemphasizes the cross. Third, Rahner argues that all grace is *gratia Christi*. After exploring these, I will consider how the ascending aspect of Rahner's transcendental Christology can integrate with and supplement the Salmanticenses.

Rahner and God's Economic Freedom

A key problem with Rahner's method is that he begins with God's contingent economic acts and concludes to necessary facts about God in himself. In other words, Rahner blurs the lines between creation and God. The fact that the Salmanticenses, in contrast, so strongly defend God's transcendence and freedom *ad extra* makes them a valuable corrective to Rahner on this point. Whereas Rahner articulates a *de iure* Christocentrism, the Salmanticenses limit themselves to a *de facto* Christocentrism. I will now explain why I think the latter is correct.

In *Der dreifaltige Gott als transzendenter Urgrund der Heilsgeschichte* (*The Trinity*), Rahner argues against the claim of typical "textbook theology" inherited from Scholasticism that any of the divine persons could become incarnate.[71] At the time of Rahner's writing, this was a standard thesis accepted by theological manuals and regarded as *sententia communis et certa in theologia*.[72] Nevertheless, Rahner claims that the thesis is undemonstrated and is, in fact, false.[73] Rahner explains that theology cannot begin with the fact of the Son's incarnation and conclude to the possibility of incarnation for the divine persons in general. Such an inference relies on a uni-

---

71. Rahner, *The Trinity*, 28–30. See also Francesco Neri, *Cur Verbum capax hominis: Le ragioni dell'incarnazione della seconda Persona della Trinità fra teologia scolastica e teologia contemporanea*, Tesi Gregoriana, Serie Teologia 55 (Rome: Editrice Pontificia Università Gregoriana, 1999), 209–98.

72. Jesus Solano, *De Verbo incarnato* I, chap. 2, a. 2, thesis 6, no. 90, in *Sacrae theologiae summa*, 4th ed., Biblioteca de autores cristianos 62 (Madrid: Biblioteca de autores cristianos, 1961), 3:60. See also Louis Billot, *De Verbo incarnato commentarius in tertiam partem s. Thomae*, 2nd expanded and rev. ed. (Rome: Ex typographia polyglotta, 1895), 165–67; Adolphe Tanquerey, *De Verbo incarnato et redemptore*, pars 1, chap. 2, §1, no. 1054, in *Synopsis theologiae dogmaticae ad mentem S. Thomae Aquinatis hodiernis moribus accommodata*, 18th ed. (Paris: Typis Societatis sancti Joannis evangelistae, Descleé et socii, 1921), 2:678–79; and Valentino Zubizarreta, *Theologia dogmatico-scholastica*, tract. 3, sect. 1, q. 4, aa. 1–2, in *Theologia dogmatico-scholastica ad mentem S. Thomae Aquinatis*, 4th ed. corrected by the author (Vitoria: Ediciones "El Carmen," 1948), 3:373–76.

73. Rahner, *The Trinity*, 28–30. See also Rahner, "Divine Trinity," in *Sacramentum mundi*, 6:298–99.

vocal understanding of "person" in God when, in fact, the three divine persons are radically distinct and not just three instances of the same kind.

What is at stake for Rahner is, of course, the identity of "God for us" and "God in himself," as expressed in his *Grundaxiom*. He worries that holding the possible incarnation of any of the divine persons "would create havoc with theology. There would no longer be any connection between 'mission' and the intra-trinitarian life."[74] If the incarnation of the Son reveals him as the Son *per se* and not only by what Jesus says about God, then incarnation must be essentially filial and, therefore, uniquely possible to the Son.

What Rahner wants to uphold—that the Son's incarnation reveals him in his personal distinctiveness—is correct. The Trinity, the central mystery of the Christian faith, undoubtedly is a mystery of salvation. "This is eternal life, that they know thee the only true God, and Jesus Christ whom thou hast sent" (Jn 17:3). The Son incarnate communicates this mystery to the human race through his personal presence as the Father's Son and through sending the Holy Spirit. Salvation consists in nothing short of communion with the divine persons. "Our fellowship is with the Father and with his Son Jesus Christ" (1 Jn 1:3). Even so, there are good reasons for rejecting Rahner's claim that *only* the Son could have become incarnate.

First of all, Rahner asserts that there is no warrant for asserting that any divine person could become incarnate.[75] While this has the semblance of avoiding a faulty argument from silence, it is actually itself an appeal to silence. Just as Scripture does not say that the Father or the Holy Spirit could have been incarnate, it also does not say that they could *not* have been incarnate.

Absent proof to the contrary, the presumption should be in favor of God's power to act freely *ad extra*—that is, to do whatever is not logically impossible. This is how the Salmanticenses argue, *a fortiori*,

---

74. Rahner, *The Trinity*, 30.
75. Rahner, *The Trinity*, 28–29.

for the Thomistic position that the three divine persons could even assume the same created nature numerically.[76] They state:

> The chief foundation of this assertion consists in this: that up till now, no argument has been found or produced by our opponents that demonstrates that there is a logical contradiction in the same created nature's being terminated in the three divine subsistences or personhoods, ... but as long as the opposite has not been demonstrated, we must uphold and take an expansive view with respect to the divine power, which certainly can do whatever is not logically contradictory or impossible on the part of the object.[77]

My purpose here is not to discuss whether the three persons could assume the same nature numerically or to explore the details of other combinations of divine persons and created natures. I only wish to state that unless the *Son's* assumption of a *single human nature* can be proven to be the only logically possible kind of incarnation, theology must affirm that it could have been otherwise.

Rahner does not truly attempt to prove the logical impossibility of counterfactual hypostatic unions. He does, however, point out what he thinks is a logical error in the traditional view. Only if "divine person" is univocal, he says, can one infer the possibility of any divine person's incarnation from the fact of the Son's. Rahner rejects such a univocity, claiming that "the ways in which each person is a person are so different that they allow of only a *very loosely* analogical concept of person, as *equally* applicable to the three persons."[78]

Now, Aquinas does indeed state that the common *ratio personalitatis* is "the same" for the three divine persons and that this enables

---

76. *ST* III, q. 3, a. 6 (Leonine, 11:64–65); and Salmanticenses, *Cursus theologicus*, tract. 21, disp. 8, dub. 6 (Palmé, 14:108–24).

77. "Praecipuum hujus assertionis fundamentum in eo consistit; quod hactenus inventa non sit, et ab Adversariis producta ratio aliqua demonstrans implicare, quod eadem natura creata terminetur tribus subsistentiis, aut personalitatibus divinis, ... quamdiu autem oppositum non demonstratur, standum, ac proferendum est pro divina virtute, quam certum est posse efficere, quidquid non implicat, aut est objective impossibile." Salmanticenses, *Cursus theologicus*, tract. 21, disp. 8, dub. 6, §1, no. 135 (Palmé, 14:109).

78. Rahner, *The Trinity*, 29. See also Rahner, *The Trinity*, 104–6; and "Divine Trinity," in *Sacramentum mundi*, 6:298.

the inference that any of them could be hypostatically united to a created nature.[79] *Personalitas* is "personhood" or "that which characterizes one as a person," while "person" means the individual subsisting in an intellectual nature.[80] The sameness of the *ratio personalitatis* with reference to the ability to assume a created nature does not necessarily require a univocal application of "divine person" to the Father, Son, and Holy Spirit with respect to each other. The fact of being one who subsists in the divine nature can be common to the Father, Son, and Spirit, while the way that each of them is one who so subsists (i.e., the particular subsisting relation that each is) differs for each.[81]

Interestingly, the Salmanticenses do hold that "divine person" is applied analogously with respect to the Father, Son, and Spirit.[82] This is especially because "in each of the divine persons, the *ratio* of 'divine person' and the particular *ratio* of 'such-and-such a person' (e.g., 'Father') are not distinguished virtually. Therefore, the *ratio* of 'divine person' will not be able to be completely abstracted from the particular divine persons and, consequently, will not be a univocal *ratio* in respect of them."[83] In this way, they share Rahner's concern: because the divine persons are subsisting relations, one can never conceive of "divine person" so abstractly as to exclude the particular relativity of each person. If this were possible, then "divine person"

---

79. "Eadem etiam est communis ratio personalitatis in tribus personis, licet proprietates personales sint differentes." *ST* III, q. 3, a. 5, co. (Leonine, 11:63).

80. *ST* I, q. 39, a. 3, ad 4 (Leonine, 4:400).

81. On the notion of "divine person" as a relation as subsisting, see Gilles Emery, *The Trinitarian Theology of St Thomas Aquinas*, trans. Francesca Murphy and Gilles Emery (Oxford: Oxford University Press, 2007), 114–19.

82. See the whole discussion in Salmanticenses, *Cursus theologicus*, tract. 6, *De sacrosanctissimae Trinitatis mysterio*, disp. 10, dub. 5 (Palmé, 3:434–44).

83. "In quavis ex personis divinis non distinguuntur virtualiter ratio personae divinae, et peculiaris ratio talis personae, v. g. Patris: ergo ratio personae divinae non erit omnino abstrahibilis a peculiaribus personis divinis: et per consequens neque erit ratio univoca respectu illarum." Salmanticenses, *Cursus theologicus*, tract. 6, disp. 10, dub. 5, §3, no. 119 (Palmé, 3:439). The Salmanticenses' point is directly logical and semantic, even though it relies on ontology.

would be a universal, like a genus or species.[84] The divine simplicity prevents this.

In analogical predication the common *ratio* includes the particularities of the individuals to which it applies, even though it includes them implicitly or in a confused way. In contrast, univocal predication demands that the common *ratio* not include the contradictory particularities of individuals so as to be completely generic. Thus "animal" can be predicated univocally of a man and a donkey because by itself "animal" includes neither "rational" nor "irrational," nor "this man" nor "this donkey." Conversely, because "divine person" means a relation subsisting in the divine nature, it can never completely exclude the particularities of these relations, which are distinct only by being opposed to one another. Instead, the *ratio* of "divine person" must include the *rationes* of "paternity," "filiation," and "passive spiration" at least implicitly or in a confused way.

Hence, affirming that the Father is a divine person means affirming that he is *paternity* as subsisting in the divine nature. Because of the divine simplicity, the Father is really identical with the divine essence. There is no composition in the Father to serve as the real foundation for a virtual distinction between being a relation subsisting in the divine nature and being paternity subsisting in the divine nature. But the three persons *are* really distinct from one another. Father and Son are both relations subsisting in the divine nature, but the former is paternity and the latter filiation. Since the Father is not the Son and yet each is a divine person, the common name and *ratio* of "divine person" can only apply to them by analogy. This does not mean, however, that one person fits the *ratio* of "divine person" eminently while the others participate in it only to a lesser degree, as can happen in other instances of analogical naming.[85]

84. Salmanticenses, *Cursus theologicus*, tract. 6, disp. 10, dub. 5, §2, nos. 110–18 (Palmé, 3:436–39). See also the explanation by Pablo de la Concepción in *Tractatus theologici*, tract. 6, disp. 3, dub. 2, §6, no. 44 (haeredes Pauli Monti, 2:46).

85. Salmanticenses, *Cursus theologicus*, tract. 6, disp. 10, dub. 5, §3, no. 120 (Palmé, 3:439–40). See also Pablo de la Concepción, *Tractatus theologici*, tract. 6, disp. 3, dub. 2, §6, no. 45 (haeredes Pauli Monti, 2:46).

Although the Salmanticenses hold that "divine person" is used analogously for the three persons, they do not agree with Rahner that this term is so "very loosely analogical" as to threaten the inference that any of the divine persons could become incarnate. The relations constituting the three persons differ irreducibly—which is why the persons are really distinguished at all—but it is still meaningful to say that each is a divine person—that is, that each *subsists* in the divine nature.[86] This being the case, each is a true subject—not merely a relation as relation but a relation *as subsisting*. Therefore, each terminates the single divine nature, and so there seems to be no reason why each could not terminate a created nature. The *ratio personae* is analogous with respect to the Father, Son, and Spirit, but it remains a common *ratio*.

As noted above, Rahner does not demonstrate that paternity or passive spiration logically excludes the assumption of human nature. Instead, he begins with the fact of the Son's hypostatic union as a non-appropriated reality, a presence in the world that is personally unique to him, and concludes that this makes the Son's personal property of filiation a necessary aspect of incarnation. If it is the Son—the unique subsisting relation of filiation—who alone has assumed human nature, then this must *not* be possible to the Father or the Holy Spirit.

In other words, Rahner begins with what is contingent (the hypostatic union), notes that it is *de facto* unique to the Son, and then concludes that it must be uniquely possible to the Son *de iure*. This is consistent with Rahner's *Grundaxiom* and method in Trinitarian theology: he starts with the economy and concludes to God in himself. The problem is that Rahner follows this method so rigidly that he denies any other possible economy of salvation (though he ad-

---

86. See the Salmanticenses' discussion in *Cursus theologicus*, tract. 6, disp. 10, dub. 5, §§4–7 (Palmé, 3:440–44), where they argue that although "divine person" has an analogous *ratio* with respect to the three divine persons, it is still predicated of each of them (as it were) *quidditative*, not only *denominative*. This is the Scholastic way of saying that "divine person" is not just a label used to point out the Father, Son, and Spirit as a group, but that it really does say something meaningful about what the three are.

mits God's freedom not to create or not to reveal himself). As Guy Mansini, OSB, puts it, Rahner "often enough ... proceeds as did St. Anselm, seeking necessary reasons for the facts of the economy of salvation where St. Thomas sought merely the intelligibility of the facts."[87]

The Salmanticenses, in contrast, exemplify respect for the contingency of the economy: "Now if you ask why the person of the Son specifically rather than the others assumed our nature, the response is that no reason can be assigned for this *a priori* besides God's will, on which the carrying out of the mystery depended."[88] However, this does not mean that the Salmanticenses think there are *no* special reasons for the incarnation of the Son in particular.[89] Far from it, since after the above quotation they immediately add several, which they describe as "quite beautiful" (*pulchras satis*).[90] The point is that these are reasons of *fittingness*, not an argument that can be advanced *a priori* and far less one that imposes necessity.

It is true that the Son's eternal birth from the Father makes it highly appropriate that he be the one to be born in time. Nevertheless, the fact that the Son is the Father's immanent self-expression does not mean that the Father could only express himself econom-

---

87. Mansini, "Quasi-Formal Causality and 'Change in the Other,'" 306.

88. "Si autem inquiras, cur specialiter persona potius Filii, quam aliae, naturam nostram assumpserit? Respondetur nullam hujus a priori rationem posse assignari, quam Dei voluntatem, a qua mysterii executio dependit." Salmanticenses, *Cursus theologicus*, tract. 21, disp. 8, dub. 2, §1, no. 37 (Palmé, 14:27).

89. A criticism sometimes leveled against Aquinas and aptly responded to by Dominic Legge in *The Trinitarian Christology of St Thomas Aquinas* (Oxford: Oxford University Press, 2017), 123–28.

90. These are: First, the Word is the exemplar, the wisdom, through whom all things were made and so is fittingly the incarnate wisdom through whom they are elevated and restored. Second, the Son is a kind of mediator between the Father and the Spirit and so is fittingly the mediator between God and human beings. Third, it is fitting for the Father's Word and likeness to repair the divine likeness that human beings lost through disordered desire for knowledge. Fourth, clarity of expression is preserved when it is the Son of God who becomes the Son of man (a concern of Anselm's). Fifth, the Son proceeds from the Father and with him spirates the Spirit, and so he is the only divine person who can both be sent and send another, meaning that the Son's coming into the world both is a mission from the Father and results in the mission of the Spirit for our sanctification.

ically through the incarnate Son, as Rahner claims.[91] The analogy between eternal and temporal generation and the analogy between the Son as the uncreated Image of God and God's created image in human beings remain analogies. Therefore, there is nothing in the notion of assuming a human nature that logically contradicts the Father's paternity. As Aquinas explains, "The temporal filiation whereby Christ is called the Son of Man does not constitute his person, as does his eternal filiation, but is a certain consequence of his temporal nativity. Hence, if the term 'filiation' were applied to the Father or the Holy Spirit in this way, no confusion of the divine persons would follow."[92] Similarly, "being innascible befits the Father with reference to eternal birth, but a birth in time would not exclude this."[93]

Now, since filiation regards a person, not a nature, and one cannot participate in what he possesses eminently, the Salmanticenses hold with Aquinas that Christ's assumed human nature does not make him an adopted son of God.[94] Christ is the Father's natural Son, not a son of the whole Trinity by adoption. In this way, they agree with Rahner that the Son's personal properties come into the world with him. Nevertheless, they do not agree that this property would necessarily have to be bound up with any possible incarnation. Instead, the filial property of the Son, which precludes his being an adopted son even as incarnate, characterizes the incarnation precisely because God has willed it so: "It is clear that the grace of union intended by God and that *de facto* exists demanded as such

---

91. Rahner, *The Trinity*, 31–33.

92. "Filiatio temporalis, qua Christus dicitur Filius Hominis, non constituit personam ipsius, sicut filiatio aeterna: sed est quiddam consequens nativitatem temporalem. Unde, si per hunc modum nomen filiationis ad Patrem vel Spiritum Sanctum transferetur, nulla sequeretur confusio divinarum personarum." *ST* III, q. 3, a. 5, ad 1 (Leonine, 11:63). Here Aquinas is alluding to an argument put forward by Anselm, who denied the possibility of the Father's or the Spirit's incarnation, in *Epistola de Incarnatione Verbi*, chap. 10, in *S. Anselmi Cantuariensis archiepiscopi opera omnia*, ed. Franciscus Salesius Schmitt (Rome, 1940), 2:25–26.

93. "Patri convenit esse innascibilem secundum nativitatem aeternam: quod non excluderet nativitas temporalis." *ST* III, q. 3, a. 5, ad 3 (Leonine, 11:63).

94. *ST* III, q. 23, a. 4 (Leonine, 11:267–68); and Salmanticenses, *Cursus theologicus*, tract. 21, disp. 23, dub. 1 (Palmé, 16:406–41).

being terminated in the person of the Word not with reference to the general concept either of subsistence or of divine personhood but determinately as such a person is the natural Son of God."[95] Here there is continuity with Rahner's real concern. While the Salmanticenses hold with Aquinas and the general Scholastic tradition that any of the divine persons could become incarnate, they do not think that this threatens the radical diversity of the three divine persons or the fact of the incarnation as God's self-communication. The Son does not assume human nature simply as a generic divine person (*secundum conceptum communem personalitatis divinae*) but precisely as the Son (*ut talis persona est Filius Dei naturalis*). The second person of the Trinity *is* the subsisting relation of filiation, and so when this person becomes the term of an assumed human nature, he does so as the Father's natural Son.[96] While Rahner takes this to mean that the incarnation must be filial, the Salmanticenses only take it to mean that the incarnation *of the Son* must be filial.

This also means that, following Aquinas, the Salmanticenses distinguish between the incarnation as the assumption of a human nature and the incarnation as a divine mission. The Son's incarnation is his visible mission, but the notion of incarnation does not *per se* entail that of divine mission. Thus, Aquinas states, "We say that the Son is sent with reference to his incarnation by the fact that he is from another. The incarnation would not be enough for the notion of mission without this."[97] Therefore, the fact that the Father cannot be sent does not mean that he could not become incarnate, and the

---

95. "Liquet gratiam unionis a Deo intentam, et de facto existentem petivisse per se terminationem ad personam Verbi non secundum conceptum communem, aut subsistentiae, vel personalitatis divinae, sed determinate ut talis persona est Filius Dei naturalis." Salmanticenses, *Cursus theologicus*, tract. 21, disp. 33, dub. 3, §1, no. 70 (Palmé, 16:472). Cf. Salmanticenses, *Cursus theologicus*, tract. 21, disp. 8, dub. 2, §2, no. 42 (Palmé, 14:31).

96. Salmanticenses, *Cursus theologicus*, tract. 21, disp. 8, dub. 2 (Palmé, 14:27–54).

97. "Mitti autem dicitur Filius secundum incarnationem, eo quod est ab illo: sine quo incarnatio non sufficeret ad rationem missionis." *ST* III, q. 3, a. 5, ad 3 (Leonine, 11:63). See Salmanticenses, *Cursus theologicus*, tract. 6, disp. 19, dub. 2, §1 (Palmé, 3:730–31).

fact that the Spirit is from the Father and the Son does not rule out the possibility of his incarnation.

As Mansini points out, quasi-formal causality undergirds Rahner's claim that only the Son could become incarnate.[98] This is how Rahner explains in ontological terms his identification of the Trinity as encountered economically with the immanent Trinity. If the Son and humanity can be compared on the analogy of formal and material principles, then there is a unique complementarity between them, just as the human soul (formal principle) is uniquely apt to inform the human body (material principle).[99] Similarly, Rahner describes Christ's humanity as a *Realsymbol* of the Son and the human body as a *Realsymbol* of the soul.[100] This aptitude runs both ways, which is why Rahner considers human but not angelic nature to be capable of assumption into hypostatic union. If there is a (quasi) formal-material complementarity between the Son and human nature, then just as another divine person could not assume, another kind of nature could not be assumed.[101] This makes sense from a Rahnerian perspective, since the logical possibilities for how God could relate to the world must be grounded in the character of the divine persons themselves. One element of this is the ontologically exclusive aptitude of the Son to assume and of humanity to be assumed.

Now the Salmanticenses also speak of quasi-formality in their explanation of the hypostatic union when they write:

The Word as terminating the humanity does not conserve it by efficient causality. For this kind of conservation, just like production, is from an extrinsic efficient principle and depends on the influence of the Word together with and inseparably from the other divine persons. Rather, [the Word] conserves [the humanity] quasi-formally by giving himself to it

---

98. Mansini, "Quasi-Formal Causality and 'Change in the Other,'" 298, 301–3.
99. Mansini, "Quasi-Formal Causality and 'Change in the Other,'" 297–98.
100. Rahner, "The Theology of the Symbol," in *TI*, 4:236–45, 245–52; and *The Trinity*, 31–33.
101. As Mansini observes; "Quasi-Formal Causality and 'Change in the Other,'" 298n24.

and taking to himself the place of a created subsistence, without which a humanity cannot naturally be conserved. Hence, just as a proper created subsistence does not conserve [its] humanity by efficient causality but quasi-formally in a terminating manner (for it is necessary in this way for the humanity's conservation), so also the uncreated subsistence does not conserve it through an active influence but with a proportional *ratio*, i.e., by completing and terminating the nature, in such a way such that it is conserved inseparably by all the divine persons.[102]

In this passage, the terminology and meaning partly agree with Rahner, given that the Salmanticenses use quasi-formality as a way to distinguish the Son's unique relation to his humanity from its production and conservation in being by the whole Trinity as efficient cause. Nevertheless, the Salmanticenses and Rahner disagree on what this quasi-formality is.

The Salmanticenses analyze the hypostatic union according to the traditional Thomistic notion of a mixed relation. The *act* of assuming a human nature, viewed in terms of efficient causality, is common to the whole Trinity, as are all acts *ad extra*. This act gives rise to a relation (the hypostatic union), of which the Word alone is the personal terminus. The relation itself is mixed—real in the humanity assumed and merely conceptual in the divine person. Thus, the Salmanticenses specify that the Word is uniquely related to his assumed humanity as the formal terminus of this relation.[103] The re-

---

102. "Verbum in quantum terminat humanitatem, non conservat illam effective: hujusmodi enim conservatio, sicut et productio, est a principio effectivo extrinseco, et dependet ab ipso Verbo simul, et indivise cum aliis personis influente. Sed conservat illam quasi formaliter dando se ipsam; et subrogando se ipsum loco subsistentiae creatae, sine qua humanitas nequit naturaliter conservari. Unde sicut subsistentia propria creata non conservat humanitatem effective, sed quasi formaliter terminative: est enim hoc modo necessaria, ut humanitas conservetur: ita subsistentia increata illam non conservat per influxum activum, sed proportionali ratione, videlicet complendo, et terminando naturam, ut conservetur indivise ab omnibus divinis personis." Salmanticenses, *Cursus theologicus*, tract. 21, disp. 5, *De actione Incarnationis, sive assumptiva, et ejus termino*, dub. 1, §2, no. 45 (Palmé, 13:496).

103. This is similar to how Paul de Letter justifies Rahner's use of quasi-formal causality: "[God] terminates the relation of the soul's real union with him without being himself the subject of a real relation of union with the soul." See de Letter, "Divine Quasi-Formal Causality," *Irish Theological Quarterly* 27, no. 3 (1960): 223. The problem is

sult is that his humanity, although a complete nature, does not subsist in its own right but instead depends on the divine person.[104] In other words, the Son's humanity is that whereby he is a man, but it is not that whereby he subsists or is a person.[105]

Because the Son terminates the union, the use of *quasi formaliter* as a way to distinguish his unique influence is warranted since, as terminus, the Son alone communicates to the assumed humanity the perfection of being his. In this, the person of the Son acts *quasi formaliter terminative*, performing the function that a created subsistence otherwise would. The analogy for the Salmanticenses is, therefore, the following: the Word is to his assumed humanity as a created subsistence is to its humanity. They even explain that the Word does not function in this way through an active influence (*per influxum activum*). This is very different from Rahner's view, which uses "quasi-formal" in a way more akin to the relationship of an individual soul to its body. Thus, Rahner affirms that the Son's quasi-formal relation to his assumed humanity makes his incarnation the only possible hypostatic union, while the Salmanticenses deny this.

Another difference is that Rahner views the incarnation as an instance of the broader quasi-formal divine self-communication to the world and so makes the Holy Spirit a quasi-formal cause of the justified soul, whereas the Salmanticenses take the usual Scholastic view that uncreated grace results from created grace produced by God as efficient cause. The Salmanticenses anticipate Rahner's critique, however, and emphasize that the divine indwelling does not consist *only* in the fact that the justified enjoy created gifts.[106] The

---

that, as Mansini shows in the places cited, Rahner is not applying "quasi-formal" in *only* this sense but in a way that more strongly emphasizes the exclusive, ontological complementarity of the quasi-form (the Son) and quasi-matter (humanity).

104. Cf. the Salmanticenses' discussion in *Cursus theologicus*, tract. 21, disp. 8, dub. 1, §1, no. 3 (Palmé, 14:3).

105. See Michael Gorman, *Aquinas on the Metaphysics of the Hypostatic Union* (Cambridge: Cambridge University Press, 2017), 36–38, 46–52.

106. On the Salmanticenses' doctrine of the divine indwelling, see especially Enrico di Santa Teresa, "Dio in noi secondo i Salmanticesi," *Vita Carmelitana* 6 (1943): 64–78; and Wenceslao Carlos Flores Gómez, *Las misiones trinitarias en los teólogos tomistas*

justified possess the divine persons *directly*, even though this occurs by means of created grace. This is because the habit of sanctifying grace together with charity does not stop in itself or in created divine gifts but extends to the divine persons themselves.[107] In other words, when God justifies a soul, he changes the soul (not himself), but this is precisely so that the justified person can know, love, and so possess *God himself* in a new way.[108] In fact,

by means of sanctifying grace and its gifts, the divine persons are not in the rational creature as the one known in the one knowing and the one loved in the one loving in just any way whatever but as the one known in the one who knows with the knowledge that is sufficient for the perfect love of friendship specifically and as the one loved in the one loving through the aforementioned love. Therefore, it is not just that they will be there through a mere objective and affective presence exclusive of a true, real, and personal presence.[109]

This is to say that the justified person knows and loves God as *truly, really, and personally present within*, not only as the external object of knowledge and love. What God effects in the soul is an "inseparable presence" of friends.[110] The friendship itself may be created, but the soul's three divine friends are not. If, *per impossibile*, God were not present in all things by his essence, presence, and power, the di-

---

españoles del siglo XVII: Aportaciones y límites a la cuestión de la inhabitación (Toledo: Instituto teológico San Ildefonso, 2017), 294–96.

107. Salmanticenses, *Cursus theologicus*, tract. 14, disp. 1, cap. 1, §3, no. 20 (Palmé, 9:12).

108. Salmanticenses, *Cursus theologicus*, tract. 6, disp. 19, *De missione divinarum personarum*, dub. 5, §4, no. 98 (Palmé, 3:760).

109. "Media gratia sanctificante, et ejus donis personae divinae non sunt utcumque in creatura rationali, tanquam cognitum in cognoscente, et amatum in amante, sed tanquam cognitum in cognoscente ea cognitione, quae sit sufficiens ad perfectissimum amorem amicitiae secundum speciem, et tanquam amatum in amante per praedictum amorem: ergo non solum erunt ibidem per solam praesentiam objectivam, et affectivam excludentem veram, realem, ac personalem praesentiam." Salmanticenses, *Cursus theologicus*, tract. 6, disp. 19, dub. 5, §2, no. 84 (Palmé, 3:755).

110. "Ex se exigat unionem inter amicos non solum secundum affectum ... sed etiam per inseparabilem praesentiam." Salmanticenses, *Cursus theologicus*, tract. 6, disp. 19, dub. 5, §2, no. 84 (Palmé, 3:755).

vine persons would still dwell in the souls of the just.¹¹¹ Moreover, the invisible missions are a cause of further created grace, not only its effect.¹¹²

Actually, the way in which Rahner prioritizes the Holy Spirit's presence in the soul via quasi-formal causality runs the risk of minimizing the Son's invisible mission and the Father's personal presence in the justified soul, which, in turn, would fail to do justice to the scriptural witness: "If a man loves me, he will keep my word, and my Father will love him, and we will come to him and make our home with him" (Jn 14:23). Rahner himself professedly wants to avoid this risk, insisting that the Father and the Son are also personally present in the justified soul.¹¹³ However, Rahner does not explain how this is possible if the Spirit becomes the soul's quasi-form. Possibly, the Father and Son would be present only indirectly, through their presence in the Spirit by perichoresis.¹¹⁴ Alternatively, if each divine person were an accidental quasi-form of the soul, it becomes difficult to prioritize the Holy Spirit.¹¹⁵ By not applying quasi-formal causality to the Spirit, the Salmanticenses allow for the presence of all three divine persons in the justified soul as the personally present objects of supernatural knowledge and love.

Further, it is worth noting that the Salmanticenses maintain that the missions of the Son and Spirit necessarily entail each other: The Son cannot be sent without sending the Spirit, and vice versa.¹¹⁶ In

---

111. Salmanticenses, *Cursus theologicus*, tract. 6, disp. 19, dub. 5, §1, no. 77 (Palmé, 3:752).

112. See Salmanticenses, *Cursus theologicus*, tract. 6, disp. 19, dub. 3, §1, no. 37 (Palmé, 3:738).

113. Rahner, "Concept of Uncreated Grace," in *TI* 1:345n5.

114. A concern that Neil J. Ormerod raises in "Two Points or Four?—Rahner and Lonergan on Trinity, Incarnation, Grace, and Beatific Vision," *Theological Studies* 68, no. 3 (September 2007): 667–68.

115. The closest we could get in this case would be to say that the Father and the Son become accidental quasi-forms, like the Spirit, but that they depend on the Spirit's presence in the way that some accidents (e.g., color) depend on the presence of others (dimensive quantity), although all of them inhere directly in the subject. To the best of my knowledge, Rahner never explains his theory in these terms.

116. Salmanticenses, *Cursus theologicus*, tract. 6, disp. 19, dub. 2, §2 (Palmé,

this way, they are immune to Rahner's critique of theology that "accepts the incarnation and the descent of the Spirit as two facticities connected by a rather extrinsic bond."[117] For the Salmanticenses, the missions of the Son and Spirit are inseparable (though distinct) because the persons themselves are sent.[118] Therefore, while the precise form that the present economy has taken is not the only form it could have taken, the Salmanticenses do agree with Rahner that any divine *self*-communication would have to include all three persons in their distinction and mutual relativity: The Father could not be sent, and the Son and Spirit can only be sent (in some way) together.

Next, in response to Rahner's concern that the Son's incarnation not be revelatory in only a verbal manner (i.e., only on the basis of Christ's statements about the Father, about himself as Son, and about the Holy Spirit), it would be a mistake to isolate verbal statements entirely from personal experience. It is natural for human beings to come to know one another through words and deeds that disclose their personal character. This applies to Christ as well.[119] The fact that Christ's words about himself contribute to our ability to recognize him as the Son does not lessen the encounter's personal character: it just makes it human (see, e.g., Mt 11:27; Mt 16:16–17; Mt 21:34–38; Mt 24:36; Mt 26:64; Mk 14:61–62; Mk 15:39; Lk 22:70; Jn 1:14; Jn 3:16; Jn 20:27; Acts 9:20; Gal 1:15–16).

Along the same lines, one should not forget the fact that God providentially saw fit to prepare for his Son's coming by progressive revelations in the Old Testament. For example, God fosters an ex-

---

3:731–33). Once again, the Salmanticenses are building on Aquinas. See *ST* I, q. 43, a. 5, ad 3 (Leonine, 4:450).

117. Rahner, *The Trinity*, 85.

118. Salmanticenses, *Cursus theologicus*, tract. 6, disp. 19, dub. 2, §2, no. 19 (Palmé, 3:731–32); and dub. 3, §2, no. 45 (Palmé, 3:740–41).

119. For a metaphysical account, see Gorman's comments about Christ's assuming not just a "human nature" but a whole "human reality," including his various accidents. The assumption of a human nature includes the assumption of concrete circumstantial attributes. These attributes along with Christ's words and deeds contribute to the revelation of his personal identity as the Father's Son. See Gorman, *Aquinas on the Metaphysics of the Hypostatic Union*, 45–46.

pectation of divine sonship in the Christ, the anointed successor of David. Thus, God says through the prophet Nathan, "I will be his father, and he shall be my son" (2 Sm 7:14; 1 Chr 17:13; Ps 2:7). While such promises refer directly to the adoptive filial status enjoyed by all of David's successors, they also prepare for the eventual recognition of David's ultimate successor, the Christ, as the Father's natural Son. This is why, at the Annunciation, Gabriel alludes to God's oath to David (2 Sm 7:8–16; Lk 1:28–33), referring to Jesus as "the Son of the Most High" (Lk 1:32) and "the Son of God" (Lk 1:35).

In other words, God fostered within his chosen people a sensitivity to divine sonship as a quality of the future redeemer. This shows that the filial character of the Son's incarnation does not render verbal revelations superfluous. God expected that Jesus would be recognized as the Son by his deeds and words because they would correspond to a deeply entrenched expectation among the chosen people. The verbal revelations of Jesus as the Father's "beloved Son" at Jesus' baptism (Mt 3:17; Mk 1:11; Lk 3:22) and transfiguration (Mt 17:5; Mk 9:7; Lk 9:35; 2 Pt 1:17) confirm this.

Similarly, it does not seem possible for the justified person to have an internal experience of sanctification unambiguously attributable to the Holy Spirit in his personal distinction. In reality, it is on the basis of numerous verbal statements about the Spirit as God's gracious gift that the Church attributes to the Spirit a special role in sanctification and, indeed, recognizes his divinity and relativity to the Father and the Son (e.g., Lk 11:13; Jn 3:34; Jn 4:10; Jn 14:16; Jn 20:22; Acts 8:18–20; Acts 11:15–17; Acts 15:8; Rom 5:5; 1 Cor 12:8; 2 Cor 1:22; 2 Cor 5:5; 1 Jn 3:24).

In any case, it is not my purpose here to argue a detailed theology of revelation or of grace. All I meant to show was that it should be presumed—against Rahner—that the Father or the Spirit could also have become incarnate and that God's presence in the world, whether in the incarnation or in grace, should not be conceived of in terms of a rigid quasi-formal causality that would limit God's economic freedom.

The Salmanticenses show that one can maintain a large piece of what Rahner most wants to maintain—that God is not hiding himself behind the scenes but actually revealing himself in the economy—without needing to limit the possibilities of the incarnation. The *Son's* incarnation has an essentially filial character. If the Father or the Spirit had assumed human nature, the resulting incarnation would be quite different.[120] Theology should affirm God's absolute power to have acted economically otherwise than he has, but it should also remain fairly agnostic about what other economies would look like.

To this extent, the Salmanticenses' *de facto* Christocentrism aligns with Rahner's *de iure* Christocentrism but without unduly limiting God's freedom to act *ad extra*. Both Rahner and the Salmanticenses hold that the economy is shaped from the beginning by being ordered to the Son incarnate as its end.[121] Just as a different kind of incarnation would look profoundly different, a world not ordered to the incarnate Son would look profoundly different. The Salmanticenses can truly say with Rahner that God has made the present world to communicate himself personally in the Son incarnate, who sends the Spirit.

Actually, in this area, the Salmanticenses are more faithful to one of Rahner's key principles than Rahner himself is. This is Rahner's stress on the fact that the *recipient* of divine self-communication is included in the notion of communication.[122] For Rahner, this means that human nature must be precisely what God would make if he wanted to communicate himself personally *ad extra*. For the Salmanticenses, it means only that because God has wanted to communicate himself personally *ad extra* through the incarnate Son as redeemer, he has made the world as he has. This is to say that the incarnate redeemer is the reason why God has disposed the rest of the economy as he has.

---

120. Cf. Aquinas's remark in *ST* III, q. 3, a. 5, ad 2 (Leonine, 11:63).
121. Cf. what Legge says about Aquinas in *Trinitarian Christology of Aquinas*, 126–27.
122. See, e.g., Rahner, *The Trinity*, 88–89.

However, this does not entail that God could not have made a different world with markedly different kinds of creatures who would more fittingly receive divine self-communication in a way other than through the Son's assumption of human nature, or that God could not have chosen a different proximate end for his creation that would have shaped the economy differently.[123] Because Christ the redeemer is the *finis cuius gratia* of the world God has actually made, he colors its theological intelligibility, though without replacing or destroying the natural constitutions or ends proportionate to various creatures. For example, marriage is natural to human beings, but according to the Salamanca view it can be said that God devised human sexual distinction in the first place so that it would signify the union of Christ with his Church. Again, eating has a natural purpose, but God also gave human beings the ability to eat so that Christ could give himself to us in the Eucharist. Wheat and grapes have their own built-in teleologies, but these are subsumed into the service of higher human ends, which are, in turn, subsumed into a divine purpose through the Christian sacrament of the altar. Even the very existence of human beings is ordered to the redeemer as final cause. So while it is perfectly correct to define man as a "rational animal" in terms of his natural constitution, we might well call him the animal God made for personal union and, in fact, the animal God made to die for. The present economy and human capacity to receive God's self-communication in this economy are correlative, but there is no reason to rule out the possibility that God could have enacted a different economy with creatures capable of receiving his self-communication in a different way.

Therefore, Rahner's Christocentric emphases are better articulated within a *de facto* Christocentrism than in his own *de iure* view. This is precisely what the Salmanticenses allow us to do. They avoid Rahner's error of limiting God's freedom to act economically while preserving some of his key concerns, especially the Son incarnate as

---

123. Cf. *De motivo Incarnationis*, dub. 2, §2, no. 50 (Palmé, 13:314).

Rahner and the Cross

This section and the following need only be brief. In short, Rahner sees Christ's death as following the pattern of human death in general and as essentially the capstone to his human life of perfect responsiveness to the Father.[124] Rahner insists that Christ's acceptance of the cross does not change God's mind. Christ's acceptance of the cross is an expression of the divine mercy and makes it concretely present in the world (the cross is a *Realsymbol*), but he does not offer something to God that God accepts as outweighing human sin. This, Rahner fears, would be a mythological view of the paschal mystery simply unacceptable in the modern world.

As I will summarize in the next chapter, Hans Urs von Balthasar offers the most important critique of Rahner's soteriology. The main problem is that Rahner applies a general theology of death to Christ when he should have taken Christ's death as unique (although not divorced from the general experience). Consequently, Rahner struggles to account for the scriptural witness, which stresses the themes of atonement, sacrifice, propitiation, and the necessity of Christ's suffering and death. The Bible never makes Christ's death simply the seal or guarantor of his life but instead portrays his life as oriented to his "hour" for human salvation.

Besides the avoidance of a "mythological" presentation of salvation, Rahner thinks that undue emphasis on the cross as atoning sacrifice may undermine the primacy of Christ as the apex of divine self-communication. In other words, because he stresses that Jesus is the goal of the world from the start, Rahner fears that stressing the cross would also put Jesus in the position of coming into the world as a response to human sin and, thus, not the goal of a process independent of sin. Rahner endorses Scotus on this point.

---

124. Rahner, *On the Theology of Death*, 57–58, 63–67; *Foundations of Christian Faith*, 279–80, 296–97; and "Jesus Christ and Christology," 32–41.

Here the Salmanticenses have a clear contribution to make, since their whole theory is meant to show the compatibility of the Scotistic emphasis on Christ's primacy in God's intention with the Thomistic intuition that Christ's coming is essentially God's response to human sin. Put into Rahnerian terms, the Salmanticenses' view is that because human transcendence includes an element of freedom—that is, because the capacity to receive divine self-communication can be exercised in the mode of acceptance or of rejection—God preferred to communicate himself to the world in a way that included the overcoming of humanity's initial rejection.

This would make Christ the apex of divine self-communication precisely as the one who has definitively overcome human rejection of this gift. This makes redemption from sin an essential aspect of Christ's coming, not just a secondary consequence of it. Emphasizing the cross does not have to undermine the primacy of Christ as the goal of the world and apex of divine self-communication.

Rahner and *gratia Christi*

When addressing the Salmanticenses' view of original justice in relation to Christ, I explained how they hold together two elements: that, like all other works *ad extra*, original justice was ordered to Christ as *finis cuius gratia* and that Christ was not, therefore, the head of Adam in the state of original justice. In other words, the Salmanticenses distinguish between grace given in view of Christ or with an order to Christ as final cause and grace that is properly *gratia Christi*, whether this means grace merited by Christ or grace given physically through his humanity.

This distinction is helpful when applied to Rahner's view of created grace. One of the problems in Rahner's account, as just noted, is a lack of emphasis on the cross. The other side of this is a view of the development of the spirit-matter world toward God, culminating in Christ, that does not sufficiently account for an economic rupture, as in the case of original sin. Rahner tends to stress the continuity of God's self-communication as a single process, and he tends to stress this because he wants to hold that Christ is the apex of this process.[125]

The Salmanticenses give us a way of affirming Christ as the apex of such a process while also accounting for the loss of original justice as a real loss. Viewed in itself, the state of original justice was meant to continue, and so the fall was a real interruption of the trajectory God had given to humanity. Viewed from the larger perspective of God's overall plan, however, the permission of sin and the resulting loss were themselves ordered to the coming of Christ. This is possible because the grace of original justice was given for the sake of Christ but was not itself *gratia Christi*. Thus, with Rahner, the Salmanticenses hold that Christ governs the whole plan of God for history as *finis cuius gratia*, but they do not flatten out the complexities of the economy to the point of simply making all grace *gratia Christi*.

Similarly, the Salmanticenses acknowledge a dependence (again, in the order of final cause) of the grace of the angels on Christ, but they do not, as Rahner does, hold that the angels' original grace was *gratia Christi*. Christ did not merit the essential grace of the angels (Heb 2:16), but in God's overall providential plan, Christ is indeed the goal of the angels' grace. The advantage of this view is that the economy of angels and human beings is unified by its end, which is ultimately God in himself and proximately the Word incarnate. Now it is true that the angelic and mundane realms necessarily have God as their source and end and would to this extent be unified no matter what. Nevertheless, the actual dispensation, in which God has willed a much closer association of angels and human beings and has directed them to Christ, is a *de facto* arrangement.

In contrast, Rahner's desire to hold to Christ's primacy as the culmination of divine self-communication to the world forces him to associate the angelic realm *per se* with the mundane, since he sees

---

125. See especially Rahner, "Theological States of Man," in *Sacramentum mundi*, 6:174; "Salvation: IV. Theology: C. Soteriology," in *Sacramentum mundi*, 5:435–36; and Rahner and Vorgrimler, *Dictionary of Theology*, s.v. "Christocentrism."

no other way to extend the significance of Christ to the angels.[126] The Salmanticenses' view allows for a purely spiritual realm in which the angels have their own prerogatives and concerns, but it also acknowledges their friendship with and ministry to human beings along with their subordination to Christ. In other words, Rahner's desire to unify the realms of spirit and matter in light of Christ's universal significance can be pursued in line with the Salmanticenses by maintaining the unifying influence of Christ as *finis cuius gratia* without thereby having to hold to an intrinsic ontological unity of the angelic and mundane realms. In the case of both original justice and the grace of the angels, then, the Salmanticenses offer a corrective to Rahner while preserving his main emphasis on Christ as the primarily intended goal of the process of divine self-communication.

Rahner, the Salmanticenses, and Ascending Christology

I have just presented three ways in which the Salmanticenses can assist Rahner. Now I will look at how Rahner can assist the Salmanticenses. In particular, I will show that the ascending aspect of Rahner's transcendental Christology has some valuable insights that can be integrated with those of the Salmanticenses.

First of all, it must be kept in mind that Rahner does not think that the ascending aspect of his transcendental Christology allows one to conclude *a priori* that the incarnation has occurred or even, strictly, that it is possible.[127] The ascending approach only establishes a framework of expectation, of looking for a singular union of God

---

126. Rahner, *The Trinity*, 90. That these realms are distinct comes across in the profession of Lateran Council IV: "Credimus et simpliciter confitemur, quod unus solus est verus Deus ... creator omnium invisibilium et visibilium, spiritualium et corporalium, qui sua omnipotenti virtute simul ab initio temporis, utramque de nihilo condidit creaturam, spiritualem et corporalem, angelicam videlicet et mundanam, ac deinde humanam quasi communem ex spiritu et corpore constitutam." Lateran Council IV, *De fide Catholica* (Tanner, 1:230).

127. Rahner, "On the Theology of the Incarnation," in *TI*, 4:110; and "Jesus Christ and Christology," 4–7.

and man as the ultimate expression of human transcendence. Only the encounter with Jesus results in the knowledge that this union has actually occurred.

There is apologetic value in Rahner's ascending approach, but when Christ is recognized for who he is, he is encountered precisely as the one who is from above. It is true that divine self-communication to humanity is only complete if it includes the human acceptance of that communication and that, therefore, we must attend to Jesus' human openness to God. However, we cannot ascribe a distinct human subjectivity to Christ, since this would be a form of Nestorianism, which Rahner professedly wishes to avoid.[128] Jesus' human openness is always the human openness of the second person of the Trinity.

Further, the divinization of Christ's humanity follows on the fact of that humanity's assumption into hypostatic union, not vice versa. This means that the conformity of the Son's human will to his divine will is a consequence of the hypostatic union, not a condition for it (Heb 10:5). Therefore, as man, Christ wills to be God in the sense that the hypostatic union he possesses is agreeable to his will, but his human will is not a principle that contributes to the production of the union.[129] The latter would entail adoptionism. As man, Christ wills to be who he is, but he is not who he is *because* he wills it.

There are not two subjects in Christ (Nestorianism), nor do Christ's human acts result in his becoming divine (adoptionism). Therefore, there is one divine subject in Christ possessing divine and human principles of action, and the human principle of action (human nature) must be radically dependent on the divine principle of action (divine nature) and the divine subject (the person). The result is that ascending Christology ultimately depends on descending Christology, just as what is human ultimately depends on what is di-

---

128. Nevertheless, there is at least a Nestorian tendency in Rahner's later thought, as Thomas Joseph White shows in *The Incarnate Lord: A Thomistic Study in Christology*, Thomistic Ressourcement Series 5 (Washington, D.C.: The Catholic University of America Press, 2015), 91–100.

129. Cf. what Aquinas says about the Trinity's notional acts in *ST* I, q. 41, a. 2 (Leonine, 4:422–23).

vine. "No one has ascended into heaven but he who descended from heaven, the Son of man" (Jn 3:13).

One can, however, affirm Rahner's ascending approach in the order of discovery: Jesus' human openness to God and experience of God may attract and resonate with us before we come to know him as the Son incarnate and may even lead us to recognize him as such (cf. Jn 4:1–42). But in the actual encounter with Christ, when we recognize him for who he is, we find that he is not first of all a man seeking God (Mt 7:8), but God seeking man (Mt 18:11). He is a man who wills union with God only because he is first God who wills union with man (cf. 1 Jn 4:19).

A pleasing illustration of this can be found in Christ's relationship to the Jerusalem temple. From a young age, his human devotion to his "Father's house" is recognized as significant (Lk 2:49). This is why Mary keeps this mystery "in her heart" and meditates on it and why St. Luke records the event in his Gospel (Lk 2:51). In his public ministry, Jesus' zeal for the temple impresses his disciples (Jn 2:17) and becomes a chief point of controversy surrounding him (Mt 26:61; Mk 14:58; Acts 6:14). This is an example of Jesus' reverence for the Father, a supreme expression of the gift of fear of the Lord.[130] This affect of reverence, a component of human openness to the divine, does not remain general but instead is expressed precisely in Jesus' cultural and religious setting: It centers on the temple. The sensitivity that Jesus, being a devout Jew, bears toward God's holiness is what ends up revealing him as the Father's Son.

In this way, Jesus' human receptivity to God does not contribute to the hypostatic union but results from it, and yet, at the same time, that human receptivity remains important both in itself and in relation to us. In itself, Jesus' human receptivity is needed because the hypostatic union involves a complete humanity. The uncreated grace of union does not obviate the need for the assumed humanity to be

---

130. On this point, see Dylan Schrader, "Christ's Fear of the Lord according to Thomas Aquinas," *The Heythrop Journal* (early access, 2017), https://doi.org/10.1111/heyj.12487.

perfected and sanctified through created gifts.[131] In relation to us, Jesus' human receptivity to God identifies him as an exemplary man worth attending to in divine matters, attracts others to him, and ultimately contributes to the disclosure of his identity as the Son once it becomes evident that only the incarnate Son could show such filial reverence for the Father.

The apologetic value of such an ascending approach integrates well with the Salmanticenses' *de facto* Christocentrism. Christ and humanity belong together in God's plan. They combine as *finis cuius gratia* and *finis cui* to form the overall end that God envisioned for the world. Because of this complementarity, Christ is the answer to humanity's questioning. He was not the only possible answer, but in the real world all people are ordered to him as their proximate end, and he is ordered to them as their redeemer. Human transcendence is not only an ontological openness to God but also a moral openness to God's *plan*. In this providential plan, Christ (*finis cuius gratia*) and the human race (*finis cui*) belong together.

Further, Christ himself enters into the *finis cui*.[132] He, too, is a man and, thus, a beneficiary of the incarnation, even its chief beneficiary. He is "the first-born among many brethren" (Rom 8:29). But Christ is first-born precisely as redeemer. In its fallen state, humanity is open and searching for God not only because of its innate transcendence but also because of evil. Wonder about God includes wonder about why he permits evil and what his response to it might be. Humanity's powerlessness to heal itself of the wound of sin means that the search for an "absolute savior," as Rahner speaks of, is also a search for the divine physician. Searching humanity comes to recognize in a confused way that it needs a cross it cannot bear.

Christ is the most sensitive of all to the need for the cross (Lk 24:26) and the only one who can bear it. His human docility to divine providence reveals him as redeemer and even as divine. *Because*

---

131. See Legge, *Trinitarian Christology of Aquinas*, 136–43.
132. *De motivo Incarnationis*, dub. 1, §6, no. 32 (Palmé, 13:295), and dub. 1, §7, no. 40 (Palmé, 13:303).

he is the man with such insight into humanity's need, he must be God who can fill that need. Only one who possessed divine joy by nature could become the "man of sorrows" by choice (Is 53:3). In this way, Rahner's ascending Christology adds apologetic value to the Salmanticenses by characterizing the human openness of Christ as revelatory of his divinity.

CONCLUSION

Karl Rahner rightly highlights Jesus as the culmination of God's self-communication to the world and, therefore, as the goal of creation. However, he fails to account for God's freedom to have realized a quite different providential order and ends up blurring the distinction between God and the world, especially by holding to a quasi-formal view of grace. The focus on self-communication also causes Rahner to lose sight of the value of the cross.

The Salmanticenses offer a way of holding to Christ's primacy while simultaneously respecting divine transcendence and the contingent character of the incarnation as it has been realized in the economy, including its essential reference to Christ's passion and cross for the sake of human salvation. At the same time, the ascending aspect of Rahner's approach can integrate with the Salmanticenses, emphasizing Jesus' own human openness to the Father in the Holy Spirit. In the final chapter, I will turn to Hans Urs von Balthasar to show how a recovery of the Salmanticenses can also benefit a Christocentrism very different from Rahner's.

6

Cruciform Center

Hans Urs von Balthasar and the Salmanticenses

For Rahner, incarnation means that the Son becomes creation at its peak. For Hans Urs von Balthasar, it is the Son's plunge into creation's infernal depths. For Rahner, the cross is incidental to the incarnation, but for Balthasar, Christ's cross and descent into hell are the completion of his incarnation. Balthasar's emphasis on the redemptive character of the incarnation resonates with the Salmanticenses, who also hold that Christ is the goal of creation precisely as redeemer. However, like Rahner, Balthasar limits God's economic freedom, articulating a *de iure* Christocentrism based on the Son's intra-Trinitarian obedience to the Father and the extension of that into the world as *kenosis*.

In this chapter, I will first explain Balthasar's Christocentrism. Then, I will show how the Salmanticenses are a corrective to Balthasar's limitation of God's economic freedom. Finally, I will explore how Balthasar's emphasis on kenosis within a dramatic-aesthetic approach can enliven the Salmanticenses' own view.

THE SHAPE OF BALTHASAR'S
CHRISTOCENTRISM

Central to Hans Urs von Balthasar's theology is the drama of divine freedom, which gives rise to and rescues human freedom. "The creation of finite freedom by infinite freedom is the starting point of all theo-drama."[1] At the heart of this interplay is Christ, the God-man, in whom divine and human freedom meet. "As the center of the world, he is the key to the interpretation not only of creation, but of God himself."[2] This theme remains consistent throughout Balthasar's many writings.

When Balthasar speaks of Christ as center and interpretive key, he always has in mind Jesus of Nazareth in all his concrete circumstances, since this is how the Son has actually chosen to glorify the Father and thus reveal himself, too, as the Father's Son in the unity of the Spirit. One of Balthasar's methodological choices is thus to avoid speculating about possible worlds.[3] For him, pure possibles are worth discussing only insofar as they "[keep] open the realms of the real freedoms, divine and human, in their interrelatedness."[4] Given that God has freely chosen to make human freedom, to create a space for it, counterfactuals are nothing but the obverse side of realized free choices. Therefore, anything we say about a hypothesis according to which God would not have created the world or would not have decreed the incarnation is theologically valuable only to help us understand what God has actually done.

In particular, Balthasar wants to avoid two extremes: saying that God's choice of the present order of history is arbitrary and say-

---

1. Hans Urs von Balthasar, *Theo-Drama: Theological Dramatic Theory*, trans. Graham Harrison, (San Francisco: Ignatius Press, 1990), 2:271.
2. Hans Urs von Balthasar, *A Theology of History*, trans. not given (San Francisco: Communio Books / Ignatius Press, 1994), 20. Cf. Balthasar, *My Work in Retrospect*, trans. not given (San Francisco: Communio Books / Ignatius Press, 1993), 22–23, 60.
3. See especially Balthasar, *Theo-Drama*, 2:268–70.
4. Balthasar, *Theo-Drama*, 2:270.

ing that God could realize nothing but the present order.[5] The existence of sin in the present order of history is a special difficulty, and Balthasar also wants to avoid the impression that sin is "the necessary precondition for love's epiphany."[6] Instead, for finite freedom to be itself, to be open to multiple possibilities, God must give it space to act by adopting a kind of latency—a hiddenness, as it were—while still accompanying human action.[7] Given humanity's actual abuse of its freedom by sinning, God manifests the center of his single plan for history through the death, descent, and resurrection of the Son.[8]

The singularity of God's plan means, for Balthasar, that although Jesus' coming is in one sense a response to human sin, it has always featured centrally in God's choice. "God the Father set [the history of salvation] in motion with the express intention of leading up to the Son."[9] This means not only the old covenant but also the entire drama of human freedom. In fact,

> the Son's action is what history is for, his uniqueness sets it free to attain its proper character. The very fact that there could be any such thing as a Paradise, a Fall, a Flood, a Covenant with Abraham, a Law, a prophetic history, all has its meaningful center in the appearance of the Son, although the Son obediently submits to the pattern of what has been and what is. History is subject to the Son and the Son to history. But the subjection of history to the Son subserves the Son's subjection to history, which in turn is only an expression of his subjection to the will of the Father.[10]

Balthasar expressly intends this rule to apply not just to sacred history in the strict sense but to human history as such: "We may therefore say that [the] 'natural law,' and consequently the whole of human history, is, like salvation history in the narrower sense, related to the life of Christ as promise to fulfillment; only with this difference, that it is mediated through salvation history."[11]

---

5. Balthasar, *Theo-Drama*, 2:268–69.
6. Balthasar, *Theo-Drama*, 2:269.
7. Balthasar, *Theo-Drama*, 2:271–75, 282–84.
8. Balthasar, *Theo-Drama*, 2:275–82.
9. Balthasar, *Theology of History*, 61–62.
10. Balthasar, *Theology of History*, 62.
11. Balthasar, *Theology of History*, 64.

God, then, plans and provides for the whole of human history—including creation and the fact of human sin—with a view to Christ, whose coming is an act of obedience to the Father. The difference between salvation history and history as a whole is whether the relation to Christ is direct or indirect, but both are ultimately referred to Christ. Thus, "the life of the Son is related to the whole of history as the world of ideas which gives it its norms and its meaning. Indeed, his life, though it does not cause, is nevertheless the very condition for the possibility of there being a Fall, and so of there being a Paradise or indeed any creation at all, if it were to be for man's good."[12] In this way, Christ is the precondition in the divine plan for everything else and also, therefore, the exemplar and interpretive key for that plan.

It may seem that Balthasar is therefore a Scotist, since he maintains the primacy of Christ in God's plan for history.[13] Actually, he rejects the Scotistic view and in this differs essentially from Rahner. In fact, Balthasar's rejection of the Scotistic view comes across most strongly in his critique of Rahner's soteriology.

Balthasar's vivid reply to Rahner in *Cordula oder der Ernstfall* (*The Moment of Christian Witness*; 1966) is well-known.[14] If love of neighbor counts as love of God *simpliciter*, if Christ's cross is a result of God's will to save but not a cause of salvation, and if Christ himself is only the culmination of a process of divine self-communication that goes on everywhere, then we have lost the basic biblical message that "God shows his love for us in that while we were yet sin-

---

12. Balthasar, *Theology of History*, 64–65.
13. Juniper B. Carol classifies Balthasar as a Scotist in *Why Jesus Christ?*, 461. Edward T. Oakes is more careful, saying only that Balthasar "leans to" the Scotistic view. Edward T. Oakes, *Pattern of Redemption: The Theology of Hans Urs von Balthasar* (New York: Continuum, 1994), 220, 226. See also the discussion in Junius Johnson, *Christ and Analogy: The Christocentric Metaphysics of Hans Urs von Balthasar* (Minneapolis: Fortress Press, 2013), 124–32.
14. See especially Hans Urs von Balthasar, *The Moment of Christian Witness*, trans. Richard Beckley (San Francisco: Communio Books / Ignatius Press, 1994), 100–113, 119–30. See also Balthasar, *Mysterium Paschale: The Mystery of Easter*, trans. Aidan Nichols (San Francisco: Ignatius Press, 2000), 146–47n106; and Balthasar, *Theo-Drama*, 4:273–84.

ners Christ died for us" (Rom 5:8). The result is that, rather than emphasizing the uniqueness of Jesus Christ and the Christian message, Christians find common ground with atheists in a "bland and shallow humanism."[15] As Karen Kilby observes,

> Rahner is concerned to avoid any suggestion that Jesus' death changes God's mind (which would appear mythological and unworthy of belief to the modern person) and uses a general theology of death to help understand the meaning of Jesus' death. Balthasar is concerned on the other hand to point us to the full and very particular drama of the Passion.... The significance of Jesus' death is to be brought out not by relating it to some more general and familiar phenomenon, but precisely by highlighting its *unfamiliarity*, its distinctiveness, and its uniqueness.[16]

For Balthasar, it is not first and foremost the incarnation that matters (as in Rahner)—it is the cross.

Thus, given that the Son incarnate is the most significant element in God's plan for history,

> it was in view of him that the venture of having any such thing as a world and world history could be made at all; in view of him and his Church that such a thing as the creation of man and woman could take place (Eph 5:31–32); in view of him and his mother that the expulsion of sinners from God's Paradise could be justified (Gen 3:15). Just as there is a true sense in which sin caused the Cross, and Christ would not have come as Redeemer if the guilt of mankind had not called on him to make good in this way the pledge given at the creation, so in another and deeper sense the Cross is the condition for the possibility not only of sin but of existence and predestination itself.[17]

---

15. Balthasar, *Moment of Christian Witness*, 126.
16. Karen Kilby, "Balthasar and Karl Rahner," in *The Cambridge Companion to Hans Urs von Balthasar*, ed. Edward T. Oakes and David Moss, Cambridge Companions to Religion (Cambridge: Cambridge University Press, 2004), 264. The same criticism of Rahner on this point is found in John W. Williams, "Karl Rahner on the Death of Christ," *Journal of the Evangelical Theological Society* 14, no. 1 (1971): 41–50.
17. Balthasar, *Theology of History*, 65–66.

Balthasar, of course, is well aware of the Scholastic discussion over the rationale for Christ's incarnation.[18] In fact, in support of the claim quoted above, he cites Godoy.[19]

In Balthasar's 1955 essay, "Kleiner Lageplan zu meinen Büchern" ("A Short Guide to My Books"), he describes his own view this way: "Christ is the concrete first Idea of the creating God—not in the Scotist sense—and thereby the goal of the world."[20] Similarly, in his 1969 *Theologie der drei Tage* (*Mysterium Paschale: The Mystery of Easter*), Balthasar distances himself from agreement "with the Scotists when they describe the Passion as an accidental addition in terms of the principal aim of the Incarnation, the glorification of the Father by the Son who unites all things in himself" as well as from Suárez's attempt to harmonize the Thomistic and Scotistic views.[21]

18. See especially Balthasar, *The Theology of Karl Barth: Exposition and Interpretation*, trans. Edward T. Oakes (San Francisco: Communio Books / Ignatius Press, 1992), 327–34.

19. The quotation—actually two passages from Godoy that Balthasar combines—is: "Ordine intentionis prius fuit volitus Christus, non solum quoad substantiam Incarnationis, sed etiam quoad circumstantiam proximae passibilitatis, et ut actualis Redemptor, quam res ordinis naturalis, et pertinentes ad ordinem gratiae, et permissio peccati [in genere causae finalis; posterius tamen in genere causae materialis].... Per passionem meruit nobis, ut essemus, siquidem nostra substantia ... fuit praedestinationis nostrae effectus, et consequenter fuit praemium meriti passionis, et mortis Christi." Godoy, *Disputationes theologicae in tertiam partem*, tract. 1, disp. 8, §6, no. 115 (Hertz, 1:142); and tract. 14, disp. 57, §4, no. 51 (Hertz, 3:392). I have given the Latin text as found in Godoy. Balthasar omits the part in brackets. As it appears in Balthasar's work, this quotation contains the unfortunate typographical error of *possibilitatis* in place of *passibilitatis*, which leads Balthasar to render the relevant part: "nicht nur was das Allgemeine der Menschwerdung angeht, sondern auch die besondere Weise ihrer unmittelbaren Ermöglichung und sein Erscheinen als der Erlöser gerade dieser Welt," an error carried through into the English translation: "not only as regards the Incarnation in general, but in the particular manner in which it was immediately made possible." Hans Urs von Balthasar, *Theologie der Geschichte: Ein Grundriss, neue Fassung*, new ed. (Einsiedeln: Johannes Verlag, 1959), 50–51; and Balthasar, *Theology of History*, 66. Godoy, however, is referring to the fact that Christ became incarnate in flesh actually liable to suffering, a standard challenge to the Scotistic position. Balthasar also cites the second part of this passage from Godoy in *Theology of Karl Barth*, 327.

20. Balthasar, *My Work in Retrospect*, 23. Balthasar makes a similar comment rejecting the Scotistic view in *Dare We Hope "That All Men Be Saved"?*, trans. David Kipp and Lothar Krauth, 2nd ed. (San Francisco: Ignatius Press, 2014), 184–85. Cf. also Balthasar, *Moment of Christian Witness*, 107.

21. Balthasar, *Mysterium Paschale*, 11, 41n2.

Instead, Balthasar argues that the Son's incarnation is essentially—not accidentally—ordered to the passion. In this way, "the Cross is the centre of the world's history, for it transcends the categories of 'elect' and 'non-elect'.... It is the mid-point, too, of all creation and predestination, inasmuch as we were predestined, in Christ's blood, to be children of God 'before the foundation of the world' (Ephesians I, 4ff)."[22] It is not just Christ who is the precondition for creation and the permission of the fall: it is the cross. Everything is ordered to Christ's coming, but Christ's coming is itself ordered to the cross. In his examination of the Fathers, Balthasar explains that East and West are in close agreement that "the Incarnation happened for the sake of man's redemption on the Cross."[23] Thus, "the Incarnation is ordered to the Cross as to its goal."[24] In fact, the incarnation itself is already kenosis, and so contains within it the same downward trajectory as the cross.[25]

Here one must keep in mind what Balthasar says about possible worlds, as noted above. The drama God has actually chosen to enact has real value precisely because God has chosen it. "Once we have avoided these two extremes [either that God's choice of worlds is arbitrary or else that God had to make the present world if he would make one], there is nothing hindering us from extolling the world God actually chose as the best, *because* it has been chosen by God, in his absolute freedom, as the adequately clear embodiment of the 'idea' of the freely obedient Son."[26] A merely possible world, of course, has no actual value. As Balthasar recognizes and avoids, God is not drawn by some outside good. Instead, he creates it.

To be sure, Balthasar upholds God's freedom not to create the

---

22. Balthasar, *Mysterium Paschale*, 16. Of course, despite the determination by divine freedom that Christ will suffer on the cross, Jesus remains free in his obedient acceptance of it. Balthasar, *Mysterium Paschale*, 17–20.
23. Balthasar, *Mysterium Paschale*, 20.
24. Balthasar, *Mysterium Paschale*, 22.
25. Balthasar, *Mysterium Paschale*, 23–26, 89–91.
26. Balthasar, *Theo-Drama*, 2:269.

world—God alone is necessary in the absolute sense.²⁷ If, however, God does make a world with free creatures, the Son (even prescinding from the question of his incarnation) must be its "ground and goal."²⁸ This is because, being God from God, the Son is the exemplar of received freedom: "Every worldly dramatic production must take its bearings from, and be judged by, the ideal nature of this coincidence of freedom and obedience [*Gehorsam*] or of self-being and consciously acknowledged dependence."²⁹ Further, it is because God is a Trinity, because otherness exists in him, that God also has the freedom to make something other than himself.³⁰ Creation is the first kind of *kenosis*, grounded in the Trinity's interpersonal relations, which, with Sergei Bulgakov (1871–1944), Balthasar characterizes as "selflessness."³¹ In this way, the Son is the necessary exemplar of any possible creation.

If the present order is "best" in the sense of being chosen by God, Balthasar also holds that God's choice is not arbitrary. If this is the case, then there must be something about the configuration of the real world in comparison with worlds God could have made that renders the present one a more fitting choice. The drama we are in must have some feature, besides the mere fact of being real, to recommend it over other possible dramas.

For Balthasar, that element of fittingness is Christ's cross. It is the cross that allows human freedom, even in its very aberration and distance from God, to be reconciled from within divine freedom itself. The Son's personal character, as the one who receives from and obeys the Father, can be manifested most especially by the cross.

But could God have redeemed humanity in some way other than

---

27. Balthasar, *Theo-Drama*, 2:261.
28. Balthasar, *Theo-Drama*, 2:268.
29. Balthasar, *Theo-Drama*, 2:268. For the German text, see *Theodramatik*, vol. 2.1 (Einsiedeln: Johannes Verlag, 1976), 243–44.
30. Hans Urs von Balthasar, *The Glory of the Lord: A Theological Aesthetics*, trans. Brian McNeil, ed. John Riches (San Francisco: Ignatius Press, 1989), 7:213–14. See also the extended discussion in Balthasar, *Theo-Drama*, 5:61–109.
31. Balthasar, *Glory of the Lord*, 7:213–14.

Christ's death, descent, and resurrection? To begin with, Balthasar again emphasizes that such speculation may miss the point, only distracting us from what God has actually done.[32] Christ's death, descent, and resurrection are normative precisely because God has chosen them. Balthasar goes beyond this, however, by reflecting on what redemption must mean in terms of the opposition between divine and human freedom. If human freedom rejects God and thus finds itself lost, divine freedom can save it only by embracing human freedom without allowing it to become unfree.[33] In other words, God must let *himself* be freely lost and freely rescued so that lost humanity can be rescued in him. Other schemata are only our own imaginings, which end up envisioning redemption as something that God merely does to humanity in an extrinsic way. This is not redemption in the full sense, which requires, instead, the embrace and internalization of finite freedom mentioned above.[34] This can only happen through the Son's death, which Balthasar takes to be not just the act of dying but the state of *being dead* as well as the biblical "death" that is distance from God.[35] This entrance into alienation from God on Christ's part is an act of radical solidarity with sinners. "Christ no longer wishes to distinguish between himself, the innocent, and his guilty brothers. He does not even want God to distinguish."[36]

With this in mind, the *kenosis* of creation is possible to God only because he foresees and plans for "the second and truest kenosis, that of the Cross, in which he makes good the uttermost consequences of

---

32. Balthasar, *Mysterium Paschale*, 137.

33. See Hans Urs von Balthasar, "Trinity and Future," in *Elucidations*, trans. John Riches (San Francisco: Ignatius Press, 1998), 81–83.

34. Balthasar, *Mysterium Paschale*, 137.

35. Balthasar, *Mysterium Paschale*, 148–81; *Glory of the Lord*, 7:229–30; and Balthasar, *Theo-Drama*, 4:487–88. See also Alyssa Lyra Pitstick, *Light in Darkness: Hans Urs von Balthasar and the Catholic Doctrine of Christ's Descent into Hell* (Grand Rapids, Mich.: Eerdmans, 2007), 304–5.

36. Hans Urs von Balthasar, "Christ the Redeemer," in Hans Urs von Balthasar and Adrienne von Speyr, *To the Heart of the Mystery of Redemption*, trans. Anne Englund Nash (San Francisco: Ignatius Press, 2010), 35. See also the discussion in Balthasar, *Glory of the Lord*, 7:136–42.

creation's freedom, and goes beyond them."[37] In other words, "free creation gives creatures genuine freedom and implies necessarily the risk of their going astray; such a risk can only be assumed responsibly if the God of love is able to gather in such lostness to himself. This is possible in no other way than by God's going in powerlessness to share in man's lostness, but out of obedience to God."[38] The intra-Trinitarian selflessness or obedience of the Son, which allows God to create in the first place, also guarantees that God can reconcile estranged creatures through the Son's obedience unto death.[39]

This is to say that if finite freedom turns from God and plunges humanity into death, the Son's obedience must embrace death as well: "Here the obedience of the Son of God represents the concrete universal idea of the relationship between heaven and earth in the form of crucified love; thus, in the highest contingency of free, divine love-creativity, it also attains that maximal 'necessity' (that is, omitting nothing) of a God-world relationship *qua major cogitari nequit*."[40] The reference to Anselm's *Proslogion* is illuminating.[41] In fact, Balthasar develops an idea of the incarnation's conditioned necessity quite similar to Anselm's: God need not create, but if he does create and free creatures go wrong, God's inability to fail at his purpose necessitates the incarnation.[42] For Balthasar, this is possible because the

---

37. Balthasar, *Glory of the Lord*, 7:214.

38. Balthasar, "Trinity and Future," 82. Cf. Hans Urs von Balthasar, "The Incarnation of God," in *Elucidations*, trans. John Riches (San Francisco: Ignatius Press, 1998), 65–68; and Balthasar, "Only If," in *Convergences: To the Source of Christian Mystery*, trans. E. A. Nelson (San Francisco: Ignatius Press, 1983), 136–40.

39. For Balthasar, the Son's obedience to the Father in allowing himself to be made incarnate is through the Spirit. See especially Hans Urs von Balthasar, *Theo-Logic: Theological Logical Theory*, trans. Graham Harrison (San Francisco: Ignatius Press, 2005), 3:48–50. This is one implication of Balthasar's "Trinitarian Inversion," that the Son's being made incarnate must also be mediated to him through the Spirit. See also the discussion in Rodney A. Howsare, *Balthasar: A Guide for the Perplexed* (London: T & T Clark, 2009), 127–29.

40. Balthasar, *Theo-Drama*, 2:271.

41. Balthasar refers to Christ's love and Christ himself as *id quo maius cogitari nequit* also in *Moment of Christian Witness*, 75, 95.

42. See especially Anselm, *Cur Deus homo?* I, chap. 16 (Schmitt, 2:74–75); II, chap. 5 (Schmitt, 2:99–100); II, chap. 6 (Schmitt, 2:101); and II, chap. 17 (Schmitt, 2:122–26). A key difference between Anselm and Balthasar is, of course, that Balthasar includes

Trinity's inner life itself already involves the "risk" of total surrender to another person.[43] Once again, the pattern of creation and redemption is founded on the distance in unity of the Father, Son, and Spirit.

Just as the *kenosis* of creation is possible because God is a Trinity, so too does Jesus' kenotic descent into God-forsakenness become the normative revelation of God's Trinitarian life: "This 'infinite distance,' which recapitulates the sinner's mode of alienation from God, will remain forever the highest revelation known to the world of the diastasis (within the eternal being of God) between Father and Son in the Holy Spirit."[44] Balthasar takes this to mean that only the Son—not the Father or the Holy Spirit—could become incarnate.[45] This is because Balthasar conceives of the assumption of a human nature precisely as an act of obedient *kenosis*, which preexists in the Trinity's inner life. The Father has no one to obey because he does not receive his will from another. The Spirit binds the Father and the Son together and so cannot distance himself from them. Only the Son, who goes forth from the Father but who remains bound to him by the Spirit, can push that self-same procession into creation through his incarnation.

As Balthasar repeats frequently, the Son's mission is his procession from the Father under a different mode. It is a mission he obediently accepts and, in this way, glorifies the Father, who is his source.[46] Thus, Balthasar sees obedience as a positive characteristic, one distinctive of the Son and therefore attributable to his divine person *via eminentiae*.

The application of the concept of obedience to the divine person is, of course, a figure of speech—an anthropomorphism. But, in the final

---

Christ's descent into the being-dead of God-forsakenness (spiritual death) in what accomplishes redemption, whereas Anselm includes only Christ's loving obedience unto the act of dying (physical death), with Christ's descent into the limbo of the Fathers as a triumphal application of redemption.

43. Balthasar, *Theo-Drama*, 5:244–46.
44. Balthasar, *Theo-Drama*, 3:228.
45. Balthasar, *Theo-Drama*, 3:226, 530.
46. Hans Urs von Balthasar, *The Christian State of Life*, trans. Mary Frances McCarthy (San Francisco: Ignatius Press, 1983), 77.

analysis, all human speech about God is anthropomorphic, and this figure has been made definitive and proper by the Incarnation of the Son (Phil 2:7).... The obedience of which the Son of God gave us an example in his human nature is by no means merely something that is grounded in his human nature and intended as an example for us insofar as we are creatures.... On the other hand, it is understandable that the world was created on the model of the Son ... because the filial mode of God's eternal love is the most proper, the most exemplary one for the right relationship between God and creature.... "If there were no interior, infinite communication and glorification in God himself, the substructure for the incarnation of a divine person would be lacking.... The Incarnation appears, not as an extraordinary event, but as the flower springing from a root buried in the trinitarian process, as the unfolding of a seed contained therein."[47]

The Son's human obedience, then, reveals who he is as Son—it is the mark of his divine personality translated into human existence. It is his "filial attitude, which looks to the Father in everything and wills to be in everything only the representation and brightness (Heb 1:3) of the paternal nature."[48] In this way, the Father's begetting the Son is the ground for the possibility of creation and simultaneously the ground for the redemption of errant creation through the Son's obedience unto death on a cross. Thus, for Balthasar, God preferred a world with the cross over one without it precisely because the cross (including the whole death-descent-resurrection event) manifests the Son's personal character *par excellence*. A greater obedience, *kenosis*, and distance in unity cannot be imagined.

Thus, the Son's death, descent, and resurrection are "the all-embracing event which establishes the possibility of human freedom and history."[49] This death-descent-resurrection event is like a "Platonic idea" in relation to all the possibilities of human freedom.[50] Balthasar's theology is thus Christocentric in the sense that

---

47. Balthasar, *Christian State of Life*, 78–79. The final quotation is from Matthias Joseph Scheeben, *The Mysteries of Christianity*, trans. Cyril Vollert (St. Louis, Mo.: Herder, 1954), 359.
48. Balthasar, *Christian State of Life*, 78.
49. Balthasar, "Trinity and Future," 84–85.
50. Balthasar, "Trinity and Future," 85. See also Johnson, *Christ and Analogy*, 118–21.

the Son can be the only possible "ground and goal" of any divine work *ad extra*.[51] In the concrete world, this means that the Son's death, descent, and resurrection are normative for a proper understanding of creation and of God himself. In this vein, Balthasar approvingly expounds St. Maximus the Confessor (ca. 580–662) to the effect that "the Incarnation—more precisely, the drama of Cross, grave, and Resurrection—is not only the midpoint of world history but the foundational idea of the world itself."[52] The result is that "by [God's] absolute free will, pain and death are eternally the language of his glory."[53]

Therefore, Christocentrism for Balthasar is not only *de facto* but *de iure*. It is not merely because the Son has, in fact, become incarnate and has, in fact, suffered death for human salvation that we look to him to learn the truth about creation and about God himself. Instead, Balthasar's Christocentrism entails a conditioned necessity. If God risks making free creatures, he also commits himself to redeeming them through the assumption of the created nature. This necessity extends not only to the fact of a redemptive incarnation but to the incarnation *of the Son* and, specifically, his death, descent, and resurrection.

One criticism that Balthasar levels against Rahner's approach is precisely that it cannot account for these concrete aspects of Christ's mission. Jesus is not only the God-man: he is the Son, with a given individual human nature, who lived, suffered, died, and rose. If all that mattered were God's self-communication, there would be no way to explain why the Son rather than the Father or the Holy Spirit should become incarnate, or why the incarnation should be limited to the assumption of one individual nature.[54] Most seriously,

---

51. Balthasar, *Theo-Drama*, 2:268.
52. Hans Urs von Balthasar, *Cosmic Liturgy: The Universe according to Maximus the Confessor*, trans. Brian E. Daley (San Francisco: Communio Books / Ignatius Press, 2003), 134. Cf. *Cosmic Liturgy*, 120.
53. Balthasar, *Theo-Drama*, 5:246.
54. Balthasar, *Theo-Drama*, 3:224. Rahner addresses the latter point in various places, as shown in the previous chapter, e.g., in "On the Theology of the Incarnation," in *TI* 4:110–11.

Rahner applies a general theology of divinization and a general theology of death to Jesus, both of which end up minimizing the dramatic power of the cross.

Again, Balthasar is concerned that Christology not become "the superabundant expression of anthropology."[55] Because the Word made flesh is unique, we cannot apply any overarching category of thought to him. God's assumption into *personal* union of a nature that is at an infinite distance from himself is not explainable by a general rule found elsewhere in creation. Instead, it becomes the singular standard for understanding the relationship of creatures to God.[56]

Besides Balthasar's concern with Rahner's reduction of Christology to anthropology, the debate between Erich Przywara, SJ (1889–1972), and Karl Barth (1886–1968) over the *analogia entis* features in the background.[57] Przywara argued for *analogia entis* as the basic form of Catholic thought. By this he meant that creation in its very creatureliness points to God as the transcendent source of creation and, therefore, that creatures bear a certain similarity (within an even greater dissimilarity) to God. Barth, however, in continuity with classic Reformed thought, insisted on fallen humanity's total

---

55. Balthasar, *Theo-Drama*, 3:224.
56. See Joseph Palakeel, *The Use of Analogy in Theological Discourse: An Investigation in Ecumenical Perspective*, Tesi Gregoriana, Serie Teologia 4 (Rome: Editrice Pontificia Università Gregoriana, 1995), 106–8; and Johnson, *Christ and Analogy*, 149–51.
57. Among other resources touching on this debate, see John R. Betz's introduction, in Erich Przywara, *Analogia Entis: Metaphysics: Original Structure and Universal Rhythm*, trans. John R. Betz and David Bentley Hart, Retrieval and Renewal: Ressourcement in Catholic Thought (Grand Rapids, Mich.: Eerdmans, 2014), 1–115; Keith L. Johnson, *Karl Barth and the Analogia Entis*, T & T Clark Studies in Systematic Theology 6 (London: T & T Clark, 2010); Thomas Joseph White, ed., *The Analogy of Being: Invention of the Antichrist or Wisdom of God?* (Grand Rapids, Mich.: Eerdmans, 2011); and Palakeel, *Analogy in Theological Discourse*. For Balthasar in particular, see also Manfred Lochbrunner, *Analogia Caritatis: Darstellung und Deutung der Theologie Hans Urs von Balthasars*, Freiburger theologische Studien 120 (Freiburg: Herder, 1981), 102–110; and Johnson, *Christ and Analogy*, 139–55. Balthasar's correspondence with Przywara and Barth is collected in Manfred Lochbrunner, *Hans Urs von Balthasar und seine Theologenkollegen: Sechs Beziehungsgeschichten* (Würzburg: Echter Verlag, 2009). The discussion is complex, and I simplify it greatly for my purposes here.

inability to control its access to God and, therefore, God's own prerogative to speak for himself in revelation and faith. In this, Barth privileged justification through Jesus Christ (*analogia fidei*) rather than creation as the basis for our idea of God, fearing that a concept of being derived from creatures and applied to God amounts, in the end, to idolatry.

There were conciliatory attempts to develop the notion of *analogia entis* in the light of Barth's critique. Gottlieb Söhngen (1892–1971), for example, argued that the Catholic view of the *analogia entis* has always actually existed within an *analogia fidei*. Balthasar, too, was extremely interested in showing that Barth's own theology was not as inimical to Catholic thought as previously supposed, that Barth's condemnation of the *analogia entis* might be the result of a misunderstanding, and that divine revelation and thus any theology, including Barth's, actually presupposes an *analogia entis*.[58]

Of greater relevance to our present purpose is Balthasar's identification of Christ as the "concrete *analogia entis*." He uses this expression in his 1950 *Theologie der Geschichte* (*A Theology of History*), but he develops it at length in the trilogy (1961–87).[59] There he explains that Christ not only joins uncreated and created being without identifying them but also eternally joins similitude and dissimilitude, proximity and distance, in his very personal identity as the Son. Balthasar understands the Son to be at an infinite distance from the Father and yet tethered to him by the bond of the Spirit. This distance is itself the ground for the possibility of creation, which makes the Son the exemplar of creation's relationship to God. In other words, all creaturely reality is modeled on the Son (analogy of attribution). The Son, in turn, exemplifies and bestows the right

---

58. Balthasar, *Theology of Karl Barth*, 86–167. Keith Johnson shows, however, that Balthasar's interpretation is based on only a partial picture of Barth and argues instead that Barth understood the *analogia entis* perfectly well and only began to reject it less vociferously when Catholic theologians refined what they meant by the idea in response to his critiques. Johnson, *Karl Barth and the Analogia Entis*, 193–201.

59. Balthasar, *Theology of History*, 69n5; Balthasar, *Theo-Drama*, 3:220–29; and Balthasar, *Theo-Logic*, 2:311–16. See also Lochbrunner, *Analogia Caritatis*, 283–87.

relation between creatures and God (proportion). Finally, in his incarnation, the Son sets up the following parallel within himself: humanity is to divinity as the Son is to the Father (analogy of proportionality).[60] In all these ways, Balthasar sees the general rule for the relation of creatures to God concretized historically in Jesus Christ.

It is important to note, further, that in Balthasar's thought, Christ is the concrete *analogia entis* precisely in his mission.[61] This includes, "above all, the capacity to suffer to the very extreme."[62] The Son can be the concrete *analogia entis* because he alone "knows what it means to live in the Father ... and he alone can know the full significance of being abandoned by him."[63] The recapitulation that Christ effects through his death, descent, and resurrection, then, "transfigures" the infinite distance between God and creatures into the Trinity itself (distance in unity).[64] Therefore, Christ must be the starting point, so that the analogy "that occurs as event in *Verbum-Caro* becomes the measure of every other analogy, whether philosophical or theological."[65]

Therefore, Balthasar's Christocentrism is a dynamic Christocentrism of redemption. The Son's obedient procession from the Father is the ground of any possible creation and the model for finite freedom. The Son's very identity—and thus that of the Father from whom he comes and of the Spirit who binds them together—is revealed most of all not in the incarnation *per se* but in the descent of the incarnate Son into the lowest limits of creaturely alienation from the Father. God thus allowed his creatures to disobey so that he could manifest the Son's even more radical obedience in reconciling them. Methodologically, this makes Jesus' death, descent, and

---

60. Balthasar, *Theo-Logic*, 2:316.
61. In addition to the passages from the trilogy just cited, see Balthasar, *Cosmic Liturgy*, 129–36; and the discussion in Hans Urs von Balthasar, *Love Alone Is Credible*, trans. D. C. Schindler (San Francisco: Communio Books / Ignatius Press, 2004), 83–90.
62. Balthasar, *Theo-Logic*, 2:314.
63. Balthasar, *Theology of History*, 69.
64. Balthasar, *Theo-Logic*, 2:315–16.
65. Balthasar, *Theo-Logic*, 2:314.

resurrection the hermeneutic key to the mystery of God and to creation itself. Having thus outlined Balthasar's Christocentrism, I will now give some reasons why a recovery of the Salmanticenses would be profitable for his thought.

THE SALMANTICENSES AND BALTHASAR

The Salmanticenses agree more with Balthasar than with Rahner in several key ways. First, the Salmanticenses' providential frame for the discussion is closer to Balthasar's dramatic approach than to Rahner's ontological approach. The Salmanticenses and Balthasar both discuss the incarnation primarily as an exceptional event planned by God, whereas Rahner focuses on the incarnation as the high point of a more general process. The Salmanticenses and Balthasar concentrate on freedom, while Rahner emphasizes the intrinsic possibilities of being. Second, the Salmanticenses and Balthasar highlight the cross. They see Christ primarily as redeemer from sin in God's plan. Rahner, in contrast, gives first place to the divine self-communication that occurs in Christ, the God-man, and sees redemption as a secondary aspect of this self-communication. Third, Rahner takes the strict Scotistic view and claims that Christ's coming is not primarily a response to sin, while the Salmanticenses and Balthasar hold that it is. Fourth, the Salmanticenses and Balthasar consequently claim that God permitted sin in the first place with a view to Christ the redeemer.

Even so, there is an area where the Salmanticenses can clarify and correct Balthasar's thinking and another where Balthasar's approach can supplement that of the Salmanticenses. Therefore, I will first examine how Balthasar limits God's economic freedom and how the Salmanticenses can avoid this tendency while preserving some of Balthasar's insights. Then I will explore how Balthasar's emphasis on *kenosis* can flesh out the Salmanticenses' understanding of the incarnation as an act of divine mercy.

Balthasar and God's Economic Freedom

One of Balthasar's methodological choices is to focus on the concrete world history and the unity of God's plan for it. Thus, he characterizes the Thomistic and Scotistic views as follows: "Actually Thomas and Scotus differ only in the fact that Thomas sees God's one concrete plan for the world: God had always willed the Incarnation from all eternity, but he had also foreseen from eternity man's sinful fall and thus willed the Incarnation as our redemption."[66] As this book shows, this estimation is misleading. Balthasar is right that Thomas emphasizes the concrete unity of the divine plan but wrong that Scotus does not. Scotus begins with the decree of Christ's predestination, which is the decree of Christ as he has actually come. Scotus accepts that God's decree of Christ and his foreknowledge of sin are both eternal. What he argues is that Christ's predestination is logically prior to and thus independent of God's foreknowing sin.

Scotus's *signa rationis* are meant to clarify the logical relationships among the objects of God's single effective decree. In fact, as evidenced in the second chapter, the strength of Scotus's arguments forced Thomists to clarify their position, often by enumerating their own *signa rationis*. There are elements in God's eternal plan that depend on others and are, thus, logically subsequent to them. For example, God's predestining Peter is logically prior to his foreknowing (with *scientia visionis*) Peter's merits. Christ's being predestined, in turn, is prior to Peter's being predestined. Appealing to the chronological co-eternity of all these in God's plan is not enough to resolve whether predestination gives rise to merits or vice versa. Similarly, the co-eternity of God's decree of the incarnation and his foreknowledge of sin is not enough to settle whether the incarnation essentially depends on sin or not. Some kind of conceptual ordering is needed.

The Salmanticenses share Balthasar's interest in preserving the unity of God's providential plan. They employ *signa rationis* and

---

66. Balthasar, *Theology of Karl Barth*, 327.

causal perspectives to delineate the relationships of dependence among the elements of God's plan, but they do this in a measured way, avoiding an excessive multiplication of conceptual stages that obscures the unity of God's plan and even the divine simplicity. The Salmanticenses share Balthasar's commitment to the singularity of the divine drama *ad extra*.

Most of the Scholastic discussion approaches the motive of the incarnation in a linear fashion. This is especially evident in hard-line positions such as those of Juan de Rada and Gabriel Vásquez. Even Francisco Suárez's attempt to harmonize Thomism and Scotism ultimately failed because he tried to fit both views into the same step-by-step schema by multiplying conditionals. In contrast, the Salmanticenses' approach is not linear but three-dimensional. In the fourth chapter, I used the analogy of a gemstone to explain this. The stone can be viewed from various vantage points, and yet the whole thing holds together and can be chosen simultaneously. The same applies to God's choice of the incarnation. From one angle, sin is first; from another, redeemed humanity; from another, Christ the redeemer. When God actualizes a given order of history, each element is chosen precisely as first from its own perspective and yet only in relation to the other elements. They are not related merely because they are chosen together, but are chosen together *as related*.

From one perspective Christ is first; from another he is last. Yet all perspectives bear a reference to him, and the whole order of history is chosen for him, so that Christ is the defining characteristic of the concrete order, the one in whom "all things hold together" (Col 1:17). This does not mean, as some strict Scotists would have it, that God has essentially willed Christ in the same way as if he had willed nothing else together with Christ. Rather, God has willed Christ as the lynchpin of the whole providential order, but by this very fact he has willed him only with reference to those things he willed to be essentially referred to Christ.

Now the image of a gemstone is clearly different from Balthasar's theatrical imagery. The former is static and inert, while the latter is dynamic and lively. Still, the same point can be articulated using the analogy of a play, as Balthasar does, to emphasize the planned-yet-free nature of world history. In this analogy, the lead role belongs to Christ, but this role by its very nature is situated in a relational context, with human beings as Christ's co-actors. In fact, the appearance of Christ even depends (in the Salmanticenses' view) on the sin in the first act of another key player (Adam). This does not make that original sin scripted in the sense of intended by God as the playwright, but it does mean that it is *permitted and accounted for*. The drama featuring Christ as the lead actor could then be viewed either as the real, grand production that the playwright always wanted or as the salvaging of a production that otherwise would have been spoiled by Adam's misstep at the beginning. Both perspectives are correct.

For Balthasar, it is also the case that God, as the faithful and ultimately successful playwright, *commits* himself to salvaging the production if he decides to put it on in the first place. Any fatal error will have to be made good for, lest the whole drama be in vain. The Salmanticenses disagree because, while they align with Balthasar's focus on the concrete world history, they also hold to a greater freedom of God *ad extra*.

The Salmanticenses insist that we can say very little about what other sorts of providential plans God would have made for other possible worlds and that determinate affirmations tend to take us beyond theology into divination. In this way, the Salmanticenses apply Balthasar's principle of focusing on the concrete even more rigorously than he does. Balthasar takes the Son's incarnation, cross, and descent as the *only* way for redemption to occur and as the best possible way of revealing the Son's personal character.[67] The Salmanticenses give us a way of saying that God's whole plan for the world is directed to the Son and his cross without imposing a necessity of means on this plan.

67. Balthasar, *Mysterium Paschale*, 148–81; *Glory of the Lord*, 7:229–30; and Balthasar, *Theo-Drama*, 4:487–88.

As I have observed, the Salmanticenses even assert: "Just as communicating himself hypostatically could be fitting to God, focusing on the nature of the good inclining to its communication, so also not communicating himself hypostatically could be fitting to God in an order to other ends, most lofty and hidden to us, such as he could think up in his wisdom."[68] In providential terms, the *ratio boni* is truly and properly understood in relation to the *ratio finis*. Thus, theology cannot rule out the possibility of other ends God could have chosen that would be better served by the Son's *not* becoming incarnate. At the same time, the Salmanticenses teach that the hypostatic union is the greatest good in terms of union (as uniting infinite and finite), in terms of giftedness (as bestowing utmost benefit on the creature), and in terms of being itself (specifically and physically surpassing all other created goods).[69] Therefore, the hypostatic union is the greatest created perfection in the actual providential order, and it remains the greatest perfection from the perspective of union, giftedness, and ontological goodness.

Some of the criticisms raised in the section on Rahner's version of the claim that only the Son could become incarnate apply here as well, but Balthasar's focus is decidedly soteriological.[70] For him, if God creates finite freedom, he commits himself to its redemption if it should go astray, and only the incarnate Son can achieve this redemption. Therefore, only the Son could become incarnate and, indeed, would *have to* become incarnate in the event of sin.[71] He

---

68. "Sicut se communicare hyposthatice [sic] posset esse Deo conveniens attenta natura boni inclinantis ad sui communicationem: ita se non communicare hypostatice posset esse Deo conveniens in ordine ad alios fines altissimos, et nobis occultos, quos ipsius sapientia posset excogitare." *De motivo Incarnationis*, dub. 2, §2, no. 50 (Palmé, 13:314).

69. Salmanticenses, *Cursus theologicus*, tract. 21, disp. 4, *De unione hypostatica*, dub. 3 (Palmé, 13:469–83).

70. For a brief comparison, see Vincent Holzer, "Karl Rahner, Hans Urs von Balthasar, and Twentieth-Century Catholic Currents on the Trinity," in *The Oxford Handbook of the Trinity*, ed. Gilles Emery and Matthew Levering (Oxford: Oxford University Press, 2011), 314–23.

71. See Balthasar, "Trinity and Future," 82; "The Incarnation of God," 65–68; and Balthasar, "Only If," 136–40.

alone is God who can be at a distance from God (the Father) while remaining tethered to him in God (the Spirit). Thus,

> if it is possible for one Person in God to accept suffering, to the extent of God-forsakenness, and to deem it his own, then evidently it is not something foreign to God, something that does not affect him. It must be something profoundly appropriate to his divine Person, for—to say it once again—his being sent (*missio*) by the Father is a modality of his proceeding (*processio*) from the Father.[72]

For Balthasar, the Son just *is* "eternal, infinite freedom in the mode ... of readiness, receptivity, obedience."[73] This is his personal, intra-Trinitarian characteristic, which is why he alone is capable of being sent into the world to embrace and rescue finite freedom.[74]

Like Rahner, Balthasar begins with the actual economy of redemption in Christ and, like Rahner, instead of limiting himself to studying its intelligibility, Balthasar tends to draw necessary conclusions. Because freedom is so important for Balthasar's dramatic method, his methodological and ontological errors are correlative. Methodologically he begins with contingency and concludes to necessity, while ontologically he blurs the distinction between the world and God. For example, in a different context, Balthasar writes, "Creation's gratuitousness (which also implies that it is *not* necessary) is grounded in the more fundamental gratuitousness of the divine life of the Trinity."[75] Here, creation's gratuity (non-necessity) is taken to be indicative of a gratuity (presumably an analogous non-necessity) in God himself. Taken at face value, this seems to mean that the Father somehow did not have to communicate the divine essence to the Son and that, consequently, the Son could have not existed and not possessed it.[76] This is an instance where

---

72. Balthasar, *Theo-Drama*, 3:226.
73. Balthasar, *Theo-Drama*, 2:267.
74. Balthasar, *Theo-Drama*, 3:529–31.
75. Balthasar, *Theo-Drama*, 5:507.
76. Cf. Balthasar, *Theo-Drama*, 5:93–94, 245–46. Balthasar, of course, would not say that the Son could have not existed but only that he eternally exists as the grateful recipient of the Father's giving of himself. Still, it is hard to conceive of the Father's generating

Balthasar's focus on God as an event (freedom) leads to confusion.

What develops is a kind of vicious circle. Beginning with God's economic freedom, Balthasar concludes that the Trinity's notional acts are free. Then, because the Son's being generated is free, obedience (freedom in the mode of reception) must *necessarily* be his personal characteristic. If this is the case, then human redemption—which can only occur through finite freedom's being brought, even in its errancy, to the interior of infinite freedom—must occur through the Son's obedience, which means the extension of his being into the world through the further *kenoses* of incarnation and cross. The result is that God is economically necessitated to this particular plan of redemption.

Why does Balthasar fall into this? Besides Barth's influence and Balthasar's concern for ecumenism and the real possibility of universal salvation,[77] there is his scriptural starting point. Balthasar is so committed to the Son's human life in all its details being revelatory of his personal identity as Son, so committed to the Son's visible mission as an extension of his procession, that Balthasar finds even the limits of the traditional *communicatio idiomatum* too restrictive. For Balthasar, the Son can only obey the Father as man because he first obeys him as God. Otherwise, the Son's economic obedience would merely be super-added to his divine person and so would fail to be either revelatory or salvific. Instead, Balthasar thinks, there must be something about the Son's divine personality that lends itself to being expressed through obedient *kenosis* in the world.

Now in addition to the issue mentioned above that intra-Trinitarian obedience implies the non-necessity of the notional acts, another problem is that intra-Trinitarian obedience would actually threaten the depth of the Son's *kenosis* for human redemption. As John Zizioulas observes,

---

the Son as being a *gift* warranting *gratitude* unless there is also some way of affirming that it did not have to occur.

77. On these, see especially White, *The Incarnate Lord*, 382–92.

revelation, *kenosis*, suffering, death, etc. are *freely* undertaken by God for our sake, precisely because they are not his natural condition, being extraneous to him. The economy manifests God's freedom precisely by showing that God is free to become what he is not rather than what he is in his own being. By projecting what God has done for our sake in the economy into what he is eternally in his Trinitarian being we implicitly undermine his freedom to become what he eternally is not.[78]

In other words, transposing God's economic acts directly onto his immanent life tends to make his free acts into necessary ones. Emphasizing God's freedom *ad extra* stresses his freedom to condescend to what he is *not*, to enter contingently into the realm of the contingent. Therefore, if the Son became man by virtue of an immanent obedience to the Father, then either the Son would not be free with respect to this act *ad extra* or else the Son would be perfected in his own immanent, personal character by an act *ad extra*. Both possibilities preclude true *kenosis*. In the former case, the Son's emptying is not a *self*-emptying. In the latter, it is ultimately self-serving. Christ would be losing his life not so much for our sake but precisely so that he could save it.

If the Son's divine personality hinged on his human acts, then these human acts would no longer be a merciful condescension but instead something aimed at the Son's own perfection. Therefore, maintaining the *de facto* but not *de iure* shape of the economy emphasizes God's economic acts, especially the Son's incarnation, as an expression of free love for creatures. It is because the Son did *not* have to become incarnate by intrinsic impulse or the Father's eternal command and because his personal identity is *not* perfected by becoming incarnate that his incarnation is a true *kenosis*.

Conflating fittingness and necessity is a risk of Balthasar's aesthetic approach. The method tends to make *decuit* into *debuit*. After all, it is certainly true that the way God has chosen to act tells us

78. John Zizioulas, "Trinitarian Freedom: Is God Free in Trinitarian Life?" in *Rethinking Trinitarian Theology: Disputed Questions and Contemporary Issues in Trinitarian Theology*, ed. Giulio Maspero and Robert J. Woźniak (New York: T & T Clark, 2010), 205–6.

something about him. What the Salmanticenses remind us is that this does not make freedom into necessity. The drama reveals the playwright, but a quite different drama might also have revealed him. In fact, this is what one would expect, given that the playwright far surpasses his work in depth of meaning. Further, the enacted drama is not influenced by the playwright alone. Its expressive power is shaped by the players themselves, whose specific characteristics are taken into account.

Thus, the Son's human obedience is revelatory and salvific, but we cannot make human obedience into divine obedience. The Son receives his will from the Father inasmuch as he receives the divine nature from him, but this does not make him immanently *obedient* to the Father.[79] Nor can the Son divest himself of divine being or suffer a kind of temporary damnation. Others have offered detailed critiques of Balthasar on these points.[80] Here I am interested in a derivative problem: if we posit a firmer line (methodologically) between fittingness and necessity as well as (ontologically) between the world and God and, therefore, maintain greater economic freedom on God's part, how can we hold that the Son's human obedience reveals him precisely as the Son? In other words, do firmer lines still allow the drama of salvation to be a *divine* drama? After all, if the Son's role is as fungible as I seem to have made it, it apparently no longer affects him personally and, therefore, no longer remains truly redemptive.

The Salmanticenses' *de facto* Christocentrism is helpful in sorting through this issue. They recognize a kind of conditional necessity for the incarnation, though of a weaker form than Balthasar's. For them, if God chooses to redeem the human race *by means of condign satisfaction*, the God-man is necessary, seeing as only he could offer a sacrifice of infinite value on humanity's behalf.[81] Further, the need

---

79. See Pitstick, *Light in Darkness*, 291–93; and Legge, *Trinitarian Christology of Aquinas*, 239–40.

80. See, for example, White, *The Incarnate Lord*, 288–305, 380–437; and the whole of Pitstick, *Light in Darkness*.

81. Salmanticenses, *Cursus theologicus*, tract. 21, disp. 1, dub. 5, §§1–3 (Palmé, 13:72–88).

of redemption in this mode adds a fittingness for *the Son* to become incarnate (as opposed to the Father or the Spirit). For the Salmanticenses, this consists especially in the fact that the Son is "between" the Father and the Spirit and so is fit to be the mediator between God and man.[82] His coming can be a mission (from the Father) that results in a mission (of the Spirit). This resonates with Balthasar's schema of redemption, where the Son distances himself from the Father, embraces humanity, and yet remains tethered to the Father in the Spirit in a kind of redemptive "bungee jump." In other words, like Balthasar, the Salmanticenses do hold that the loving obedience unto death of Christ the redeemer contributes to revealing him as the Son.

Now what I just stated about the necessity and fittingness of the Son's redemptive incarnation is a commonly held Thomistic view and not original to the Salmanticenses. Their contribution lies in the idea that God willed Christ as redeemer (concretely, in the mode of condign satisfaction through death on a cross) from the first as the proximate final cause of all other works *ad extra*. In this way, although not *de iure*, Christ's paschal mystery shapes and governs the entire actual order of history. This resonates with Balthasar's emphasis that "the Incarnation—more precisely, the drama of Cross, grave, and Resurrection—is not only the midpoint of world history but the foundational idea of the world itself."[83] Further, because Christ is the *finis cuius gratia*, he never becomes only a means of human redemption. He is not deprived of the lead role, nor does redemption become anything less than personal union with God (the last end) through Christ (the proximate end).

The Salmanticenses, then, offer us a way to affirm a dramatic, kenotic, cruciform Christocentrism without positing intra-Trinitarian obedience and without imposing economic necessity on this exact means of redemption. God does not commit himself to the

---

82. Salmanticenses, *Cursus theologicus*, tract. 21, disp. 8, dub. 2, §1, no. 37 (Palmé, 14:27–28).

83. Balthasar, *Cosmic Liturgy*, 134. Cf. *Cosmic Liturgy*, 120.

redemptive incarnation or to the Son's death by virtue of creating. Both redemption and redemption specifically through the Son's death are super-gratuitous, a pure outpouring of divine mercy. The Son's human obedience is a free condescension on behalf of disobedient humanity, not an act that perfects his divine personality. At the same time, this condescension is not an afterthought in God's plan and does not reduce Christ to a means. This is because God set the world in motion for the sake of the redeemer, who is first in his providential plan. *Stat crux dum volvitur orbis!* In other words, God made the world to receive cruciform mercy through the Son. On this point, Balthasar can also assist the Salmanticenses.

Balthasar, the Salmanticenses, and Divine Mercy

Balthasar's emphasis on *kenosis* can help flesh out the Salmanticenses' account of the incarnation as an act of mercy. Above, I stressed God's economic freedom—that is, his freedom to condescend to what he is not—as the ground of true *kenosis*. What are the economy's logical limits that would establish the bounds of a possible *kenosis* on God's part? First, I observe that human beings are the lowest intelligent creatures. God could have made other creatures than he has, including human beings as we know them. For example, he could have made rational animals of more than two sexes or with different external senses. Yet it seems impossible to unite spiritual intelligence with anything less than an animal body of some sort. This makes humanity (rational animality) the lowest possible intelligent nature and, therefore, the lowest possible nature capable of assumption into hypostatic union. Second, given that humanity consists in the union of a spiritual soul with a body as its substantial form, the severing of soul and body in death is the greatest physical evil possible for human beings.[84]

---

84. Short of annihilation, that is. Nevertheless, even in this case annihilation would be not so much a physical evil suffered by a human being as the ceasing-to-be of a human being. Just as creation is not a change, strictly speaking, neither is annihilation.

Therefore, the Son has *de facto* chosen to become the lowest kind of being he could become and to suffer the worst kind of physical destruction such a being could suffer. Further, he chose to peer into moral evil—which for him held no veneer of goodness—and to experience utmost physical and emotional suffering leading up to his death. All this remains true even if Christ was never bereft of the vision of the Father.[85]

In the Salmanticenses' view, we cannot explain Christ's *kenosis* (either in the incarnation itself or in its extension to the lowest possible limit of suffering and death on the cross) by appealing to it as the only possible means of redemption. In this, they disagree with Balthasar. Nevertheless, Balthasar's emphasis on *kenosis* as Christ's solidarity with sinners resonates with the Salmanticenses' view of the incarnation as motivated by mercy. Mercy is, after all, *misericordia*—taking another's misery to heart and so seeking to alleviate it. Thus, mercy properly belongs to one who is in a superior state and who condescends to someone in an inferior state, as when one who has food gives to someone who is hungry. In his omnipotence, God can exercise the *act* of mercy without actually *feeling* another's misery as his own.[86] As the Salmanticenses hold, following Aquinas, God could have saved the human race even by bestowing redemptive grace while asking no satisfaction for sins, and yet without violating justice.[87]

Still, Christ's incarnation together with his condign satisfaction for sins through suffering and death is a *far better* way for God to redeem us. This is because Christ's incarnation allows for the *human* mercy of God and the subsequent human atonement for sins. By assuming a human nature, the Son made himself capable of experiencing human misery as his own. "He had compassion [ἐσπλαγχνίσθη] on them, because they were like sheep without a shepherd" (Mk

85. See White, *The Incarnate Lord*, 328–39.
86. In fact, all acts of God *ad extra* can be called acts of mercy insofar as they are a benefit bestowed by a superior upon an inferior. Balthasar, *Dare We Hope*, 121–23.
87. *ST* III, q. 46, a. 2, ad 3 (Leonine, 11:437); and Salmanticenses, *Cursus theologicus*, tract. 21, commentary on *ST* III, q. 1, a. 2, no. 2 (Palmé, 13:10–11).

6:34). The positive divine act (the sending of Christ) gives rise to the receptive human act (Christ's visceral experience of the suffering of others as his own) and the subsequent positive human act (Christ's human will to alleviate it). "He had to be made like his brethren in every respect, so that he might become a merciful and faithful high priest in the service of God, to make expiation for the sins of the people" (Heb 2:17).

In fact, as man, Christ is also the greatest recipient of divine mercy, since he has received the greatest unmerited benefit from God (the grace of union). God's election of him as an individual man is *ante praevisa merita* in the strictest sense—not subsequent to consideration of any human acts, even Adam's sin. From the most significant causal perspective (*finis cuius gratia*), God, in fact, permits Adam's sin precisely because he intends Christ the redeemer. This also means that Christ enters into the incarnation's *finis cui*, which is to say that, as man, he enjoys God's mercy. This, too, is an aspect of *kenosis*, which can be viewed as the Son's emptying himself in the assumption of human nature but can also be viewed as the elevation of the assumed humanity to a kind of infinite dignity.[88] Christ's habitual grace, grace of headship, and merits are all possible because of the grace of union. This singular act of divine mercy founds the whole economy of salvation. All the mercy in the mystical body derives from the original mercy experienced by Christ the head.

Now God could have preserved all human beings from sin through the grace of Christ, as he did in Mary's case.[89] This preservation would *also* have been an act of mercy.[90] Instead, he chose to redeem Mary in the most perfect way and others in a less perfect

---

88. Cf. *ST* I, q. 25, a. 6, ad 4 (Leonine, 4:299).

89. *De motivo Incarnationis*, dub. 1, §4, no. 20 (Palmé, 13:282).

90. Pancheri argues that difficulties with the Scotistic view (e.g., the apparent separation of the fact of Christ's being predestined from the concrete modality of his coming) could be resolved by the notion of a general preservative redemption. In this way, Christ would be redeemer whether atoning for sin or preventing it, since in either case he would bestow a supernatural gift remedying creaturely peccability. Pancheri, *Universal Primacy of Christ*, 47–49.

way. We cannot compare the present order to a merely possible order in which everyone would have been preserved from sin and then assign a determinate reason why the present order is certainly preferable to that possible order. What theology *can* do, however, is explore the intelligibility of the present order. This is the approach that the Salmanticenses take. It is why they distinguish their disputation's first doubt (about the present order) from its second (about another merely possible order).

Because what God first intends is the God-man as redeemer of the human race, he wills that anyone, insofar as that person is human, should fall under Christ's headship and enjoy the fruits of his redemption. This is God's antecedent will to save. However, God's intention for the redeemer itself gives rise to the permission of sin, the permission of final impenitence, and, in short, everything good and bad that actually occurs. This is God's consequent will, where the mystery of evil lurks. This is an area where Balthasar is especially helpful. His emphasis on the aesthetic and dramatic aspects of the incarnation illuminates how Christ and his cross address the problem of evil.

Although good has no need of evil *per se*, human beings tend to appreciate goods more when they are contrasted with evils. For instance, we experience heightened vigor after convalescence and tend to be more grateful for the goods we have when their loss is narrowly avoided. Likewise, we often have greater insight into the good when it is contextualized by risk, loss, struggle, and triumph. These characterize the present order, in which God has chosen to impart mercy in a costly way (1 Pt 1:18). God has chosen to repair ruin rather than prevent it, and this choice becomes more intelligible from a dramatic or aesthetic perspective. It is the drama of the Lord's cross that reveals the mysterious depth of divine mercy *par excellence*: "All things become clear: what sin and lostness are. Why God allowed them to become reality. How he can bear them in himself and overcome them in his patience: by the pain of God in which the eternal love pours out its blood from wounds which transcend all inner worldly hurts."[91] In this way, Christ's *kenosis* manifests how divine providence directs all works and permissions to the union of the redeemer (*finis cuius gratia*) and the redeemed (*finis cui*). This consummate union, "the stature of the fulness of Christ" (Eph 4:13), answers the *why* of evil.

At the same time, Christ's *kenosis* does not unduly subordinate him to us.[92] Mercy is the act of a superior toward an inferior. His *kenosis* is a condescension for our sake, but Christ remains the *finis cuius gratia*. He is also our exemplar and our king, with the authority to command acts of mercy in imitation of himself (Mt 5:7; Mt 18:21–35; Mt 25:31–46; Lk 6:36; Jn 13:15).[93] Thus, Christ, the Church's head, directs the mystical body in acts of mercy in a visible way, while the Holy Spirit, the Church's heart, vivifies them from within in a hidden way.[94] "Receive the Holy Spirit. If you forgive the sins of any, they are forgiven; if you retain the sins of any, they are retained" (Jn 20:22c–23).

This also means that the cross is not incidental but essential to the life of the Christian wayfarer, just as it was essential to Christ's life (Mt 16:24; Lk 9:23).[95] Each Christian must empty himself, and this *kenosis* is itself a gift of divine mercy. The cross is the means divine providence has given to us to become like Christ. Accepting the cross also impels us to acts of mercy toward our neighbor. The cross is never self-serving. It only perfects through love of God and neighbor. "Now I rejoice in my sufferings for your sake, and in my flesh I complete what is lacking in Christ's afflictions for the sake of his body, that is, the church" (Col 1:24). In fact, the cross has only really been taken up when it has been taken up for someone else

---

91. Balthasar, "Trinity and Future," 84.

92. See Reginald Garrigou-Lagrange, "Motivum Incarnationis fuit motivum misericordiae," *Angelicum* 7, no. 3 (1930): 293–94.

93. Note that in the discourse on the sheep and the goats, Christ emphasizes that on the basis of their mercy or lack thereof, his followers will be judged by him *as man*.

94. ST III, q. 8, a. 1, ad 3 (Leonine, 11:127); and Salmanticenses, *Cursus theologicus*, tract. 21, disp. 16, dub. 1, §2, no. 6 (Palmé, 14:563).

95. Reginald Garrigou-Lagrange, *Christ the Savior: A Commentary on the Third Part of St. Thomas' Theological Summa*, trans. Bede Rose (St. Louis, Mo.: Herder, 1957), 101.

(Mt 16:25; Mk 8:35; Lk 9:24). Just as the cross is normative for the Church, so is mercy. It is even normative for the world under the present providence, since the merciful Christ is the end of all things.

CONCLUSION

While Balthasar is much closer to the Salmanticenses than Rahner, he commits the same methodological overreach as Rahner, beginning with the economy and concluding to supposed qualities of God's intra-Trinitarian life. For Balthasar, this means a kind of proto-obedience of the Son to the Father within the immanent Trinity, which also entails that only the Son could become incarnate. The Salmanticenses offer a way of holding, with Balthasar, that the Son incarnate is the goal of the created order precisely in his paschal mystery, but they do so without denying other possibilities and without positing obedience or *kenosis* within the Trinity itself. As I attempted to show in the final section of this chapter, Balthasar's aesthetic-dramatic approach also harmonizes nicely with the logical rigor of the Salamanca theory, particularly in terms of divine mercy.

Conclusion
That Primordial Mercy

Recovering the Scholastic discussion over the motive of the incarnation has much to offer the conciliar emphasis on Christ's centrality. This discussion began in earnest in the twelfth century, reached a turning point at the end of the thirteenth with Aquinas and Scotus, deepened from the fourteenth through sixteenth centuries, and continued through the seventeenth century until the waning and end of Scholasticism prior to the neo-Scholastic movement.

The Salmanticenses, who produced their great *Cursus theologicus* at the height of early modern Scholasticism, are especially worth looking to. They engage thoroughly with their predecessors and contemporaries and draw broadly from Scripture and the Fathers. They show themselves familiar with the most important arguments and objections to their own theory. In short, they outstrip many of their peers in the breadth and rigor of their work. At the same time, the Salmanticenses also exemplify a certain elegance, a simplicity in their principles. By combining key distinctions, particularly the aspects of final cause *cuius gratia* and *cui* along with a two-stage view of God's "decision-making process," they avoid the confusion and excess sometimes found in Baroque Scholasticism. In the same conceptual moment, God wills the world for Christ (*finis cuius gratia*) and Christ for the world (*finis cui*).

Karl Rahner and Hans Urs von Balthasar, whom I examined in the final chapters of this book, represent two different, postconciliar views on Christ's centrality. Both end up affirming a near-necessity in the incarnation. Rahner finds it practically unthinkable that God would elevate humanity to grace without the incarnation, whereas Balthasar holds that God can only redeem through the incarnation and thus commits himself to it in the event of sin. Both hold that only the Son can become incarnate. In contrast, the Salmanticenses take the view that God can and did bestow grace that was not *gratia Christi*, that God could have redeemed humanity in a way other than through Christ's cross, and that any of the divine persons could have become incarnate. While the Rahnerian and Balthasarian approaches amount to a *de iure* Christocentrism, the Salmanticenses offer a *de facto* Christocentrism.

Rahner sees Christ as central because he is what the whole spirit-matter cosmos aspires to. Balthasar sees Christ as central because he empties himself so completely as to make room for the whole errant creation within himself. Rahner emphasizes the incarnation *per se*, while Balthasar emphasizes the cross. Yet both visions blur the line between God and creation. This ontological blurring is tied up with a methodological overreach. In Rahner, the ontological blurring takes the form of divine self-communication (uncreated grace) via quasi-formal causality. For Balthasar, the ontological blurring occurs in the Son's kenotic descent to the point of real alienation from the Father, which is itself possible because obedience is the Son's intra-Trinitarian characteristic to begin with. In both Rahner and Balthasar, the methodological overreach is a tendency to begin with God's contingent, economic acts and conclude to necessary truths about God's immanent life in a way unwarranted by revelation. In other words, it is a tendency to confuse fittingness with necessity.

This is where the Salmanticenses are the most helpful of all. Their providential perspective is rooted in Thomistic principles. They are committed to God's transcendence and freedom *ad extra*. These principles lead them to hold with St. Thomas that the incarnation is essentially redemptive. At the same time, they also affirm

Christ's primacy in the divine plan. Thus, they teach that Christ is the first willed and intended by God, that all other works of nature and grace are directed to him as their proximate end, and that his coming is itself essentially a work of mercy, ordered to the cross for human salvation. In this way, the Salmanticenses share Rahner and Balthasar's chief Christocentric emphases but without their ontological and methodological problems.

The Salmanticenses show that a Thomistic Christocentrism is possible. Because Christ is the proximate end of all God's other works, he colors the whole order of history in the way that a final cause influences what is willed for its sake. "All things were created through him and for him" (Col 1:16). But because Christ's coming is essentially meant to save humanity from sin, the theological intelligibility of the present order depends on Christ *as redeemer*. The God-man's intrinsic value cannot be sundered from the divine mercy. Out of myriad possibilities beyond theology's reckoning, divine mercy has chosen the present order in which to take on flesh and express itself through the human mercy of the God-man. Jesus' compassion toward sinners has been the condition for the world's creation. God has wed Christ to the lapsed universe as its rescuer, Lord, and king. In this way, the savior is the heart of God's plan for history, the key to its meaning from a providential perspective.

If this book has contributed in some small way to a renewed appreciation of the Salmanticenses, then it has succeeded. They, for their part, direct us to their master, St. Thomas Aquinas, whose disciples they strove to be. He, in turn, points us to the one of whom he wrote well, Jesus Christ, the "King of kings and Lord of lords" (Rev 19:16), "the first and the last" (Rev 22:13), who "came not to call the righteous, but sinners" (Mk 2:17). To him be glory forever. Amen.

Bibliography

ANCIENT AND PATRISTIC WORKS

Ambrose. *De Incarnationis dominicae sacramento*. Edited by Otto Faller. In CSEL 79:223–81. Vienna: Tempsky, 1964.

———. *Explanatio psalmorum xii*. Edited by M. Petschenig. CSEL 64. Vienna: Tempsky, 1919.

Andrew of Crete. *Oratio X in venerabilem pretiosae et vivificae crucis Exaltationem*. Edited by J.-P. Migne. In PG 97:1017–36. Paris, 1865.

Aristotle. *Categoriae vel praedicamenta: Translatio Boethii*. Edited by L. Minio-Paluello. Bruges: Desclée de Brouwer, 1961.

———. *The Complete Works of Aristotle: The Revised Oxford Translation*. Edited by Jonathan Barnes. Bollingen Series 71.2. 2 vols. Princeton, N.J.: Princeton University Press, 1984.

———. *Physica (translatio vetus)*. Edited by Fernand Bossier and Jozef Brams. Aristoteles Latinus 7.1. Leiden: Brill, 1990.

———. *Physica*. Edited by W. D. Ross. Scriptorum classicorum bibliotheca Oxoniensis. Oxford: Clarendon Press, 1950. Reprinted 2009.

Athanasius. *Oratio de Incarnatione Verbi*. Edited by J.-P. Migne. In PG 25:95–198. Paris, 1857.

———. *Orationes I et II contra Arianos*. Vol. 1.1.2 of *Athanasius Werke*, edited by Kyriakos Savvidis. Berlin: De Gruyter, 1998.

Augustine. *De civitate Dei*. Edited by B. Dombart and A. Kalb. CCSL 48–49. Turnout: Brepols, 1955.

———. *De libero arbitrio*. Edited by William M. Green. In CCSL 29:211–321. Turnhout: Brepols, 1970.

———. *De nuptiis et concupiscentia*. Edited by Karl F. Urba and Joseph Zycha. CSEL 42:207–319. Vienna: Tempsky, 1902.

———. *De praedestinatione sanctorum*. Edited by J.-P. Migne. In PL 44:959–92. Paris, 1865.

———. *De Trinitate libri XV*. Edited by W. J. Mountain and F. Glorie. CCSL 50 and 50A. Turnhout: Brepols, 1968.

———. *Enarrationes in psalmos I-L*. Edited by E. Dekkers and J. Fraipont. CCSL 38. Turnhout: Brepols, 1956.

———. *In Iohannis evangelium tractatus CXXIV*. 2nd ed. Edited by R. Willems. CCSL 36. Turnhout: Brepols, 1990.

———. *Sermon 8 de verbis Apostoli (Sermon 174)*. Edited by J.-P. Migne. In PL 38:939–45. Paris, 1865.

———. *Sermon 9 de verbis Apostoli (Sermon 175)*. Edited by J.-P. Migne. In PL 38:945–49. Paris, 1865.

———. *Sermon 29 de verbis Domini (Sermon 105)*. Edited by J.-P. Migne. In PL 38:618–25. Paris, 1865.

Biblia sacra cum glossa ordinaria. Edited by Fulgensis Strabus, Nicholas of Lyra, Paul Burgensus, Matthias Toringus, François Feuardent, Jean Dadré, and Jacques de Cuilly. 6 vols. Venice, 1603.

Cyril of Alexandria. *De SS. Trinitate dialogi VII*. Edited by J.-P. Migne. In PG 75:657–1124. Paris, 1863.

———. *Divi Cyrilli patriarchae Alexandrini [...] opus insigne, quod Thesaurus inscribitur*. Translated by Georgius Trapezontius. Basel: Apud Andream Cratandrum, 1524.

———. *Thesaurus de sancta et consubstantiali Trinitate*. Edited by J.-P. Migne. In PG 75:9–656. Paris, 1863.

Cyril of Jerusalem. *S. Patris nostri Cyrilli Hierosolymorum Archiepiscopi opera quae supersunt omnia*. Edited by Guilielmus Carolus Reischl. Munich: Sumptibus Librariae Lentnerianae, 1848.

Epiphanius of Salamis. *Ancoratus und Panarion haer. 1–33*. Vol. 1 of *Epiphanius*, edited by Karl Holl. Berlin: De Gruyter, 2013.

Gregory the Great. *In librum primum Regum expositionum libri VI*. Edited by P. P. Verbraken. In CCSL 144:49–614. Turnhout: Brepols, 1963.

Gregory of Nazianzus. *Discours 27–31*. Edited by Paul Gallay and Maurice Jourjon. In SC 250. Paris: Éditions du Cerf, 1978.

Gregory of Nyssa. *Oratio in diem natalem Christi*. Edited by J.-P. Migne. In PG 46:1127–50. Paris, 1863.

Hilary of Poitiers. *De Trinitate*. Edited by P. Smulders. CCSL 62 and 62A. Turnhout: Brepols, 1979–80.

Irenaeus of Lyon. *Contre les hérésies: Livre III*. Edited by Adelin Rousseau and Louis Doutreleau. 2 vols. SC 210–11. Paris: Éditions du Cerf, 1974.

———. *Contre les hérésies: Livre IV*. Edited by Adelin Rousseau, Louis Doutreleau, and Charles Mercier. 2 vols. SC 100. Paris: Éditions du Cerf, 1965.

———. *Contre les hérésies: Livre V*. Edited by Adelin Rousseau, Louis Doutreleau, and Charles Mercier. 2 vols. SC 152–53. Paris: Éditions du Cerf, 1969.

Jerome. *Commentarius in Ecclesiasten*. Edited by Marc Adriaen. In CCSL 72:249–361. Turnhout: Brepols, 1959.

Bibliography

John Chrysostom. *In Epistolam ad Hebraeos homilia V.* Edited by J.-P. Migne. In PG 63:45–54. Paris, 1862.

———. *In Matthaeum homilia LXVI al. LXVII.* Edited by J.-P. Migne. In PG 58:625–32. Paris, 1862.

John Damascene. *La foi orthodoxe: 45–100.* Edited by Bonifatius Kotter, Georges-Matthieu de Durand, and Pierre Ledrux. SC 540. Paris: Éditions du Cerf, 2011.

John Scottus Eriugena. *Homilia in prologum S. Evangelii secundum Joannem.* Edited by J.-P. Migne. In PL 122:283–96. Paris, 1865.

Leo the Great. *Tractatus.* Edited by Eddy Gouder, Michel Gueret, and Paul Tombeur. CCSL 138 and 138A. Turnhout: Brepols, 1987.

Pseudo-Augustine. *De spiritu et anima.* Edited by J.-P. Migne. In PL 40:779–852. Paris, 1865.

———. *The Pseudo-Augustinian Hypomnesticon against the Pelagians and Celestinans.* Vol. 2, *Text Edited from the Manuscripts.* Edited by John Edward Chisholm. Fribourg: The University Press, 1967–80.

Pseudo-Basil. *Homilia in sanctam Christi generationem.* Edited by J.-P. Migne. In PG 31:1457–76. Paris, 1857.

Pseudo–John Chrysostom. *In Ascensionem Domini nostri Jesu Christi sermo II.* Edited by J.-P. Migne. In PG 52:793–96. Paris, 1862.

Tertullian. *De carne Christi.* Edited by A. Kroymann. In CCSL 2:871–918. Turnhout: Brepols, 1954.

Theodoret. *Haereticarum fabularum compendium.* Edited by J.-P. Migne. In PG 83:335–556. Paris, 1864.

Theophylact. *Enarratio in evangelium Joannis.* Edited by J.-P. Migne. In PG 123:1127–1348. Paris, 1864.

MEDIEVAL AND SCHOLASTIC WORKS

Abelard, Peter. *Theologia "scholarium."* Edited by E. Buytaert and C. Mews. Opera theologica 3. CCCM 13. Turnhout: Brepols, 1987.

Albert the Great. *Commentarii in tertium librum Sententiarum.* Vol. 28 of *B. Alberti Magni, Ratisbonensis episcopi, Ordinis praedicatorum, opera omnia,* edited by Steph. Caes. Aug. Borgnet. Paris: Apud Ludovicum Vivès, 1894.

———. *Quaestio de conceptione Christi.* In *Alberti Magni opera omnia,* edited by Henryk Anzulewicz and Wilhelm Kübel, 25.2:258–63. Münster: Aschendorff, 1993.

Alexander of Hales. *Doctoris irrefragabilis Alexandri de Hales Ordinis Minorum Summa theologica seu sic ab origine dicta "Summa fratris Alexandri"* [...]. 4 vols. Ad Claras Aquas (Quaracchi): Ex typographia Collegii S. Bonaventurae, 1924–48.

———. *Glossa in quattuor libros Sententiarum Petri Lombardi, nunc demum reperta atque primum edita, studio et cura PP. Collegii S. Bonaventurae.* 4 vols. Bibliotheca Franciscana scholastica medii aevi 12–15. Ad Claras Aquas (Quaracchi): Ex typographia Collegii S. Bonaventurae, 1951–57.

———. *Quaestiones disputatae "antequam esset frater."* Bibliotheca Franciscana scholastica medii aevi 19. Ad Claras Aquas (Quaracchi): Ex typographia Collegii S. Bonaventurae, 1960.

Anselm of Canterbury. *Cur Deus homo?* In *S. Anselmi Cantuariensis archiepiscopi opera omnia*, edited by Franciscus Salesius Schmitt, 2:37–133. Rome, 1940.

———. *Epistola de Incarnatione Verbi.* In *S. Anselmi Cantuariensis archiepiscopi opera omnia*, edited by Franciscus Salesius Schmitt, 2:1–35. Rome, 1940.

Bernard of Clairvaux. *Sermones: I.* Vol. 4 of *S. Bernardi opera*, edited by J. Leclercq and H. Rochais. Rome: Editiones Cistercienses, 1966.

Bibliotheca Casinensis seu codicum manuscriptorum qui in tabulario Casinensi asservantur series, vol. 2. Edited by the Monks of the Order of Saint Benedict. Monte Casino: Ex typographia Casinensi, 1875.

Billuart, Charles-René. *F. C.-R. Billuart Summa sancti Thomae hodiernis academiarum moribus accommodata.* New ed. 8 vols. Paris: Apud Victorem Palmé, 1872.

Bonaventure. *Breviloquium.* In *Doctoris seraphici S. Bonaventurae S. R. E. episcopi cardinalis opera omnia*, 5:199–291. Ad Claras Aquas (Quaracchi): Ex typographia Collegii S. Bonaventurae, 1891.

———. *Collationes in hexaëmeron: Redactio A.* In *Collationes in hexaëmeron et Bonaventuriana quaedam selecta*, 1–275, Bibliotheca Franciscana scholastica medii aevi 8. Ad Claras Aquas (Quaracchi): Ex typographia Collegii S. Bonaventurae, 1934.

———. *Collationes in hexaëmeron: Redactio B.* In *Doctoris seraphici S. Bonaventurae S. R. E. episcopi cardinalis opera omnia*, 5:329–449. Ad Claras Aquas (Quaracchi): Ex typographia Collegii S. Bonaventurae, 1891.

———. *Commentarii in tertium librum Sententiarum.* Vol. 3 of *Doctoris seraphici S. Bonaventurae S. R. E. episcopi cardinalis opera omnia* […]. Ad Claras Aquas (Quaracchi): Ex typographia Collegii S. Bonaventurae, 1887.

———. *De reductione artium ad theologiam.* In *Doctoris seraphici S. Bonaventurae S. R. E. episcopi cardinalis opera omnia*, 5:317–25. Ad Claras Aquas (Quaracchi): Ex typographia Collegii S. Bonaventurae, 1891.

Cajetan, Tommaso de Vio. *Commentary on the* Summa theologiae. In vols. 4–12 of *Opera omnia iussu impensaque Leonis XIII. P. M. edita.* Rome: Ex Typographia Polyglotta S. C. de Propaganda Fide, 1888–1906.

Capréolus, Jean. *Defensiones theologiae divi Thomae Aquinatis in tertio Sententiarum.* Vol. 5 of *Johannis Capreoli Tholosani Ordinis praedicatorum, Thomistarum princeps defensiones theologiae divi Thomae Aquinatis*, edited by Ceslas Paban and Thomas Pègues. Tours: Sumptibus Alfred Cattier, 1904.

Catarino, Ambrogio. *F. Ambrosii Catharini Politi Senensis de praescientia, providentia, et praedestinatione Dei, libri duo. Eiusdem de eximia praedestinatione Christi. Item, de statu futuro puerorum, qui sine sacramento, et in antiquo peccato de-*

functi sunt, tractatus. Paris: Ex officina Carolae Guillard, sub sole aureo, via ad divum Iacobum, 1541.

Chatton, Walter. *Reportatio super librum primum Sententiarum.* Vols. 1–2 of *Reportatio super Sententias,* edited by Joseph C. Wey and Girard J. Etzkorn. Studies and Texts 141 and 142. Toronto: Pontifical Institute of Mediaeval Studies, 2002.

Duns Scotus, John. *Lectura in tertium librum Sententiarum.* Vols. 20–21 of *Doctoris subtilis et Mariani B. Ioannis Duns Scoti Ordinis Fratrum Minorum opera omnia* [...] *studio et cura Commissionis Scotisticae ad fidem codicum edita.* Vatican City: Typis Vaticanis, 2003–2004.

———. *Ordinatio.* Vols. 1–10 of *Doctoris subtilis et Mariani B. Ioannis Duns Scoti Ordinis Fratrum Minorum opera omnia* [...] *studio et cura Commissionis Scotisticae ad fidem codicum edita.* Vatican City: Typis Vaticanis, 1950–2007.

———. *Quaestiones in tertium librum Sententiarum.* Vols. 14–15 of *Joannis Duns Scoti doctoris subtilis, Ordinis Minorum, opera omnia* [...]. New ed. Paris: Apud Ludovicum Vivès, 1894.

———. *Reportata Parisiensia: Liber tertius.* In *Joannis Duns Scoti doctoris subtilis, Ordinis Minorum, opera omnia* [...], new ed., 23:234–530. Paris: Apud Ludovicum Vivès, 1894.

Ferrara, Francesco Silvestri de. Commentary on the Summa contra Gentiles. Vols. 13–15 of *Opera omnia iussu impensaque Leonis XIII. P. M. edita.* Rome: Ex Typographia Polyglotta S. C. de Propaganda Fide, 1918–30.

Frassen, Claude. *Scotus academicus seu universa Doctoris subtilis theologica dogmata.* New ed. Vol. 7. Rome: Ex typographia Sallustiana, 1901.

Godoy, Pedro de. *Illustrissimi, ac reverendissimi D. D. F. Petri de Godoy Ordinis praedicatorum: Salmanticensis academiae in sacra theologia magistri: Eiusdemque universitatis quondam cancellarii: Diu vespertina, et primaria cathedra moderatoris: concionatoris regii: Et nunc episcopi Oxomensis disputationes theologicae in tertiam partem divi Thomae.* 3 vols. Venice: Apud Ioannem Iacobum Hertz, 1686.

Gonet, Jean-Baptiste. *Clypeus theologiae Thomisticae contra novos eius impugnatores.* 6 vols. Paris: Apud Ludovicum Vivès, 1875–76.

Guerric of Igny. *Sermons: I.* Edited by John Morson, Hilary Costello, and Placide Deseille. SC 166. Paris: Éditions du Cerf, 1970.

Guerric of Saint-Quentin. *Quaestiones de quolibet.* Edited by Walter H. Principe and Jonathan Black. Studies and Texts 143. Toronto: Pontifical Institute of Mediaeval Studies, 2002.

Henry of Ghent. *Summae quaestionum ordinariarum theologi recepto praeconio solennis Henrici a Gandavo.* 2 vols. Paris: Venumdatur in aedibus Iodoci Badii Ascensii, 1520.

———. *Tractatus super facto praelatorum et fratrum (Quodlibet XII, quaestio 31).* Vol. 17 of *Henrici a Gandavo opera omnia,* edited by L. Hödl and M. Haverals. Leuven: Leuven University Press, 1989.

John of St. Thomas. *Admodum reverendi et eximii patris Joannis a S. Thoma Ordinis praedicatorum, doctoris theologi in Complutensi academia professoris primarii, supremi fidei censoris cursus philosophicus Thomisticus secundum exactam, veram et genuinam Aristotelis et doctoris angelici mentem.* New ed. 3 vols. Paris: Ludovicus Vivès, 1883.

———. *Admodum reverendi et eximii patris Joannis a S. Thoma Ordinis praedicatorum, doctoris theologi in Complutensi academia professoris primarii, supremi fidei censoris cursus theologicus in Summam theologicam D. Thomae.* New ed. 10 vols. Paris: Ludovicus Vivès, 1883–86.

Juan de la Anunciación. *Collegii Complutensis Fr. Discalceatorum B. M. de Monte Carmeli, artium cursus, ad breviorem formam collectus, et novo ordine, atque faciliori stylo dispositus.* 5 vols. London: Sumptibus Petri Chevalier, 1670.

Juan de Campoverde. *Tractatus de Incarnatione Verbi divini divisus in tres tomos.* 3 vols. Alcalá de Henares: Apud Iulianum Franciscum Garcia Briones, typographum Universitatis Complutensis, 1711–12.

Licheto, Francesco. Commentary on Scotus's *Quaestiones in tertium librum Sententiarum.* In *Joannis Duns Scoti doctoris subtilis, Ordinis Minorum, opera omnia* [...], new ed., vols. 14–15. Paris: Apud Ludovicum Vivès, 1894.

Lorca, Pedro de. *Commentariorum, ac disputationum in tertiam partem D. Thomae, tomus primus, continens priorum viginti sex quaestionum expositionem.* Alcalá de Henares: Apud viduam Andrea Sanchez de Ezpeleta, 1616.

Lynch, Dominic. *Summa philosophiae speculativae iuxta mentem et doctrinam D. Thomae et Aristotelis.* 4 vols. Paris: Sumptibus Antonii Bertier, 1666–86.

Mastri, Bartolomeo. *R. P. F. Bartholomaei Mastri de Meldula Ordinis Minorum conventualium S. Francisci theologi disputationes theologicae in tertium librum Sententiarum.* Latest ed. Venice: Apud Paulum Balleonium, 1698.

Medina, Bartolomé de. *Expostitio in tertiam D. Thomae partem usque ad quaestionem sexagesimam complectens tertium librum Sententiarum.* Salamanca: Typis haeredum Mathiae Gastii, 1580.

Mendoza, Alfonso de. *Fratris Alphonsi Mendozae, ex Ordine eremitarum D. Augustini, in florentissima Salmanticensium academia, sacrae theologiae magistri et vesperarii professoris, quaestiones quodlibeticae et relectio de Christi regno ac dominio.* Salamanca: Excudebat Petrus Lassus, sumptibus Francisci Martini, 1596.

Molina, Luis de. *Ludovici Molinae e Societate Iesu S. theologiae doctoris, et professoris commentaria, in primam D. Thomae partem.* 2 vols. London: Sumptibus Ludovici Prost haeredis Roville, 1622.

———. *Ludovici Molina liberi arbitrii cum gratiae donis, divina praescientia, providentia, praedestinatione et reprobatione concordia.* Edited by Johann Rabeneck. Societatis Iesu selcti scriptores. Oña: Collegium maximum S. I., 1953.

Natalis, Hervaeus. *De quattuor materiis sive Determinationes contra magistrum Henricum de Gandavo.* Edited by L. M. de Rijk. 2 vols. Studia artistarum 30 and 35. Turnhout: Brepols, 2011–13.

Pablo de la Concepción. *Tractatus theologici juxta miram D. Thomae et Cursus Salmanticensis ff. Discalceatorum B. Mariae de Monte Carmeli primitivae observantiae doctrinam.* 2nd ed. 4 vols. Parma: Apud haeredes Pauli Monti, sub signo fidei, 1725.

Peter of Aquila. *Quaestiones in quatuor Sententiarum libros.* In *Petri Aquilani cognomento Scotelli ex Ord. min. in doctrina Ioan. Duns Scoti spectatissimi quaestiones in quatuor Sententiarum libros, ad ejusdem doctrinam multum conferentes.* Edited by M. Constantius a Sarnano. Venice: Apud Hieronymum Zenarius, 1584.

Peter Auriol. *Scriptum super primum Sententiarum.* Edited by Eligius M. Buytaert. 2 vols. Franciscan Institute Publications, Text Series 3. St. Bonaventure, N.Y.: Franciscan Institute, 1952–56.

Peter Lombard. *Magistri Petri Lombardi Parisiensis episcopi Sententiae in IV libris distinctae.* 3 vols. Spicilegium Bonaventurianum 4–5. Grottaferrata (Rome): Editiones Collegii S. Bonaventurae ad Claras Aquas, 1981.

Rada, Juan de. *Controversiae theologicae inter S. Thomam et Scotum super tertium librum Sententiarum.* Vol. 3 of *Controversiae theologicae inter S. Thomam et Scotum super quatuor libros Sententiarum.* Cologne: Apud Ioannem Crithium sub signo Galli, 1620.

Robert Grosseteste. *De cessatione legalium.* Edited by Richard C. Dales and Edward B. King. Auctores Britannici medii aevi 7. London: Oxford University Press, 1986.

———. *Exiit edictum.* In "Robert Grosseteste Bishop of Lincoln (1235–1253) on the Reasons for the Incarnation," by Dominic Unger, *Franciscan Studies* 16, no. 1/2 (1956), 18–23.

———. *Hexaëmeron.* Edited by Richard C. Dales and Servus Gieben. Auctores Britannici medii aevi 6. London: Oxford University Press, 1982.

Rupert of Deutz. *De glorificatione Trinitatis et processione Spiritus sancti.* Edited by J.-P. Migne. In PL 169:9–202. Paris, 1854.

———. *Ruperti Tuitiensis commentaria in evangelium sancti Iohannis.* Edited by Hrabanus Haacke. CCCM 9. Turnhout: Brepols, 1969.

———. *Ruperti Tuitiensis de gloria et honore Filii hominis super Matthaeum.* Edited by Hrabanus Haacke. CCCM 29. Turnhout: Brepols, 1979.

———. *Ruperti Tuitiensis de sancta Trinitate et operibus eius, libros XXXIV–XLII: De operibus Spiritus sancti.* Edited by Hrabanus Haacke. CCCM 24. Turnhout: Brepols, 1972.

Salmanticenses. *Cursus theologicus Collegii Salmanticensis Fr. discalceatorum B. Mariae de Monte Carmeli [...] Summam theologicam angelici doctoris D. Thomae complectens.* New corrected ed. 20 vols. Paris: Apud Victorem Palmé, 1870–83.

——— (Discalced Carmelites of Salamanca). *On the Motive of the Incarnation.* Translated by Dylan Schrader. Early Modern Catholic Sources 1. Washington, D.C.: The Catholic University of America Press, 2019.

Suárez, Francisco. *Commentaria ac disputationes in tertiam partem D. Thomae.* Vols. 17–22 of *R. P. Francisci Suarez e Societate Jesu opera omnia.* New ed. Paris: Apud Ludovicum Vivès, 1860–78.

———. *Disputationes metaphysicae.* Vols. 25–26 of *R. P. Francisci Suarez e Societate Jesu opera omnia.* New ed. Paris: Apud Ludovicum Vivès, 1860.

———. *Opusculum II de scientia conditionata futurorum contingentium.* In *R. P. Francisci Suarez e Societate Jesu opera omnia,* new ed., 11:294–375. Paris: Apud Ludovicum Vivès, 1877.

———. *Tractatus de angelis.* Vol. 2 of *R. P. Francisci Suarez e Societate Jesu opera omnia.* New ed. Paris: Apud Ludovicum Vivès, 1856.

Thomas Aquinas. *Commentum in secundum librum Sententiarum.* Vol. 2 of *S. Thomae Aquinatis, Ordinis praedicatorum, doctoris communis ecclesiae, Scriptum super Sententiis magistri Petri Lombardi episcopi Parisiensis,* edited by Mandonnet, new ed. Paris: Sumptibus P. Lethielleux, 1929.

———. *De ente et essentia.* In *Opera omnia iussu impensaque Leonis XIII. P. M. edita,* 43:369–81. Rome: Editori di San Tommaso, 1976.

———. *Quaestio disputata de caritate.* In *Quaestiones disputatae,* edited by P. Bazzi et al., 10th ed., 2:753–91. Rome: Marietti, 1965.

———. *Quaestiones disputatae de veritate.* Vol. 22 of *Opera omnia iussu impensaque Leonis XIII. P. M. edita.* Rome: Editori di San Tommaso, 1970–76.

———. *Scriptum super libro tertio Sententiarum.* Vol. 3 of *S. Thomae Aquinatis, doctoris communis ecclesiae, Scriptum super Sententiis magistri Petri Lombardi,* edited by Maria Fabianus Moos, new ed. Paris: Sumptibus P. Lethielleux, 1933.

———. *Summa theologiae.* Vols. 4–12 of *Opera omnia iussu impensaque Leonis XIII. P. M. edita.* Rome: Ex Typographia Polyglotta S. C. de Propaganda Fide, 1888–1906.

———. *Super epistolam ad Hebraeos lectura.* In *S. Thomae Aquinatis, doctoris angelici, super epistolas S. Pauli lectura,* edited by Rafael Cai, 8th rev. ed., 2:335–506. Rome: Marietti, 1953.

———. *Super epistolam ad Romanos lectura.* In *S. Thomae Aquinatis, doctoris angelici, super epistolas S. Pauli lectura,* edited by Rafael Cai, 8th rev. ed., 1:5–230. Rome: Marietti, 1953.

———. *Super primam epistolam ad Timotheum lectura.* In *S. Thomae Aquinatis, doctoris angelici, super epistolas S. Pauli lectura,* edited by Rafael Cai, 8th rev. ed., 2:211–64. Rome: Marietti, 1953.

Vásquez, Gabriel. *Commentariorum, ac disputationum in tertiam partem S. Thomae, tomus primus.* Alcalá de Henares: Apud viduam Iusti Sanchez Crespo, 1609.

Vicente de Astorga, Juan. *Relectio de habituali Christi salvatoris nostri sanctificante gratia.* Rome: Ex typographia Pauli Diani, 1591.

William of Ockham. *Scriptum in librum primum Sententiarum: Ordinatio.* Vols. 1–4 of *Guillelmi de Ockham opera philosophica et theologica* [...]. Opera theologica 1–4. St. Bonaventure, N.Y.: Institutum Franciscanum, 1967–79.

OTHER WORKS

Adams, Marilyn McCord. "The Primacy of Christ." *Sewanee Theological Review* 47, no. 2 (2004): 164–80.

Balthasar, Hans Urs von. *The Glory of the Lord: A Theological Aesthetics*. Edited by Joseph Fessio, Brian McNeil, and John Riches. Translated by Oliver Davies, Erasmo Leiva-Merikakis, Andrew Louth, Francis McDonagh, Brian McNeil, John Saward, Martin Simon, and Rowan Williams. 7 vols. San Francisco: Ignatius Press, 1982–89.

———. *The Christian State of Life*. Translated by Mary Frances McCarthy. San Francisco: Ignatius Press, 1983.

———. "Only If." In *Convergences: To the Source of Christian Mystery*, translated by E. A. Nelson, 135–53. San Francisco: Ignatius Press, 1983.

———. *Theo-Drama: Theological Dramatic Theory*. Translated by Graham Harrison. 5 vols. San Francisco: Ignatius Press, 1988–93. Original: *Theodramatik*. 5 vols. Einsiedeln: Johannes Verlag, 1973–83.

———. *The Theology of Karl Barth: Exposition and Interpretation*. Translated by Edward T. Oakes. San Francisco: Communio Books / Ignatius Press, 1992.

———. *My Work in Retrospect*. Translator not given. San Francisco: Communio Books / Ignatius Press, 1993.

———. *The Moment of Christian Witness*. Translated by Richard Beckley. San Francisco: Communio Books / Ignatius Press, 1994.

———. *A Theology of History*. Translator not given. San Francisco: Communio Books / Ignatius Press, 1994. Original: *Theologie der Geschichte: Ein Grundriss*. New ed. Einsiedeln: Johannes Verlag, 1959.

———. "The Incarnation of God." In *Elucidations*, translated by John Riches, 58–68. San Francisco: Ignatius Press, 1998.

———. "Trinity and Future." In *Elucidations*, translated by John Riches, 80–90. San Francisco: Ignatius Press, 1998.

———. *Mysterium Paschale: The Mystery of Easter*. Translated by Aidan Nichols. San Francisco: Ignatius Press, 2000.

———. *Theo-Logic: Theological Logical Theory*. Translated by Adrian J. Walker and Graham Harrison. 3 vols. San Francisco: Ignatius Press, 2000–2005.

———. *Cosmic Liturgy: The Universe According to Maximus the Confessor*. Translated by Brian E. Daley. San Francisco: Communio Books / Ignatius Press, 2003.

———. *Love Alone Is Credible*. Translated by D. C. Schindler. San Francisco: Communio Books / Ignatius Press, 2004.

———. "Christ the Redeemer." In *To the Heart of the Mystery of Redemption*, by Hans Urs von Balthasar and Adrienne von Speyr, translated by Anne Englund Nash, 15–42. San Francisco: Ignatius Press, 2010.

———. *Dare We Hope "That All Men Be Saved"?* Translated by David Kipp and Lothar Krauth. 2nd ed. San Francisco: Ignatius Press, 2014.

Barden, William. "A Thomist Approach towards Scotism." *Irish Theological Quarterly* 26 (1959): 368–75.

Beeke, Joel R. *Debated Issues in Sovereign Predestination: Early Lutheran Predestination, Calvinian Reprobation, and Variations in Genevan Lapsarianism*. Göttingen, Germany: Vandenhoeck & Ruprecht, 2017.

Benedict XVI. *Deus caritas est*. Encyclical Letter. December 25, 2005. In *AAS* 98 (2006): 217–52.

———. *Spe salvi*. Encyclical Letter. November 30, 2007. In *AAS* 99 (2007): 985–1027.

Benson, Joshua. "The Christology of the *Breviloquium*." In *A Companion to Bonaventure*, edited by Jay M. Hammond, J. A. Wayne Hellmann, and Jared Goff, 247–87. Brill's Companions to the Christian Tradition. Leiden: Brill, 2014.

Billot, Louis. *De Verbo incarnato commentarius in tertiam partem s. Thomae*. 2nd expanded and rev. ed. Rome: Ex typographia polyglotta, 1895.

Blanchette, Oliva. *The Perfection of the Universe According to Aquinas: A Teleological Cosmology*. University Park: Pennsylvania State University, 1992.

Bonnefoy, Jean-François. "La question hypothétique: Ultrum [sic] si Adam non peccasset [...] au XIIIe siècle." *Revista española de teología* 14 (1954): 327–68.

———. *Christ and the Cosmos*. Edited and translated by Michael D. Meilach. 1st American ed. Paterson, N.J.: St. Anthony Guild Press, 1965.

Boyer, Carlo. *Cursus philosophiae ad usum seminariorum*. 2 vols. Bilbao: Desclée de Brouwer, 1962.

Buckley, James J. "Christological Inquiry: Barth, Rahner, and the Identity of Jesus Christ." *The Thomist* 50, no. 4 (1986): 568–98.

Cai, Rafael. Introduction to *S. Thomae Aquinatis doctoris angelici, super epistolas S. Pauli lectura*, edited by Rafael Cai, 8th rev. ed., 1:v–xix. Rome: Marietti, 1953.

Capol, Cornelia. *Hans Urs von Balthasar: Bibliographie 1925–1990*. Einsiedeln: Johannes Verlag, 1990.

Carol, Juniper B. *A History of the Controversy over the "debitum peccati."* Franciscan Institute Publications, Theology Series 9. St. Bonaventure, N.Y.: Franciscan Institute, 1978.

———. "The Absolute Predestination of the Blessed Virgin Mary." *Marian Studies* 31 (1980): 178–238.

———. *Why Jesus Christ? Thomistic, Scotistic and Conciliatory Perspectives*. Manassas, Va.: Trinity Communications, 1986.

Catechism of the Catholic Church. 2nd ed. Washington, D.C.: United States Catholic Conference, 1997.

Coffey, David. "The Whole Rahner on the Supernatural Existential." *Theological Studies* 65 (2004): 95–118.

Colish, Marcia L. "Peter Lombard and Abelard: The *Opinio nominalium* and Divine Transcendence." In *Studies in Scholasticism*, VI, 1–17. Hampshire, UK: Ashgate, 2006.

Congregation for the Doctrine of the Faith. *Dominus Iesus*. Declaration. August 6, 2000. In *AAS* 92 (2000): 742–65.
Cortez, Marc. "What Does It Mean to Call Karl Barth a 'Christocentric' Theologian?" *Scottish Journal of Theology* 60, no. 2 (2007): 1–17.
Craig, William Lane. *The Problem of Divine Foreknowledge and Future Contingents from Aristotle to Suarez*. Brill's Studies in Intellectual History 7. Leiden: Brill, 1988.
Crisp, Oliver D. "The Election of Jesus Christ." *Journal of Reformed Theology* 2, no. 2 (2008): 131–50.
Cross, Richard. *Duns Scotus*. Great Medieval Thinkers. Oxford: Oxford University Press, 1999.
Cullen, Christopher M. "Alexander of Hales." In *A Companion to Philosophy in the Middle Ages*, edited by Jorge J. E. Gracia and Timothy B. Noone, 104–8. Blackwell Companions to Philosophy. Oxford: Blackwell, 2003.
Daguet, François. *Théologie du dessein divin chez Thomas d'Aquin: Finis omnium Ecclesia*. Bibliothèque thomiste 54. Paris: Librairie philosophique J. Vrin, 2003.
Dalmau, J. M. *De Deo uno et trino*. In *Sacrae theologiae summa*, 3rd ed., 2:11–441. Biblioteca de autores Cristianos 90. Madrid: Biblioteca de autores Cristianos, 1958.
de la Taille, Maurice. "Sur diverses classifications de la science divine." *Recherches de Science Religieuse* 13 (1923): 7–23, 535–42.
de Letter, Paul. "Divine Quasi-Formal Causality." *Irish Theological Quarterly* 27, no. 3 (1960): 221–28.
———. "If Adam Had Not Sinned..." *Irish Theological Quarterly* 28 (1961): 117–25.
Delio, Ilia. "Revisiting the Franciscan Doctrine of Christ." *Theological Studies* 64, no. 1 (March 2003): 3–23.
del Sagrado Corazón, Enrique. *Los Salmanticenses: su vida y su obra. Ensayo histórico y proceso inquisitorial de su doctrina sobre la Inmaculada*. Pontificia Universidad Eclesiastica de Salamanca. Madrid: Editorial de Espiritualidad, 1955.
———. "Juan Duns Escoto en la doctrina de los Salmanticenses sobre el motivo de la Encarnación." In *De doctrina Ioannis Duns Scoti: Acta Congressus Scotistici internationalis Oxonii et Edimburgi 11–17 sept. 1966 celebrati*, 461–515. Studia Scholastico-Scotistica 4. Rome: Ercolano, 1968.
———. "El colegio de San Elías y los *Salmanticenses*." In *Trayectoria histórica e instituciones vinculadas*, vol. 1 of *Historia de la Universidad de Salamanca*, edited by Luis Enrique Rodríguez-San Pedro Bezares, 687–704. Acta Salmanticensia: Historia de la Universidad 61. Salamanca: Ediciones Universidad de Salamanca, 2002.
di Santa Teresa, Enrico. "Il carattere del 'Cristocentrismo, nella tesi dei Salmanticesi sul motivo dell'Incarnazione." *Vita Carmelitana* 3 (1942): 39–56.
———. "Dio in noi secondo i Salmanticesi." *Vita Carmelitana* 6 (1943): 64–78.
Dodds, Michael J. *The Unchanging God of Love: Thomas Aquinas and Contempo-

rary Theology on Divine Immutability. 2nd ed. Washington, D.C.: The Catholic University of America Press, 2008.

Dreyer, Mechthild. "Albertus Magnus." In *A Companion to Philosophy in the Middle Ages*, edited by Jorge J. E. Gracia and Timothy B. Noone, 92–101. Blackwell Companions to Philosophy. Oxford: Blackwell, 2003.

Dumont, Stephen D. "John Duns Scotus." In *A Companion to Philosophy in the Middle Ages*, edited by Jorge J. E. Gracia and Timothy B. Noone, 353–69. Blackwell Companions to Philosophy. Oxford: Blackwell, 2003.

Emery, Gilles. *The Trinitarian Theology of St Thomas Aquinas*. Translated by Francesca Murphy and Gilles Emery. Oxford: Oxford University Press, 2007.

Farmer, Jerry T. "Four Christological Themes of the Theology of Karl Rahner." In *The Myriad Christ: Plurality and the Quest for Unity in Contemporary Christology*, edited by T. Merrigan and J. Haers, 433–62. Bibliotheca ephemeridum theologicarum Lovaniensium 152. Leuven: University Press, 2000.

Francis. *Evangelii gaudium*. Apostolic Exhortation. November 24, 2013. In *AAS* 105 (2013): 1019–1137.

Galtier, Paul. *Les deux Adam*. Paris: Beauschesne et ses fils, 1947.

Garrigou-Lagrange, Reginald. "Le principe de finalité." *Revue Thomiste* 26, no. 3 (1921): 418–23.

———. "Motivum Incarnationis fuit motivum misericordiae." *Angelicum* 7, no. 3 (1930): 289–302.

———. "De motivo Incarnationis: Examen recentium objectionum contra doctrinam S. Thomae IIIa, q. 1, a. 3." In *Acta Pont. Academiae Romanae S. Thomae Aquinatis et Religionis Catholicae*, 7–45. Nova series 10. Rome: Academia Romana S. Thomae Aquinatis, 1945.

———. *Christ the Savior: A Commentary on the Third Part of St. Thomas' Theological Summa*. Translated by Bede Rose. St. Louis, Mo.: Herder, 1957.

Goergen, Donald. "Albert the Great and Thomas Aquinas on the Motive of the Incarnation." *The Thomist* 44 (1980): 523–38.

Gómez, Wenceslao Carlos Flores. *Las misiones trinitarias en los teólogos tomistas españoles del siglo XVII: Aportaciones y límites a la cuestión de la inhabitación*. Toledo: Instituto teológico San Ildefonso, 2017.

Gorman, Michael. *Aquinas on the Metaphysics of the Hypostatic Union*. Cambridge: Cambridge University Press, 2017.

Gornall, Thomas. "A Note on Imagination and Thought about God." *The Heythrop Journal* 4, no. 2 (1963): 135–40.

———. Introduction to *Summa theologiae: Latin Text and English Translation, Introductions, Notes, Appendices and Glossaries*, 4:xix–xxvi. Cambridge: Cambridge University Press, 2006.

Goudin, Antoine. *Philosophia juxta inconcussa tutissimaque d. Thomae dogmata*. 4 vols. Pompei: Urbeveteri, 1859.

Gracia, Jorge J. E., and Timothy B. Noone, eds. *A Companion to Philosophy in the Middle Ages*. Blackwell Companions to Philosophy. Oxford: Blackwell, 2003.

Gredt, Josef. *Elementa philosophiae Aristotelico-Thomisticae*. 13th ed. reviewed and expanded by Eucharius Zenzen. 2 vols. Barcelona: Herder, 1961.
Harper, Thomas. *The Metaphysics of the School*. 3 vols. London: Macmillan, 1881.
Hausherr, Irénée. "Un précurseur de la théorie Scotiste sur la fin de l'incarnation: Isaac de Ninive (VIIe Siècle)." *Recherches de sciences religieuse* 22 (1932): 316–20.
Holzer, Vincent. "Karl Rahner, Hans Urs von Balthasar, and Twentieth-Century Catholic Currents on the Trinity." In *The Oxford Handbook of the Trinity*, edited by Gilles Emery and Matthew Levering, 314–27. Oxford: Oxford University Press, 2011.
Horan, Daniel P. "How Original Was Scotus on the Incarnation? Reconsidering the History of the Absolute Predestination of Christ in Light of Robert Grosseteste." *The Heythrop Journal* 52, no. 3 (May 2011): 374–91.
Howsare, Rodney A. *Balthasar: A Guide for the Perplexed*. London: T & T Clark, 2009.
Hunter, Justus H. *If Adam Had Not Sinned: The Reason for the Incarnation from Anselm to Scotus*. Washington, D.C.: The Catholic University of America Press, 2020.
John Paul II. *Redemptor hominis*. Encyclical Letter. March 4, 1979. In *AAS* 71 (1979): 257–324.
———. *Catechesi tradendae*. Apostolic Exhortation. October 16, 1979. In *AAS* 71 (1979): 1277–1340.
———. *Sollicitudo rei socialis*. Encyclical Letter. December 30, 1987. In *AAS* 80 (1988): 513–86.
———. *Veritatis splendor*. Encyclical Letter. August 6, 1993. In *AAS* 85 (1993): 1134–1228.
———. *Tertio millennio adveniente*. Apostolic Letter. November 10, 1994. In *AAS* 87 (1995): 5–41.
———. *Evangelium vitae*. Encyclical Letter. March 25, 1995. In *AAS* 87 (1995): 401–522.
Johnson, Junius. *Christ and Analogy: The Christocentric Metaphysics of Hans Urs von Balthasar*. Minneapolis: Fortress Press, 2013.
Johnson, Keith L. *Karl Barth and the Analogia Entis*. T & T Clark Studies in Systematic Theology 6. London: T & T Clark, 2010.
Kilby, Karen. "Balthasar and Karl Rahner." In *The Cambridge Companion to Hans Urs von Balthasar*, edited by Edward T. Oakes and David Moss, 256–68. Cambridge Companions to Religion. Cambridge: Cambridge University Press, 2004.
Knebel, Sven K. "Aureol and the Ambiguities of the Distinction of Reason." In *Philosophical Debates at Paris in the Early Fourteenth Century*, edited by Stephen F. Brown, Thomas Dewender, and Theo Kobush, 325–38. Leiden: Brill, 2009.
Lateran Council IV. *De fide Catholica*. Constitution. In *Decrees of the Ecumenical*

Councils, edited by Norman P. Tanner, 1:230–31. London: Sheed and Ward, 1990.

Legge, Dominic. *The Trinitarian Christology of St Thomas Aquinas*. Oxford: Oxford University Press, 2017.

Lochbrunner, Manfred. *Analogia Caritatis: Darstellung und Deutung der Theologie Hans Urs von Balthasars*. Freiburger theologische Studien 120. Freiburg: Herder, 1981.

———. *Hans Urs von Balthasar und seine Theologenkollegen: Sechs Beziehungsgeschichten*. Würzburg: Echter Verlag, 2009.

Losinger, Anton. *The Anthropological Turn: The Human Orientation of the Theology of Karl Rahner*. Translated by Daniel O. Dahlstrom. New York: Fordham University Press, 2000.

Lynn, William D. *Christ's Redemptive Merit: The Nature of Its Causality According to St. Thomas*. Analecta Gregoriana cura Pontificiae universitatis Gregorianae edita 115. Rome: Gregorian University Press, 1962.

Mansini, Guy. "Quasi-Formal Causality and 'Change in the Other': A Note on Karl Rahner's Christology." *The Thomist* 52, no. 2 (1988): 293–306.

March, Francis Andrew. *Latin Hymns with English Notes for Use in Schools and Colleges*. Douglass Series of Christian Greek and Latin Writers 1. New York: Harper, 1874.

Marcil, George. "Joannes de Rada and the Argument for the Primacy of Christ in His *Controversiae Theologicae*." In *Homo et Mundus: Acta Quinti Congressus Scotistici Internationalis, Salmanticae, 21–26 Septembris 1981*, 137–44. Studia Scholastico-Scotistica 8. Rome: Societas Internationalis Scotistica, 1984.

Marshner, William H. "A Logician's Reflections on the *Debitum Contrahendi Peccatum*." *Marian Studies* 29, no. 1978 (n.d.): 134–87.

Martelet, Gustave. "Sur le motif de l'Incarnation." In *Problèmes actuels de Christologie*, edited by Humbert Bouëssé, 35–80. Textes et études théologiques. Paris: Desclée de Brouwer, 1965.

Martin, Melquiades Andres. *Historia de la Teología en España (1470–1570)*. Publicaciones del Instituto Español de Historia Eclesiastica Monografias 7. Rome: Iglesia Nacional Española, 1962.

McCormack, Bruce L. *Karl Barth's Critically Realistic Dialectical Theology: Its Genesis and Development 1909–1936*. Oxford: Clarendon Press, 1995.

McDermott, John M. "The Christologies of Karl Rahner." *Gregorianum* 67, no. 1 (1986): 87–123.

———. "The Christologies of Karl Rahner – II." *Gregorianum* 67, no. 2 (1986): 297–327.

McEvoy, James. "The Absolute Predestination of Christ in the Theology of Robert Grosseteste." In *"Sapientiae Doctrina": Mélanges de théologie et de littérature médiévales offerts à Dom Hildebrand Bascour O.S.B.*, Recherches de théologie ancienne et médiévale, numéro spécial 1. Leuven: Imprimerie Orientaliste, 1980.

---. *Robert Grosseteste*. Great Medieval Thinkers. Oxford: Oxford University Press, 2000.
McIntosh, Mark A. *Christology from within: Spirituality and the Incarnation in Hans Urs von Balthasar*. Studies in Spirituality and Theology 3. Notre Dame: University of Notre Dame Press, 1996.
---. "Christology." In *The Cambridge Companion to Hans Urs von Balthasar*, edited by Edward T. Oakes and David Moss, 24–36. Cambridge Companions to Religion. Cambridge: Cambridge University Press, 2004.
Merl, Otho. *Theologia Salmanticensis: Untersuchung über Entstehung, Lehrrichtung und Quellen des theologischen Kurses der spanischen Karmeliten*. Regensburg: J. Habbel, 1947.
Moiser, Jeremy. "Why Did the Son of God Become Man?" *The Thomist* 37, no. 2 (1973): 288–305.
Neri, Francesco. *Cur Verbum capax hominis: Le ragioni dell'incarnazione della seconda Persona della Trinità fra teologia scolastica e teologia contemporanea*. Tesi Gregoriana, Serie Teologia 55. Rome: Editrice Pontificia Università Gregoriana, 1999.
Nestle, Eberhard, Barbara Aland, Kurt Aland, Johannes Karavidopoulos, Carlo M. Martini, and Bruce M. Metzger, eds. *Novum Testamentum Graece et Latine*. 4th ed. Stuttgart: Deutsche Bibelgesellschaft, 2002.
Normore, Calvin. "Future Contingents." In *The Cambridge History of Later Medieval Philosophy: From the Rediscovery of Aristotle to the Disintegration of Scholasticism 1100–1600*, edited by Norman Kretzmann, Anthony Kenny, Jan Pinborg, and Eleonore Stump, 358–81. Cambridge: Cambridge University Press, 1982.
Oakes, Edward T. *Pattern of Redemption: The Theology of Hans Urs von Balthasar*. New York: Continuum, 1994.
O'Neill, Taylor Patrick. *Grace, Predestination, and the Permission of Sin: A Thomistic Analysis*. Washington, D.C.: The Catholic University of America Press, 2019.
Ormerod, Neil J. "Two Points or Four?—Rahner and Lonergan on Trinity, Incarnation, Grace, and Beatific Vision." *Theological Studies* 68, no. 3 (September 2007): 661–73.
Palakeel, Joseph. *The Use of Analogy in Theological Discourse: An Investigation in Ecumenical Perspective*. Tesi Gregoriana, Serie Teologia 4. Rome: Editrice Pontificia Università Gregoriana, 1995.
Pancheri, Francesco Saverio. *The Universal Primacy of Christ*. Translated by Juniper B. Carol. Front Royal, Va.: Christendom Publications, 1984.
Pfisterer, Robert B. "El motivo de la Encarnación según los Salmanticenses." PhD diss., Universidad Pontificia de Salamanca, 1950.
Phillips, R. P. *Modern Thomistic Philosophy: An Explanation for Students*. 2 vols. Westminster, Md.: The Newman Bookshop, 1935.
Pitstick, Alyssa Lyra. *Light in Darkness: Hans Urs von Balthasar and the Catholic*

Doctrine of Christ's Descent into Hell. Grand Rapids, Mich.: Eerdmans, 2007.

Pomplun, Trent. "The Immaculate World: Predestination and Passibility in Contemporary Scotism." *Modern Theology* 30, no. 4 (2014): 525–51.

———. "Baroque Catholic Theologies of Christ and Mary." In *The Oxford Handbook of Early Modern Theology, 1600–1800*, 104–18. Oxford: Oxford University Press, 2016.

Potvin, Thomas R. *The Theology of the Primacy of Christ According to St. Thomas and Its Scriptural Foundations*. Edited by C. E. O'Neill. Studia Friburgensia: Works Published under the Direction of the Dominican Professors at the University of Fribourg Switzerland New Series 50. Fribourg: The University Press, 1973.

Principe, Walter H. *Alexander of Hales' Theology of the Hypostatic Union*. Vol. 2 of *The Theology of the Hypostatic Union in the Early Thirteenth Century*. Pontifical Institute of Mediaeval Studies 12. Toronto: Pontifical Institute of Mediaeval Studies, 1967.

Przewozny, B. J. "Christocentrism." In *New Catholic Encyclopedia*, ed. Berard L. Marthaler et al., 2nd ed., 3:557–59. Detroit: Gale Publishing, 2003.

Przywara, Erich. *Analogia Entis: Metaphysics: Original Structure and Universal Rhythm*. Translated by John R. Betz and David Bentley Hart. Retrieval and Renewal: Ressourcement in Catholic Thought. Grand Rapids, Mich.: Eerdmans, 2014.

Purcell, Michael. "Quasi-Formal Causality, or the Other-in-Me: Rahner and Lévinas." *Gregorianum* 78, no. 1 (1997): 79–93.

Rahner, Karl. "Eine Antwort." *Orientierung* 14, no. 12/13 (1950): 141–45.

———. "Concerning the Relationship between Nature and Grace." Translated by Cornelius Ernst. In *TI*, 1:297–317. London: Darton, Longman & Todd, 1961.

———. "Current Problems in Christology." Translated by Cornelius Ernst. In *TI*, 1:149–213. London: Darton, Longman, and Todd, 1961.

———. "Some Implications of the Scholastic Concept of Uncreated Grace." Translated by Cornelius Ernst. In *TI*, 1:319–46. London: Darton, Longman, and Todd, 1961.

———. *Theological Investigations*. Various translators. 23 vols. London: Darton, Longman & Todd, 1961–92.

———. "Personal and Sacramental Piety." Translated by Karl-H. Kruger. In *TI*, 2:109–33. London: Darton, Longman, and Todd, 1963.

———. *On the Theology of Death*. Translated by C. H. Henkey and W. J. O'Hara. 2nd English ed. Quaestiones disputatae. New York: Herder, 1965.

———. "Christology within an Evolutionary View of the World." Translated by Karl-H. Kruger. In *TI*, 5:157–92. London: Darton, Longman, and Todd, 1966.

———. "The Concept of Mystery in Catholic Theology." Translated by Kevin Smyth. In *TI*, 4:36–73. London: Darton, Longman, and Todd, 1966.

———. "Nature and Grace." Translated by Kevin Smyth. In *TI*, 4:165–88. London: Darton, Longman & Todd, 1966.

———. "On the Theology of the Incarnation." Translated by Kevin Smyth. In *TI*, 4:105–20. London: Darton, Longman, and Todd, 1966.

———. "The Theology of the Symbol." Translated by Kevin Smyth. In *TI*, 4:221–52. London: Darton, Longman, and Todd, 1966.

———. *Spirit in the World*. Translated by William V. Dych. New York: Herder, 1968.

———. "Jesus Christ: IV. History of Dogma and Theology." In *Sacramentum mundi*, 3:192–209. New York: Herder, 1969.

———. "The Unity of Spirit and Matter in the Christian Understanding of Faith." Translated by Karl-H. Kruger and Boniface Kruger. In *TI*, 6:153–77. London: Darton, Longman, and Todd, 1969.

———. "Divine Trinity." In *Sacramentum mundi: An Encyclopedia of Theology*, ed. Karl Rahner et al., 6:295–303. New York: Herder, 1970.

———. "Salvation: IV. Theology: C. Soteriology." In *Sacramentum mundi*, 5:435–38. New York: Herder, 1970.

———. "Theological States of Man." In *Sacramentum mundi*, 6:173–75. New York: Herder, 1970.

———. "'I believe in Jesus Christ': Interpreting an Article of Faith." Translated by Graham Harrison. In *TI*, 9:165–68. London: Darton, Longman, and Todd, 1972.

———. *Mary, Mother of the Lord*. Translated by W. J. O'Hara. Paperback ed. Wheathampstead, Hertfordshire: Anthony Clarke Books, 1974.

———. "Reflections on Methodology in Theology." Translated by David Bourke. In *TI*, 11:68–114. London: Darton, Longman & Todd, 1974.

———. "The One Christ and the Universality of Salvation." Translated by David Morland. In *TI*, 16:199–224. London: Darton, Longman, and Todd, 1979.

———. "Jesus Christ and Christology." In *A New Christology*, by Karl Rahner and Wilhelm Thüsing, translated by David Smith and Verdant Green, 1–41. New York: The Seabury Press, 1980.

———. "Jesus Christ in the Non-Christian Religions." Translated by Margaret Kohl. In *TI*, 17:39–50. London: Darton, Longman, and Todd, 1981.

———. *Foundations of Christian Faith: An Introduction to the Idea of Christianity*. Translated by William V. Dych. New York: The Crossroad Publishing Company, 1987.

———. "The Christian Understanding of Redemption." Translated by Hugh M. Riley. In *TI*, 21:239–54. London: Darton, Longman, and Todd, 1988.

———. *Hearer of the Word: Laying the Foundation for a Philosophy of Religion*. Translated by Joseph Donceel. New York: Continuum, 1994.

———. *The Trinity*. Translated by Joseph Donceel. Milestones in Catholic Theology. New York: The Crossroad Publishing Company, 2004.

Rahner, Karl, and Herbert Vorgrimler. *Dictionary of Theology*. Translated by Richard Strachan, David Smith, Robert Nowell, and Sarah O'Brien Twohig. 2nd ed. New York: Crossroad, 1988.

Reinstadler, Sebastian. *Elementa philosophiae scholasticae*. 7th and 8th ed. reviewed by the author. 2 vols. Freiburg: Herder, 1913.

Richard, Guy M. "Samuel Rutherford's Supralapsarianism Revealed: A Key to the Lapsarian Position of the Westminster Confession of Faith?" *Scottish Journal of Theology* 59, no. 1 (2006): 27–44.

Risi, Francesco Maria. *Sul motivo primario della incarnazione del Verbo, ossia, Gesù Cristo predestinato di primo intento per fini indipendenti dalla caduta dell'uman genere e dal decreto di redenzione*. 4 vols. Brescia: Tipografia Mucchetti & Riva, 1897–98.

Rocca, Gesualdo Maria, and Gabriele Maria Roschini. *De ratione primaria existentiae Christi et Deiparae: Novum tentamen conciliationis sententiae Thomisticae cum sententia Scotistica circa sic dictum motivum incarnationis*. Rome: Officium Libri Catholici, 1945.

Scarafoni, P. *Cristocentrismo: Riflessione teologica*. Rome: Città Nuova, 2002.

Scheeben, Matthias Joseph. *The Mysteries of Christianity*. Translated by Cyril Vollert. St. Louis, Mo.: Herder, 1954.

Schlosser, Marianne. "Bonaventure: Life and Works." In *A Companion to Bonaventure*, edited by Jay M. Hammond, J. A. Wayne Hellmann, and Jared Goff, 9–59. Brill's Companions to the Christian Tradition. Leiden: Brill, 2014.

Schrader, Dylan. "Christ's Fear of the Lord according to Thomas Aquinas." *The Heythrop Journal* (early access, 2017). https://doi.org/10.1111/heyj.12487.

Signoriello, Nunzio. *Lexicon peripateticum philosophico-theologicum in quo scholasticorum distinctiones et effata praecipua explicantur*. 2nd expanded ed. Naples: Apud officinam Bibliothecae Catholicae scriptorum, 1872.

Solano, Jesus. *De Verbo incarnato*. In *Sacrae theologiae summa*, 4th ed., 3:11–322. Biblioteca de autores cristianos 62. Madrid: Biblioteca de autores cristianos, 1961.

Spindeler, Alois. *Cur Verbum caro factum? Das Motiv der Menschwerdung und das Verhältnis der Erlösung zur Menschwerdung Gottes in den christologischen Glaubenskämpfen des vierten und fünften christlichen Jahrhunderts*. Forschungen zur christlichen Literatur- und Dogmengeschichte 18.2. Paderborn: Verlag Ferdinand Schöningh, 1938.

Sutton, Matthew Lewis. "*Mysterium Christi*: The Christologies of Maurice de La Taille and Karl Rahner." *International Journal of Systematic Theology* 10, no. 4 (October 2008): 416–30.

Tanner, Norman P., ed. *Decrees of the Ecumenical Councils*. 2 vols. London: Sheed and Ward, 1990.

Tanquerey, Adolphe. *Synopsis theologiae dogmaticae ad mentem S. Thomae Aquinatis hodiernis moribus accommodata*. 18th ed. 2 vols. Paris: Typis Societatis sancti Joannis evangelistae, Descleé et socii, 1921.

Torrell, Jean-Pierre. *Saint Thomas Aquinas*. Translated by Robert Royal. Vol. 1, *The Person and His Work*. Rev. ed. Washington, D.C.: The Catholic University of America Press, 2005.

Unger, Dominic J. "Robert Grosseteste Bishop of Lincoln (1235–1253) on the Reasons for the Incarnation." *Franciscan Studies* 16, no. 1/2 (1956): 1–36.

United States Conference of Catholic Bishops. *Doctrinal Elements of a Curriculum Framework for the Development of Catechetical Materials for Young People of High School Age*. Washington, D.C.: USCCB, 2008.

Urrutibéhéty, Chrysostome. *Christus Alpha et Omega seu De Christi universali regno*. 2nd ed. Lille, France: R. Giard Libraire, 1910.

———. *Le Motif de l'Incarnation et les principaux thomistes contemporains*. Tours: Librairie Alfred Cattier, 1921.

van Driel, Edwin Christiaan. *Incarnation Anyway: Arguments for Supralapsarian Christology*. Oxford: Oxford University Press, 2008.

Van Engen, John H. *Rupert of Deutz*. Publications of the UCLA Center for Medieval and Renaissance Studies. Los Angeles: University of California Press, 1983.

Vatican Council II. *Gaudium et spes*. Pastoral Constitution. In *Decrees of the Ecumenical Councils*, edited by Norman P. Tanner, 2:1069–1135. London: Sheed and Ward, 1990.

Weber, Robert and Roger Gryson, eds. *Biblia sacra Vulgata*. 5th ed. Stuttgart: Deutsche Bibelgesellschaft, 2007.

Weinandy, Thomas. *In the Likeness of Sinful Flesh: An Essay on the Humanity of Christ*. Edinburgh: T & T Clark, 1993.

White, Thomas Joseph. *The Incarnate Lord: A Thomistic Study in Christology*. Thomistic Ressourcement Series 5. Washington, D.C.: The Catholic University of America Press, 2015.

———, ed. *The Analogy of Being: Invention of the Antichrist or Wisdom of God?* Grand Rapids, Mich.: Eerdmans, 2011.

Williams, John W. "Karl Rahner on the Death of Christ." *Journal of the Evangelical Theological Society* 14, no. 1 (1971): 41–50.

Wong, Joseph H. "Anonymous Christians: Karl Rahner's Pneuma-Christocentrism and an East-West Dialogue." *Theological Studies* 55, no. 4 (December 1994): 609–37.

Zizioulas, John. "Trinitarian Freedom: Is God Free in Trinitarian Life?" In *Rethinking Trinitarian Theology: Disputed Questions and Contemporary Issues in Trinitarian Theology*, edited by Giulio Maspero and Robert J. Woźniak, 193–207. New York: T & T Clark, 2012.

Zubizarreta, Valentino. *Theologia dogmatico-scholastica ad mentem S. Thomae Aquinatis*. 4 vols. 4th ed. corrected by the author. Vitoria: Ediciones "El Carmen," 1948.

Index

Abel, 145
Abelard, Peter, 124
Acts of the Apostles, 2, 194–95, 203
Adam, 11–12, 16, 25, 39, 45, 48–49, 87, 106, 109n153, 110–11, 112n161, 113–14, 117, 130–32, 140, 145, 147
adoptionism, 202
Albert the Great, 15–18
Alexander of Hales, 12–14, 42, 44, 106
Álvarez, Diego, 92n97
analogia entis, 219–21
angelic nature, 14, 16–17, 57n39, 82, 189
angels, 16, 40, 65, 77, 81–82, 109–11, 141–43, 154–55, 200–201
Anselm of Canterbury, 3, 5–7, 16, 215
Anunciación, Juan de la, 60, 70n41
Aquinas, Thomas, 42, 48, 65n24, 106, 182–83, 187; cause in, 107; fall in, 25n58; *finis cuius* in, 69n38; incarnation in, 22–34, 125, 139, 145–47; Salmanticenses and, 4, 81, 115; *signa rationis* and, 47, 121–22
Araújo, Francisco de, 92n97
Aristotle, 46–47, 64, 72n47, 121–22
Astorga, Juan Vicente de, 93
Augustine, 11, 28, 34, 106
Auriol, Peter, 47

Balthasar, Hans Urs von, 5, 238–39; Christocentrism of, 207–22; freedom in, 207–8, 212–13, 222–32; incarnation in, 211–13, 215–16; mercy and, 232–37; Rahner and, 209–10, 218–19; redemption in, 206, 213–14, 221–22; Salmanticenses and, 222–37; sin in, 208; Trinity in, 216
Barth, Karl, 219–20, 228
Bernard of Clairvaux, 23, 106
Billuart, Charles-René, 150
Bonaventure, 18–21, 25, 37n87, 47–48
Bonnefoy, Jean-François, 151–52
Breviloquium (Bonaventure), 20
Bulgakov, Sergei, 213

Cain, 145
Cajetan, Tommaso de Vio, 52–53, 92n97, 96, 101n126, 140n60, 155
Capréolus, Jean, 51, 72n46
Carol, Juniper B., 39n93, 56n39, 60, 209n13
Categories (Aristotle), 72n47
cause, 63–74, 66n26, 70, 72n47, 74nn49–50, 98n119, 100, 102–3, 102n129, 121–22, 126–27, 136, 168, 178
Christocentrism: of Balthasar, 207–22; defined, 3; incarnation and, 3; of Rahner, 159–79; Thomistic, 4–5
Collationes in hexaëmeron (Bonaventure), 20–21
Colossians, Epistle to, 75, 224, 236, 240
Commentary on the Sentences (Aquinas), 22–26
Concepción, Pablo de la, 79n58
Cornejo de Pedrosa, Pedro, 92n97
cross, 175–77, 179, 198–99, 210, 213, 236

Cross, Richard, 39
Cur Deus homo? (Anselm of Canterbury), 6–7
Cursus theologicus, 59–61, 238
Cyril of Alexandria, 107–8

Daguet, François, 122–23, 143–45
Daniel, Book of, 143
David, 88, 195
De anima (Aristotle), 64
De cessatione legalium (Grosseteste), 9
De gloria et honore Filii hominis super Matthaeum (Rupert of Deutz), 7–8
de la Taille, Maurice, 119–21
De motivo Incarnationis (de la Anunciación), 60–61, 67n33, 70n41, 113, 115–16, 147
De spiritu et anima (attrib. Augustine), 11, 23
De veritate (Aquinas), 145–46

Ephesians, Epistle to, 75, 156, 210, 236
Eve, 11–12, 16

fall of man, 4, 7, 9, 12–13, 20–21, 36–40, 109n153, 110–17, 112n161, 130–31, 140, 143–47
finis causa, 66–68, 70
finis cui, 63–71, 73–74, 76, 78, 95–96, 100, 116, 118, 130, 134–43, 204, 234
finis cuius gratia, 63–78, 94–101, 103–4, 110, 116, 118, 123, 130, 134–43, 154, 197, 201, 204, 231, 234
finis effectus, 66–68, 70, 138
finis operis, 66n26, 138
finis qui, 70, 138n57
finis quo, 70
1 Corinthians, 2, 108, 148, 160, 195
1 John, 181, 203
1 Peter, 235
1 Timothy, 2, 23, 27–33, 70n59
freedom, of God: in Balthasar, 207, 212–13, 222–32; in Rahner, 164, 173, 179–98, 226; in Salmanticenses, 74, 124–25, 132, 139

Galatians, Epistle to, 70n59, 194
Galtier, Paul, 128n31

Garrigou-Lagrange, Reginald, 49, 150–51
Gaudium et Spes (Second Vatican Council), 1
Geist in Welt (Spirit in the World) (Rahner), 160
Genesis, Book of, 210
God: in Balthasar, 209–10, 214–15; economic freedom of, 180–98; free will of, 81, 96n115, 97, 139; in Grosseteste, 9; incarnation and, 3, 6; knowledge and, 120–21, 124; love of, 135; mercy of, 63; permission of sin by, 31, 54, 56n39, 63, 75–79, 87, 92–95, 97–98, 100–102, 104–6, 112n161, 113, 126–29, 134n46, 147–53; in Rahner, 160–63, 164n18, 166–68, 171–74, 177; in Rupert of Deutz, 7–8; in Salmanticenses' argumentation, 61–62, 79–82; in Salmanticenses' position, 74–78; sin and, 105–6; in Suárez, 55–56; transcendence of, 14–15. *See also* freedom, of God; incarnation
Godoy, Pedro de, 57, 150, 211
Goergen, Donald, 17
Gonet, Jean-Baptiste, 57, 86
Gorman, Michael, 194n119
grace, 52, 54, 104, 112, 126–27, 130–31, 163, 165–69, 199–200, 234
Grosseteste, Robert, 9–12, 22n53, 44, 106
Grundkurs des Glaubens (Foundations of Christian Faith) (Rahner), 160
Guerric of Saint-Quentin, 14–15

Harper, Thomas, 71n45
Hearer of the Word (Rahner), 160–61
Hebrews, Epistle to, 23, 70n59, 160, 234
Heidegger, Martin, 163
Henry of Ghent, 47
Holy Spirit, 144, 169, 177–78, 193–94
Horan, Daniel, 35–36
Humani generis (Pius XII), 163
humility, 23, 26

Immaculate Conception, 44–45, 87
incarnation, 3–4, 6, 8–12; Adam and, 106; in Albert the Great, 15; in Alexander of Hales, 12–14; in Aquinas, 22–34, 146–47; in Balthasar, 211–13, 215–16, 218; in

Index

Bonaventure, 18–21; causality and, 66–67; creation and, 163–64; in Guerric of Saint-Quentin, 14–15; mercy and, 63; modality of, 49–50, 85; "motive" of, 48; "present decree" and, 48–49; in Rahner, 163–66, 168–70, 173, 180–81, 191–92; redemption and, 66–69, 79–80, 86–88, 94–95, 103, 233–34; redemption vs., 17; in Salmanticenses position, 61–62, 76, 230–31; in Scotus, 34–41; in Silvestri, 51–52; Trinity and, 188–89
instantia rationis, 45, 120. *See also signa rationis*
Isaiah, Book of, 143

James of Venice, 46
Jesus Christ: in Aquinas, 28; in Balthasar, 208, 212, 220–21; in Cajetan, 52; causality and, 67–68; in Cyril of Alexandria, 107–8; in Grosseteste, 10–11; humanity of, 167–68, 202–4; Immaculate Conception of, 44–45; in John Paul II, 1; in Jon of St. Thomas, 54; in Licheto, 54–55; mortality of, 19; in Pancheri, 134; predestination of, 32–38, 49, 54–55, 102–4, 110; as prior to sin, 92; in Rahner, 159–79; redemption and, 80–81, 108–9; in Salmanticenses' position, 74–76; salvation and, 2; in Scholasticism, 3–4; in Scotus, 38–39; in Vásquez, 53. *See also* incarnation
John, Gospel of, 70n59, 84–85, 108, 160, 181, 193–94, 203, 236
John of St. Thomas, 54, 65, 67n30, 92n97
John Paul II, Pope, 1
Johnson, Keith, 220n58
justice, 25n58, 77, 104, 111–13, 116, 143–49, 199–201, 233

Kilby, Karen, 210

Lectura (Scotus), 34–37, 45n2
Leibniz, Gottfried, 124
Léon, Luis de, 57
Letter, Paul de, 190n103
Licheto, Francesco, 54–55, 142n63
Lombard, Peter, 22, 34

Lorca, Pedro de, 93–94
Lubac, Henri de, 162–63
Luke, Gospel of, 19, 70n59, 151, 195, 204, 236–37

Madre de Dios, Antonio de la, 57, 59–60
magisterium, 3, 173
Mansini, Guy, 186, 189, 191n103
Maréchal, Joseph, 162
Mark, Gospel of, 79n59, 135, 194, 203, 233–34, 236–37, 240
Mary, 12, 44, 87, 234–35
Matthew, Gospel of, 24, 143, 194, 203, 236–37
Maximus the Confessor, 218
Medina, Bartolomé de, 109n153
Mendoza, Alfonso de, 93–94
mercy, 4, 63, 97, 117, 198, 222, 232–37, 240
Metaphysics (Aristotle), 121–22
Molina, Luis de, 55, 119, 129–30
Molinism, 126, 129, 133
Moment of Christian Witness, The (Balthasar), 209–10

Natalis, Hervaeus, 47, 119
Nathan, 195
Nestorianism, 202
Nicene Creed, 80n59, 84, 99

ordinate volens, 50–51, 96
Ordinatio (Scotus), 37–40
original sin, 25, 44, 61, 104, 112, 115–16, 199, 225

Pancheri, Francesco Saverio, 134–36, 234n90
penitence, 63
Peter, 38, 223
Pfisterer, Robert B., 60, 86
Philippians, Epistle to, 217
Physics (Aristotle), 46
Pius XII, Pope, 163
predestination, 32–38, 49, 54–55, 98–99, 102–5, 110–12, 126–27, 148, 210–12, 223
"present decree," 30n72, 45, 48–49, 56n37, 61, 78–79, 86–87, 106, 110–11, 113, 115–16, 130–32, 152–54

Przywara, Erich, 219
Psalms, Book of, 143, 195

Quaestio de conceptione Christi (Albert the Great), 17

Rada, Juan de, 50–51, 96, 117, 224
Ragusa, Giuseppe, 92n97
Rahner, Karl, 5, 238–39; Balthasar and, 209–10, 218–19; Christocentrism of, 159–79; cross and, 175–77, 179, 198–99; freedom of God in, 164, 173, 179–98, 226; and God's economic freedom, 180–98; grace in, 163, 165–69, 199–200; incarnation in, 163–66, 168–70, 173, 180–81, 191–92; Salmanticenses and, 179–98; salvation in, 175–76, 185–86, 198; sin in, 174–75, 226–27; transcendence in, 171–72, 180; Trinity in, 168–69, 181, 184, 186–88
redemption, 103, 134n46; in Balthasar, 206, 213–14, 221–22; in Bonaventure, 19–20; fall of man and, 17; *finis cuius gratia* and, 139, 141; of Mary, 234–35; in Salmanticenses, 66–69, 78–82, 86–88, 94–95, 108–9, 112, 149–51, 231–32; sin and, 98n118
Reginald of Piperno, 27
Reportatio (Scotus), 40–41
reprobation, 109–10
revelation, 27, 83–84, 160–61, 194–95
Revelation, Book of, 143, 240
Risi, Francesco Maria, 118, 125–26, 153–57
Romans, Epistle to, 2, 14–15, 26, 35, 109, 195, 210
Rupert of Deutz, 7–8

Sagrado Corazón, Enrique, 135n49
Salmanticenses, 4–5, 45, 59, 70, 157, 200, 238–40; argumentation of, 79–116; Balthasar and, 222–37; *finis cui* in, 63–71; *finis cuius gratia* in, 63–71; God's glory in, 61; mercy and, 232–37; position of, 74–78; Rahner and, 179–205; redemption in, 66–69, 231–32; *signa rationis* in, 71–74, 125, 128–30, 133–50; sin in, 62–63

salvation, 2, 24, 50–52, 77, 80, 84, 96, 99–100, 112n161, 139–43, 167, 171–72, 174–77, 185–86, 198, 208–9
Samuel, 88
San Juan Bautista, Antonio de, 60
Santa Teresa, Domingo de, 59–60
Saul, 88
Scholasticism, 3–4, 34–35, 48–49, 73n49, 113, 124, 180, 188, 191, 211, 224, 238
Scotus, John Duns, 4–5, 34–41, 45, 47, 49–52, 62, 96–97, 119, 141n61, 198, 223
2 Corinthians, 195
2 Peter, 195
2 Samuel, 195
Second Vatican Council, 1, 4
Sentences (Lombard), 22
signa rationis, 45–48, 71–74, 93, 118–27, 129, 223. See also *instantia rationis*
signum(a) a quo, 71–74, 123–24, 130, 132–33
signum(a) in quo, 71–74, 86, 91, 95, 127, 129–30, 132–33
Silvestri de Ferrara, Francesco, 51–52
sin: in Albert the Great, 15; in Alexander of Hales, 13; in Aquinas, 23, 25–26, 28–32; in Balthasar, 208; in Bonaventure, 20; in Cajetan, 52; Christ as prior to, 92; God and, 105–6; God as willing, 150–53; grace and, 52; in Grosseteste, 9–11; Immaculate Conception and, 44–45; mercy and, 63; original, 25, 44, 61, 104, 112, 115–16, 199, 225; penitence and, 63; permission of, by God, 31, 54, 56n39, 63, 75–79, 87, 92–95, 97–98, 100–102, 104–6, 112n161, 113, 126–29, 134n46, 147–53; predestination and, 102, 104–5; in Rahner, 174–75, 226–27; redemption and, 98n118, 149–51; in Rupert of Deutz, 8; in Salmanticenses, 62–63, 78; Salmanticenses on, 63; Scotistic vs. Thomistic view of, 4; in Scotus, 38. See also fall of man
Söhngen, Gottlieb, 220
Suárez, Francisco, 55–56, 86–91, 211, 224
Summa fratris Alexandri (Alexander of Hales), 13
Summa theologiae (Aquinas), 28–33

transcendence, 14–15, 164–65, 171–72, 180
Trinitarianism, 47, 119, 169, 185, 206
Trinity, 13, 47, 166–69, 181–84, 186–89, 216, 221

Unger, Dominic J., 9n9, 10n15, 11n15
United States Conference of Catholic Bishops, 1–2
Urrutibéhéty, Chrysostome, 132, 136–37, 140–42

Vásquez, Gabriel, 53–54, 89, 92n97, 117, 152, 224

William of Ockham, 47, 119
Wong, Joseph H., 177–78
Word, 49, 93, 164, 186n90, 189–90, 200

Zeno of Elea, 46
Zizioulas, John, 228–29

ALSO IN THE
THOMISTIC RESSOURCEMENT SERIES

Series Editors: Matthew Levering
Thomas Joseph White, OP

Habits and Holiness
Ethics, Theology, and Biopsychology
Ezra Sullivan, OP

Reading Job with St. Thomas Aquinas
Edited by Matthew Levering, Piotr Roszak, and Jörgen Vijgen

To Stir a Restless Heart
Thomas Aquinas and Henri de Lubac on Nature, Grace, and the Desire for God
Jacob W. Wood

Aquinas on Transubstantiation
The Real Presence of Christ in the Eucharist
Reinhard Hütter

Bound for Beatitude
A Thomistic Study in Eschatology and Ethics
Reinhard Hütter

Analogy after Aquinas
Logical Problems, Thomistic Answers
Domenic D'Ettore

The Metaphysical Foundations of Love
Aquinas on Participation, Unity, and Union
Anthony T. Flood

www.ingramcontent.com/pod-product-compliance
Lightning Source LLC
Chambersburg PA
CBHW031237290426

44109CB00012B/334